THEORY
CONSTRUCTION

PRENTICE-HALL METHODS OF SOCIAL SCIENCE SERIES

EDITORS

Herbert L. Costner
Neil Smelser

HUBERT M. BLALOCK, JR.
University of North Carolina

THEORY CONSTRUCTION

From Verbal to Mathematical Formulations

PRENTICE-HALL, INC., Englewood Cliffs, New Jersey

TO HARRIET L. HERRING,
KATHARINE JOCHER,
GUY B. JOHNSON,
AND
RUPERT B. VANCE

© 1969 by PRENTICE-HALL, INC., Englewood Cliffs, N.J.

All rights reserved. No part of this book
may be reproduced in any form or by any means,
without permission in writing from the publisher.

13-913343-7

Library of Congress Catalog Card Number: 69-17478
Printed in the United States of America

Current printing (last digit):
10 9 8 7 6 5 4

PRENTICE-HALL INTERNATIONAL, INC., *London*
PRENTICE-HALL OF AUSTRALIA, PTY. LTD., *Sydney*
PRENTICE-HALL OF CANADA, LTD., *Toronto*
PRENTICE-HALL OF INDIA PRIVATE LTD., *New Delhi*
PRENTICE-HALL OF JAPAN, INC., *Tokyo*

Preface

As the title implies, my main purpose in writing this short book is to contribute to our understanding of the process of moving from the kinds of verbal theories that abound in the social sciences to more rigorous formulations in terms of mathematical models. At the same time, I have been very much concerned that these theories be testable and therefore rejectable on empirical grounds. I believe that it is both possible and desirable to aim very consciously toward a closer integration of theory-building efforts with quantitative empirical research.

In other disciplines there have developed subfields oriented towards these specific objectives. Perhaps the field of econometrics comes closest to what I have in mind, but there are also very comparable fields within psychology (psychometrics) and the biological sciences (biometrics). Unfortunately, the terms "sociometrics" and "sociometry" have already been given a somewhat narrower connotation, which perhaps should now be broadened to encompass a wider range of topics. The suffix *–metrics* obviously refers to the measurement process, and indeed fields such as econometrics and psychometrics are centered around problems of measurement and statistical estimation. But it would be misleading to imply that this involves a rather narrow focus of interest. One of the major tasks of the methodologist is to study the logic of the scientific method insofar as this bears on theory building, the processes of measurement and conceptualization, and the testing and estimation procedures used in evaluating theories.

My own interest in theory building was initially centered around propositional inventories. As my interest shifted more toward applied multivariate analysis and causal model building, I became much more concerned with problems of evaluating alternative theories and theory testing, rather than with the process of constructing these theories. This orientation toward testing and evaluation is very much evident in most of my previous work on causal models. In part, this is because the kinds of causal models I have thus far discussed are all exceedingly simple. For example, one-way causation was assumed throughout *Causal Inferences in Nonexperimental Research*, and none of the examples discussed in that book involved more than five variables.

As I attempted to extend this work, and as I read more of the econometrics literature, I became increasingly aware of the fact that more complex models will be needed. My work on status-inconsistency theory convinced me that the *theoretical* formulation of even such a relatively simple idea as "statistical interaction" is by no means a simple problem. And as I studied the econometricians' approaches to reciprocal causation and structural systems, it became all too apparent that existing sociological theories are rarely clearly enough specified to lend themselves to model building of the sort that we find in the economics literature. In part, this is due to much more difficult measurement problems that must be squarely faced by sociology. But I am also convinced that it is also a result of a rather unfortunate and false dichotomy between "theory" and "research" that has developed within our discipline. I have therefore decided to deal with theory building from the peculiar slant or perspective of applied multivariate analysis, knowing that others are approaching the topic less quantitatively.

The problems dealt with in this book are rather complex and technical. The technical literature on the subject is, in fact, becoming very extensive, and reading it probably requires more mathematical training than most sociologists have received. Therefore, one of my major tasks is to communicate these ideas without presupposing a knowledge of more than simple algebra and applied multiple regression analysis. It would be highly misleading, however, if I were to give the impression that the process of constructing really testable theories can be accomplished without at least some basic understanding of the kinds of rather difficult conceptual and methodological problems that are discussed throughout this book. It seems to me that there is a very great need for sociologists to take a careful look at some of the problems that lie ahead, and this cannot be accomplished without first mastering the technical literature that has been produced by scholars in some of the more advanced disciplines. In particular, I believe that sociologists have much to learn from the econometrics literature, upon which this book depends very heavily.

In addition to the authors whose works are cited throughout this book, I am especially indebted to my wife, Ann B. Blalock, and to the graduate students who have provided numerous ideas for this book. I would also like to thank the National Science Foundation for partial support of this research and Hayward R. Alker, Jr., Herbert L. Costner, O. Dudley Duncan, Arthur S. Goldberger, George C. Homans, Gerhard E. Lenski, N. Krishnan Namboodiri, and Neil J. Smelser for their helpful comments on portions of the original manuscript. I also appreciate the speedy and excellent typing assistance provided by Karon Hysom and Mary Warnock of the Institute for Research in Social Science at the University of North Carolina.

Finally, I offer my genuine appreciation to that older generation of sociologists at North Carolina to whom this book is dedicated: Harriet L. Herring, Katharine Jocher, Guy B. Johnson, and Rupert B. Vance.

HUBERT M. BLALOCK, JR.

Contents

1
INTRODUCTION　　　　　　　　　　　　　　　　　　　　　1

2
AXIOMS AND THEOREMS　　　　　　　　　　　　　　　10

　　　Covariance Statements　12
　　　A Resolution　17
　　　A More Complex Example with Feedback　21

3
RECASTING VERBAL THEORIES AS CAUSAL MODELS　　27

　　　Typologies　30
　　　Inventories of Causes　35
　　　Inventories of Effects　41
　　　Simple Chains and Loops　43

4

STATIC FORMULATIONS AND IDENTIFICATION PROBLEMS 48

    Identification of Supply and Demand Equations   50
    A General Linear Model   59
    Additional Examples   66
    Block-Recursive Systems   71
    Concluding Remarks   74

5

SINGLE-EQUATION DYNAMIC MODELS 76

    The Nature of Dynamic Models   77
    Lagged Endogenous Variables and Difference Equations   78
    Differential Equations   88
    Estimation with Least Squares   97

6

SIMULTANEOUS-EQUATION DYNAMIC MODELS 100

    Theoretical Specification of Feedback Relationships   102
    Stability Conditions   106
    Illustrations   126
    Concluding Remarks   139

7

GENERALIZATIONS AND LEVELS OF ABSTRACTION 141

    The Element-Class Perspective   142
    The Class-Subclass Perspective   144
    The Indicator Perspective   151

APPENDIX:
A

THEORY BUILDING AND THE STATISTICAL CONCEPT OF INTERACTION   155

First-order Interactions: Multiplicative Models   156
Higher-order Interactions: Atkinson's Motivation Model   162
Concluding Remarks   164

APPENDIX:
B

SOME ELEMENTARY CALCULUS   166

INDEX   178

1

Introduction

Most social scientists seem agreed on the need for more adequate theories, but there is less consensus on the processes or strategies that would be most useful in constructing such theories. My purpose in this short book is to attempt to provide some suggestions or guidelines that are sufficiently general that they can be applied in a number of diverse fields. The basic orientation will involve a causal models approach to theory construction, with the emphasis being on integrating various verbal approaches to theory building with the construction of mathematical models consisting of simultaneous equations with causal interpretations.

The notion of "theory" in sociology has several connotations which have been discussed by Homans, Merton, and Zetterberg, among others.[1] Therefore it is necessary at the outset to indicate briefly how I shall be using the concept and why it is important to study the theory-building process. First,

---

[1] See George C. Homans, "Contemporary Theory in Sociology," in *Handbook of Modern Sociology*, ed. R. E. L. Faris (Chicago: Rand McNally and Company, 1964), Chap. 25; Robert K. Merton, *Social Theory and Social Structure* (Glencoe, Illinois: The Free Press, 1957), Chaps. 1 and 2; and Hans L. Zetterberg, *On Theory and Verification in Sociology*, 3rd ed (Totowa, New Jersey: The Bedminster Press, 1965), Chap. 1.

I shall not include under the heading of theory what might be more appropriately labeled the history of social thought, or the study of sociological classics. Likewise, I shall not include what Zetterberg has termed "historical criticism," or the sociology of knowledge. That is, I shall exclude discussions of who said what, which scholars influenced sociological developments in specific epochs or countries, and the historical factors that may have influenced various schools of thought. All of these topics may be important, and in fact they may shed light on the motivational factors that influence the final theoretical product. They may also have some bearing on the psychological processes involved in gaining intuitive insights. I am not denying the importance of studying the classics of sociology, but I shall focus entirely on the content of the theory as indicated by its specific propositions.

It has been noted that theories do not consist entirely of conceptual schemes or typologies but must contain lawlike propositions that interrelate the concepts or variables two or more at a time. Furthermore, these propositions must themselves be interrelated. For example, if one proposition relates variables A and B, a second relates C and D, and a third E and F, then there must be additional propositions enabling one to make deductive statements connecting these three propositions. Ideally, one might hope to achieve a completely closed deductive theoretical system in which there would be a minimal set of propositions taken as axioms, from which all other propositions could be deduced by purely mathematical or logical reasoning. More realistically we might take the model of the completely closed deductive system as an ideal which in practice can only be approximated. One of the major problems that will be encountered in the remaining chapters is that of dealing with less than completely closed deductive systems and studying how existing theories can be built up inductively so as to approximate the ideal more closely. At the same time, we shall have to be concerned with the problem of evaluating these theoretical systems from the standpoint of testing their correspondence with reality.

It should not be necessary to dwell on the need for such theories. Social scientists are well aware, for example, that facts do not speak for themselves. One can readily point to the possibility of assembling so many miscellaneous facts on a subject that it becomes virtually impossible to make any sense out of them. But empirically-minded quantitative sociologists sometimes in effect endorse an anti-theoretical position by throwing numerous variables into a regression equation with the idea of selecting out that subset which "explains" the most variance. To be sure, this kind of dragnet approach is often useful as an exploratory device, or as insurance in case most of the variables thought to be important turn out to be only weakly related to the dependent variable. But beyond this, it can hardly be judged an efficient procedure given the limitless number of variables that can usually be brought into the picture.

If simple short-run "prediction" or estimation is taken as the goal of science, it might seem as though theoretical explanations can be avoided. Of course there are often practical situations in which such explanations are not really needed. For example, suppose one wishes to predict the performance of students in college in order to decide which ones to admit. One of the best predictors of college performance turns out to be high school performance. More generally, the best predictor of a variable at some point in time may be the value of that same variable at a previous time. As long as the basic situation does not change, the prediction may hold reasonably well. But if any of the major parameters are varied, a theoretical explanation will be needed. For example, if the college atmosphere is very different from that of the high school, then success in one setting may not predict success in the other. Instead, it will be necessary to locate, measure, and fit together the basic causal factors that affect the dependent variable. This process of finding explanatory variables is a much more difficult one, since, in effect, only a small fraction of the predictor variables will turn out to be directly related causally to the variable to be explained. Furthermore, there may be complex reciprocal relationships among all of the variables that cannot be disentangled through prediction equations alone. There must be a theory in terms of which these interrelationships can be explained.

But not all theories will be testable, regardless of how carefully they are constructed. I assume that there is general agreement, at least among sociologists, that there is still a substantial gap between existing theory, on the one hand, and actual empirical research, on the other. There is an obvious need for testable theories that are sufficiently complex to give insights beyond those that can be gained through common sense or practical experience. In this connection, two points seem worth stressing at the outset. First, the kinds of verbal theories that serve as first approximations to deductive theories are often far too simple and unclear to stand as adequate formulations; mathematical models should eventually replace or supplement such verbal theories. Second, when we come to test these deductive theories, we must anticipate a number of problems concerning the handling of "errors" produced by inadequate measurements and the omission of other variables from the system. Such errors often make the tests much more indirect and subtle than one might suppose on the basis of common-sense arguments.

The need for deductive theories, when combined with the need for testable theories that are sufficiently complex to give really new insights, poses a major dilemma for the theory builder. In order to develop deductive theories, one must ordinarily begin with very simple models that are totally inadequate to mirror the real world. By adding new variables and complications a few at a time, one can then construct more realistic theories by what amounts to an inductive process. But many social scientists are inclined to study complex phenomena of social importance: population growth, minority-group relations, delinquency, bureaucratic behavior, stratification in industrial societies, and so forth. Analyses of such phenomena obviously require one to deal with many variables. Furthermore, it would seem premature to eliminate most of these variables in favor of those few that happened to fit most easily into a simple deductive theory.

In a sense, then, our naïveté plus the complexity of the real world make it difficult to begin the process of developing useful deductive theories. The methodological task is to suggest procedures for constructing reasonably simple deductive theories that also allow for relatively large numbers of variables.

Complexity can be introduced in a number of different ways. First, one can add more and more variables. Second, he may allow for relatively more complex forms of relationships such as nonlinearity or nonadditive joint effects. Third, he can construct dynamic theories that deal with time paths, feedbacks, cycles, and so on. Fourth, he may use increasingly complex but more realistic assumptions about the omission of variables from the system producing measurement errors and unexplained variation. The task of the methodologist is to learn more about the implications of each of these complicating factors.

The social scientist is confronted with a second major dilemma. The statement of theories on a highly general level requires that concepts be defined rather abstractly. For example, on the social psychological level one may develop propositions in terms of values, goals, rewards and punishments, expectancies, and similar concepts. But if such general theories are to be applied to diverse empirical data, one must somehow link the more abstract concepts with numerous indicators or research operations. The abstract or general concepts will ordinarily be fewer in number than the indicators. For instance, there are many types of rewards or resources. Numerous situational factors may be assumed to affect expectancies or perceived probabilities, and there are numerous needs, goals, and values.

Testing the more abstract or general theories requires that the small number of abstract variables contained in these theories be linked in very explicit ways to measured variables. Since there will inevitably be large numbers of possible indicators, each of which is appropriate only under limited circumstances, one can hardly expect the theorist to specify more than a handful of particular indicators. Usually, this is done by providing illustrations of the more general concept. But the exact nature of the linkages is often left unspecified, and therefore the theory cannot be tested without making a number of ad hoc assumptions.

The resolution of this particular difficulty appears to require a division of labor between those who would construct the abstract theories and those who wish to test them. But it will also require that auxiliary theories be constructed applying the general theory to particular substantive problems and testing the general theory (indirectly, to be sure) in specific research settings.[2] Both the general theory and the auxiliary theory should be stated as explicitly as possible.

A number of problems involving both real and apparent difficulties seem closely related to these two basic dilemmas. The complex nature of reality, particularly the kind of reality with which the social scientist must deal, has led a number of scholars to the position that it is almost impossible to apply the analytic methods of the physical sciences to social phenomena. It may be denied that a social system can be taken apart and the pieces put back together again in a meaningful way. One may claim, for example, that the whole is greater than the sum of its parts. Hayward Alker, a political scientist, indicates the nature of this position in the following figurative quotation:

> At least since all the King's horses and all the King's men were unable to put Humpty Dumpty back together again, poets and scholars have often believed that biological, social, and political wholes are somehow greater than the sum of their parts. Most severely criticised among the King's men for their lack or misuse of the relevant surgical skills have been policy scientists using the logical tools of mathematics and the research procedures of the behavioral and social sciences.[3]

Alker argues that, rather than merely asserting that the pieces cannot be put together in a simple additive way, it is more constructive to specify precisely what seems to be implied by this notion of nonadditivity. He notes three respects in which simple adding may be misleading. First, the process

---

[2] The notion of an auxiliary theory designed for testing purposes is discussed briefly in Chap. 7 below and somewhat more thoroughly in H. M. Blalock, "The Measurement Problem: A Gap Between the Languages of Theory and Research," in *Methodology in Social Research*, ed. H. M. Blalock and Ann B. Blalock (New York: McGraw-Hill Book Company, 1968), Chap. 1. In essence, the auxiliary theory should contain explicit assumptions as to how each measured variable is causally linked to the unmeasured variables. It must also contain assumptions as to the extent of random measurement error or specific kinds of nonrandom errors. Tests of the main theory will of necessity involve tests of the auxiliary theory as well.

[3] Hayward R. Alker, Jr., "The Long Road to International Relations Theory: Problems of Statistical Nonadditivity," *World Politics*, 18 (July 1966), 623.

of aggregation, by which one obtains summary measures from individual scores, may not be at all simple. For example, one might have to use weighted averages rather than simple arithmetic means, if he wished to allow for the fact that some individuals are more important than others in decision-making processes. Moreover, different sets of weights would have to be used whenever the individuals or issues changed.[4]

Second, one should not necessarily assume that variables can be added, in the sense that two or more variables are presumed to have simple additive effects on a dependent variable. For example, the linear equation

$$Y = a + b_1 X_1 + b_2 X_2$$

may inadequately represent reality. Perhaps Y should be taken as a more complex function of these two variables.[5]

Third, and more subtly, it may be unrealistic to assume that equations can be added, or, on the contrary, that every equation can always meaningfully stand alone. Perhaps the above equation makes sense only when imbedded in a set of simultaneous equations, and one cannot study each equation separately, as it were. This particular question will be considered in some detail in Chap. 4.

The position I shall take in the remainder of this book is that it is far better to attempt to spell out explicitly exactly what one means by a statement such as "the whole is greater than the sum of its parts" than to use this kind of pious pronouncement to avoid the difficult task of analyzing our analytic procedures. The alternative would seem to be to attempt to describe reality in as much detail as possible so that the "true essence" of the whole can be grasped. Unfortunately, very few sociologists have been able to order miscellaneous details of complex human phenomena in meaningful ways that can be communicated to others so that knowledge can be accumulated. In short, I see no alternative to the processes of abstraction, omission of details, analysis, and synthesis. The trick is to accomplish these in such a way that we do not become dissatisfied and disillusioned with necessarily incomplete and imperfect models of reality.

Another problem stems from the fact that if they are to be simple, theories cannot contain very many variables; therefore simple theories must omit

---

[4] This question of aggregation is a highly important problem of measurement that has not been adequately studied by sociologists. Unfortunately, it cannot be discussed in the present work. For a lucid statement of the basic issues see James S. Coleman, *Introduction to Mathematical Sociology* (New York: Free Press of Glencoe, 1964), Chap. 2.

[5] This type of "nonadditivity" is usually discussed in the statistical literature in connection with the notion of statistical interaction. While I shall for the most part make use of simple additive models in the remainder of this book, nonadditive models are discussed briefly in Chaps. 3 and 7 and somewhat more thoroughly in Appendix A.

numerous explanatory factors. If so, when one uses empirical tests and prediction equations he is likely to find that he is able to explain only a relatively small fraction of the variation in a given dependent variable. Whenever one is confronted with a large percentage of unexplained variation, the error terms in his equations will be substantial. This usually means that assumptions concerning the behavior of the omitted variables, which produce the errors, become less realistic. From the empirical point of view it would be preferable to bring these variables explicitly into the equation so as to reduce the size of the error term. But from the standpoint of theory building, this could make the theory too complex at a given stage of theoretical development.

Many of these problems will be discussed in the remainder of this book. However, many highly important topics cannot, for various reasons, be covered in this brief treatment of a very complex subject. It will not be possible to discuss a wide range of approaches to the construction of mathematical models. The literature on mathematical models is becoming increasingly technical and requires at least a minimal knowledge of modern algebra, probability, and matrices. It is of course hoped that the topics and questions discussed in the remaining chapters will whet the reader's appetite for a serious study of this more advanced and technical literature, for which several very readable introductory texts are available.[6] I assume that the kinds of models I shall discuss will be relatively easier for most readers, who should already be familiar with multiple regression analysis and other topics in applied statistics. Therefore I would hope that the present attempt to provide a transition from verbal to mathematical formulations will constitute a useful starting point, but the reader should understand that I have not attempted to provide a representative sampling of all possible mathematical approaches.

Nor will problems of conceptualization and measurement be dealt with extensively, since other volumes in this series will be devoted to these topics. For the most part, I will be making the unrealistic but simple assumption that measurement problems have been effectively resolved and that there are only negligible measurement errors. However, there are ways of conceptualizing problems of measurement in terms of the kinds of causal models that will be discussed in the remainder of this book. I have discussed this general approach elsewhere, and there have been several attempts to apply this mode of attack to specific kinds of causal models.[7] At present, however,

---

[6] See especially Coleman, *Introduction to Mathematical Sociology;* John G. Kemeny, J. Laurie Snell, and Gerald L. Thompson, *Introduction to Finite Mathematics*, 2nd ed. (Englewood Cliffs, N.J.: Prentice-Hall, Inc., 1966); and Robert McGinnis, *Mathematical Foundations for Social Analysis* (Indianapolis: Bobbs-Merrill, 1965).

[7] H. M. Blalock, "The Measurement Problem." See also Paul M. Siegel and Robert W.

the sociological literature on the subject is not as extensive as might be hoped.

Closely related to problems of measurement are a large number of issues involving the choice of one's variables, the level of abstraction at which the theory is stated, and the process of moving up or down the ladder of abstraction so as to state more or less inclusive theoretical formulations. While I shall comment briefly on some of these questions in the final chapter, they are much too complex to be discussed adequately in this book. I will again make the very simple assumption that the social scientist has already resolved most of these questions, and that he has decided on the appropriate level of generality at which his theory is to be stated.

In connection with theory testing, or the evaluation of the theory in terms of the empirical evidence, I would wholeheartedly endorse the position of Glaser and Strauss that theory must be grounded in empirical data.[8] It would be highly misleading to suggest that theories are first arrived at by a deductive process and *then* tested. The actual process is much more fluid than this and undoubtedly always involves an inductive effort. One formulates the best theory he can in the light of existing evidence. He then should formalize this theory in order to spell out its implications. These implications are then checked against new data and the theory modified. In the present work I will concentrate almost exclusively on the formal aspect of this theory-building process.

Finally, it will not be possible to deal extensively with the actual procedures used in providing statistical tests or estimates of the fundamental parameters that appear in a theory. Many of these questions have been carefully studied by applied statisticians, and there is an extensive though technical literature on the subject.[9] However, it will be necessary to discuss these testing and estimating procedures in sufficient detail to study the limits they impose on the theory-building process. One of the major points that will be emphasized throughout the remaining chapters is that theories must be stated in such a way that they can be tested, and that anyone seriously interested in the theory-construction process must be well versed in the methodology of theory testing.

In brief, the plan of the book is as follows. We begin with purely verbal theoretical formulations, gradually moving to simultaneous algebraic equations appropriate in static theories, and finally to simultaneous differ-

---

Hodge, "A Causal Approach to the Study of Measurement Error," in *Methodology in Social Research*, ed. Blalock and Blalock, Chap. 2; and Peter M. Blau and O. Dudley Duncan, *The American Occupational Structure* (New York: John Wiley and Sons, Inc., 1967), Chap. 5 and passim.

[8] See Barney Glaser and Anselm Strauss, *The Discovery of Grounded Theory* (Chicago: Aldine Publishing Co., 1967).

[9] References to this literature are given in appropriate places in Chap. 4.

ential equations suitable for dynamic formulations. Since I shall assume no more than a knowledge of simple algebra and multiple regression, it will be necessary to introduce a minimal amount of elementary calculus in Appendix B in order to explain these dynamic formulations.

Chapter 2 deals with the nature of axioms and theorems and how these can be stated so as to make possible both deductive reasoning and verification. In Chap. 3 we shall be concerned with the practical question of how one may proceed from a survey of the literature to the construction of verbal theories capable of being translated into simultaneous algebraic or differential equations. Chapters 4–6 are somewhat more technical. Chapter 4 involves a discussion of certain identification problems encountered in connection with static formulations allowing for reciprocal causation. Chapters 5 and 6 deal with dynamic mathematical formulations, Chap. 5 being introductory to Chap. 6 in that the attention is confined to single differential or difference equations. Chapter 6 contains a more general discussion of stability conditions in dynamic models. Finally, Chap. 7, the concluding chapter, deals with the question of generalizability and the meaning of the notion that there are different levels of abstraction in terms of which a theory may be stated.

2

Axioms and Theorems

A deductive theory must contain both axioms and theorems. Axioms are propositions that are assumed to be true. Theorems, on the other hand, are derived by reasoning, or *deduced*, from the axioms. Let us assume that a theorist has stated a number of specific propositions, some of which he wishes to take as axioms and the remainder as theorems. The focus of this chapter will be on two very important questions: How does one decide which propositions to select as axioms? Are there any differences in the ways in which axioms and theorems should be stated, given that the theorems are to be deduced from the axioms?

A distinct though related question involves the issue of testability. Conceivably, all axioms and theorems could be more or less directly tested.[1] Usually it will not be possible to test all propositions, however. We shall be specifically concerned with theoretical systems in which the axioms are inherently untestable but at least some of the derived theorems can be tested. The argument that will be developed in the remainder of this chapter is

[1] Strictly speaking, of course, direct tests will almost always be impossible because of the necessity of making untestable assumptions regarding measurement error.

essentially as follows: Our axioms should be causal assertions that strictly speaking will be untestable because of the fact that it will never be possible to control for all "relevant" variables. For example, if we assume that a change in X causes or produces a change in Y, even if we observe covariations and temporal sequences we can never be sure that these have not been produced by some extraneous factor.[2] But if our axioms contain such causal assertions, and if we make certain additional assumptions concerning the operation of extraneous factors, we shall then be in a position to derive from our axioms testable theorems about covariances and temporal sequences.

In geometry and other branches of mathematics an axiom is a statement the truth of which is taken for granted. Of course, in the strict sense, the axioms of geometry need not apply to the real world. That is, their "truth" in terms of their empirical validity is not at issue. They are simply a set of assumptions that generate theorems, once a set of rules and definitions has been added to the theoretical system. But the notion of "axiom" has been borrowed by the empirical sciences and used in the sense of an assumption that is almost universally accepted. It is of course rare in the social sciences to find very many unquestionable assumptions, and therefore we need to recognize that the term "axiom" is used in the sense of an untested (or untestable) assumption, rather than as an assumption the truth of which is taken for granted. Obviously it would be very much to our advantage if we could discover universal propositions the truth of which was not in question. There undoubtedly are a few such propositions, such as "all men are mortal," or "all men are motivated by self-interest." The question is whether such propositions can be combined with enough more specific ones to generate deductive theories that take us very far beyond the obvious. For a considerable period of time, social scientists will have to settle for highly tentative theories based on axioms that are really nothing more than rather plausible assumptions.

Tests of the theories in these instances will involve empirical tests of the derived theorems.[3] Clearly, if the theorems prove false the theory must be modified or the axioms of the theory even abandoned. But if they are true, one cannot claim that the theory has been "verified" unless all possible competing alternatives can be rejected. In the case of causal theories, it will always be possible to state alternative explanations by the simple device of

---

[2] This point is discussed more thoroughly in H. M. Blalock, *Causal Inferences in Nonexperimental Research* (Chapel Hill, N.C.: University of North Carolina Press, 1964), Chap. 1.

[3] It is also possible that the axioms of a theory may be tested, or well established, whereas the theorems may not. See F. S. C. Northrop, *The Logic of the Sciences and Humanities* (New York: The Macmillan Company, 1947), Chaps. 8 and 13; and Coleman, *op. cit.*, Chaps. 1 and 18.

introducing additional variables. Where one allows for measurement error, a second kind of alternative explanation can always involve the possibility that results might have been different had there been no such measurement error. Therefore we shall be in the unfortunate situation of having to proceed by eliminating inadequate theories, rather than ever really establishing any of them. This is of course a very general situation that is not peculiar to the social sciences. Since we shall not be concerned with the details of testing procedures, but rather with the process of theory construction itself, it is sufficient to merely note this fact in passing.[4]

Covariance Statements

Many of the empirical generalizations found in the social science literature are stated in simple covariance form. Where both X and Y are continuous variables, the prototype statement of a covariance relationship would be of the form, "the greater the X, the greater the Y." Where both variables are attributes, the prototype statement would be of the form, "A's tend to be associated with B's." These covariance statements may or may not be testable, depending on whether each of the variables in the proposition has been measured. The question we shall deal with in the present section, however, is that of how one goes about deducing one covariance statement from another. How can one build a deductive theory on the basis of such propositions?

Let us consider a specific example of a theory, given by Zetterberg, consisting of ten propositions as follows:

1. The greater the division of labor, the greater the consensus.
2. The greater the solidarity, the greater the number of associates per member.
3. The greater the number of associates per member, the greater the consensus.
4. The greater the consensus, the smaller the number of rejections of deviants.
5. The greater the division of labor, the smaller the number of rejections of deviants.
6. The greater the number of associates per member, the smaller the number of rejections of deviants.
7. The greater the division of labor, the greater the solidarity.
8. The greater the solidarity, the greater the consensus.

---

[4] Procedures for testing relatively simple models involving one-way causation are discussed in Blalock, *Causal Inferences in Nonexperimental Research*, Chap. 3. In the case of more complex models, the reader is referred to the econometrics literature cited in Chap. 4 below.

9. The greater the number of associates per member, the greater the division of labor.
10. The greater the solidarity, the smaller the number of rejections of deviants.[5]

Zetterberg selects the last four propositions (7–10) as axioms and claims that the remainder can be deduced from this combination of four propositions.[6] He does not, however, adequately discuss the crucial question of why these particular four were selected. The reader is left with the impression that *any* set of propositions that could imply the remainder would be satisfactory. Presumably, a deductive theory which involved the smallest number of mutually consistent axioms, and which also implied all of the theorems, would be most satisfactory by virtue of the criterion of simplicity.

We cannot come to grips with this problem unless we first discuss a criticism of this approach given by Costner and Leik.[7] These authors make two main points. First, propositions of the form "the greater the X, the greater the Y" are ambiguous in that it is often not clear whether causal asymmetry is implied. Second, if one finds error or unexplained variation in an empirical attempt to test the theory, the strict deductive argument implied by an axiomatic theory (such as that relating propositions 1–10) will not apply unless one adds a set of auxiliary assumptions about the behavior of uncontrolled variables. Let us consider each of these points and then return to the question of how one chooses his axioms.

As Costner and Leik emphasize, causal asymmetry is often implied in propositions of the form, "the greater the X, the greater the Y." Sometimes a theorist is very explicit about this question. More often, it seems, the symmetry or asymmetry has to be inferred by a careful reading of an author's discussion of the proposition. I would infer, in the case of Zetterberg, that for each of these ten propositions the first variable mentioned in each pair is to be taken as causally prior. Yet, as we shall see below, this is probably not what is actually intended in the case of propositions 2 and 4, which are taken as theorems. Let us consider some additional examples.

Homans, in *The Human Group*, usually makes it clear to the reader whenever he wishes to imply a reciprocal relationship.[8] He states his propositions in several different ways, examples of which are as follows (with emphasis added):

---

[5] Zetterberg, *On Theory and Verification*, pp. 159–60. Quoted by permission of the publisher.
[6] *Ibid.*, p. 160.
[7] See Herbert L. Costner and Robert K. Leik, "Deductions from Axiomatic Theory," *American Sociological Review*, 29 (December 1964), 819–35.
[8] George C. Homans, *The Human Group* (New York: Harcourt, Brace and Company, 1950).

If the frequency of interaction between two or more persons increases, the degree of their liking for one another will increase, *and vice versa*.[9]

... persons who feel sentiments of liking for one another will express those sentiments in activities over and above the activities of the external system, *and these activities may further strengthen the sentiments of liking*.[10]

The more frequently persons interact with one another, the more alike in some respects both their activities and their sentiments tend to become.[11]

In the case of the last proposition, there is no explicit mention of reciprocal causation, but in the very next sentence (which is not, however, part of the formal proposition), Homans goes on to say: "Moreover, the more a person's activities and sentiments resemble those of others, the more likely it is that interaction between him and these others will increase."[12] Thus Homans is reasonably explicit about the direction of causality, and one would therefore infer that a single direction is implied whenever no mention is made of relationships working in both directions. For example, if the phrase "and vice versa" were omitted from the first proposition cited above, one would infer that interaction affected liking but *not* vice versa.

Consider now a series of propositions given by Ralf Dahrendorf:

The intensity of class conflict decreases to the extent that classes are open.[13]

The violence of class conflict decreases to the extent that the conditions of class organization are present.[14]

The radicalness of structure change in an association covaries with the intensity of class conflict.[15]

Since most of Dahrendorf's propositions are stated in a language similar to that used in the first two of the above propositions, the reader might infer that the third proposition has been deliberately worded so as to mean something very different. Judging from the context of the propositions, I would infer that in the case of the first two propositions, Dahrendorf is implying that the first-mentioned variable is affected by the second. The notion of "covaries with" in the third proposition would not seem to imply the same asymmetry, however. Unfortunately, different readers are likely to draw different inferences from these statements.

[9] *Ibid.*, p. 112.
[10] *Ibid.*, p. 118.
[11] *Ibid.*, p. 120.
[12] *Ibid.*, p. 120.
[13] Ralf Dahrendorf, *Class and Class Conflict in Industrial Society* (Stanford: Stanford University Press, 1959), p. 239.
[14] *Ibid.*, p. 239
[15] *Ibid.*, p. 240.

The question of causal symmetry or asymmetry is not a moot point, as will be indicated in some detail in subsequent chapters. The simple phrase "and vice versa" can be tacked onto a theoretical proposition with great ease—but it can also lead to numerous verification problems. Here it will suffice to emphasize a point made by Costner and Leik. If statements of the form, "the greater the X, the greater the Y" are *not* meant to imply causal asymmetry, it is very easy to make erroneous deductive arguments. Consider, for example, propositions 7, 8, and 1 in Zetterberg's set. Presumably, theorem 1 follows from axioms 7 and 8. But suppose 8 were reversed to read: "the greater the consensus, the greater the solidarity." We would then have a theory of the form:

7. The greater the X (division of labor), the greater the Y (solidarity).
8'. The greater the Z (consensus), the greater the Y (solidarity).
1. Therefore, the greater the X (division of labor), the greater the Z (consensus).

Most readers will undoubtedly object that proposition 1 does not obviously follow from 7 and 8', and in so doing will in effect admit that the symmetry-asymmetry question is crucial. In terms of asymmetric causal models, one might wish to distinguish between the situations:

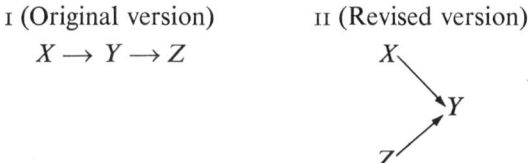

I (Original version) II (Revised version)
$X \rightarrow Y \rightarrow Z$

In model I we expect X and Z to be related, since an increase in X will produce an increase in Y, which in turn will increase Z (assuming all relationships to be positive).[16] But in model II, there is no reason to suppose a specific relationship between X and Z merely because they have a common effect Y.

The more general point is that statements of the form, "the greater the X, the greater the Y" do not really permit one to deduce implications unless they are meant to be more than mere covariance statements. In many instances common-sense applications of verbal language will not lead one astray. But as the theory becomes more and more complex, there will be increasing

---

[16] In the above diagram, and in all diagrams that follow, an arrow linking a given pair of variables indicates that there is assumed to be a *direct* causal link between these variables, with "directness" always being relative to the variables that explicitly appear in the model. For further discussion of this point see Blalock, *Causal Inferences in Nonexperimental Research*, Chaps. 1 and 2.

opportunities for ambiguities of the above type, as well as for erroneous "deductions."

There is another point about "causal chain" relationships that has been noted by several authors, including Costner and Leik.[17] If one uses a number of intervening links, and also admits that at any point in the chain other uncontrolled factors may be operating, then the correlations between nonadjacent variables may be extremely weak. If so, the assumptions one makes about the ways that disturbing influences operate become crucial.[18] Consider the following theory, as stated by Gibbs and Martin:

1. The suicide rate of a population varies inversely with the stability and durability of social relationships within that population. (Postulate 1)
2. The stability and durability of social relationships within a population vary directly with the extent to which individuals in that population conform to the patterned and socially sanctioned demands and expectations placed upon them by others. (Postulate 2)
3. The extent to which individuals in a population conform to patterned and socially sanctioned demands and expectations placed upon them by others varies inversely with the extent to which individuals in that population are confronted with role conflicts. (Postulate 3)
4. The extent to which individuals in a population are confronted with role conflicts varies directly with the extent to which individuals occupy incompatible statuses in that population. (Postulate 4)
5. The extent to which individuals occupy incompatible statuses in a population varies inversely with the degree of status integration in that population. (Postulate 5)
6. The suicide rate of a population varies inversely with the degree of status integration in that population. (Derived theorem)[19]

The theory would seem to imply that suicide rates should vary inversely with the relative frequency with which status combinations are occupied. But given the fact that at each stage there will be numerous variables operating, over and above those specified by the theory, it is by no means obvious that one can deduce even the sign or direction of the relationship between the

[17] Costner and Leik, "Deductions from Axiomatic Theory." See also O. Dudley Duncan, "Axioms or Correlations?" *American Sociological Review*, 28 (June 1963), 452.

[18] Perhaps the simplest set of such assumptions is that neglected factors produce only random disturbances. See below, Chap. 4.

[19] Jack P. Gibbs and Walter T. Martin, *Status Integration and Suicide* (Eugene, Oregon: University of Oregon Press, 1964), p. 27. See also Jack P. Gibbs and Walter T. Martin, "On Assessing the Theory of Status Integration and Suicide," *American Sociological Review*, 31 (August 1966), 533–41.

two end variables.[20] Deductions of this sort require one to commit himself on the causal asymmetry question and also to make explicit assumptions about error terms produced by variables left out of the system. Furthermore, the plausibility of the latter assumptions depends upon whether one allows for reciprocal causation or feedback, or whether he restricts himself to one-way causation.[21] Suffice it to say that the problem is not a simple one; purely verbal formulations will not enable us to deal with subtleties of this sort.

A Resolution

Let us return to the original problem of choosing one's axioms by asking what many authors seem to be doing when they state their arguments in verbal or paragraph form. In most of the attempts I have made to reconstruct or infer an author's argument, I have concluded that his rationale for stating a proposition linking two variables is that he is assuming a direct causal connection between the two. The notion of "directness" is of course relative. An author may or may not attempt to spell out intervening links, some of which he may later omit from his formal theory. But when he states a proposition of the form, "the greater the X, the greater the Y," this is usually preceded or followed by a discussion of why the predicted relationship should hold. Sometimes, this discussion implies a reciprocal causal relationship, as is the case with many of the propositions in *The Human Group*. In other instances, the author is tracing out a causal chain argument, in which causal asymmetry is definitely implied. Sometimes, unfortunately, the language may be so ambiguous that the direction of causality cannot be inferred. Rarely, however, does an author link two variables in a proposition where no causal connection whatsoever is implied.

It is often difficult to infer exactly what an author has in mind by relying solely on the way he words his propositions. Sometimes propositions are stated as though they refer to total correlations, rather than direct causal links. But if one merely says that two variables should be correlated, without spelling out the mechanisms producing this correlation, then it will be difficult to deduce additional propositions from the theory.

[20] Costner and Leik, "Deductions from Axiomatic Theory," refer to this kind of simple deduction as providing a "sign rule." In the case of a simple causal chain, one may multiply the signs of the intervening relationships; an even number of negative signs will produce a positive predicted relationship between the two "end variables," whereas an odd number of negative relationships will yield a negative predicted relationship, as in the case of the Gibbs-Martin propositions.

[21] See below, Chap. 4.

Whenever a theorist is ambiguous on this question, it will of course be easy to put words into his mouth by assuming, for example, that a failure to mention a connection between two variables indicates that there is supposed to be no direct causal link. Rather than debate the question of what the author really meant, it is advisable to go ahead with a more explicit formulation according to whatever line of theoretical reasoning seems most sensible.

Given this ambiguity in statements of the form "the greater the X, the greater the Y," and given the desirability of stating axioms in such a way that they imply direct causal links among variables, I would suggest the following two rules for stating theories in verbal form:

Rule 1: *Select as axioms those propositions that involve variables that are taken to be directly linked causally; axioms should therefore be statements that imply direct causal links among variables.*

Rule 2: *State theorems in terms of covariations and temporal sequences, thereby making them testable provided adequate measures of all variables can be obtained.*

Axioms may be stated in such a way that reciprocal causation is implied. Ideally, the relative length of time required for the feedback should also be specified. Thus, an axiom might be stated somewhat as follows: "An increase in X will produce (cause) an almost immediate increase in Y; this increase in Y will, in turn, result in a further increase in X, but with a delayed reaction." As we shall see in connection with dynamic formulations, this kind of verbal proposition could be translated reasonably easily into a set of simultaneous equations, one of which would be a differential or difference equation. (See Chap. 5.) If, in addition, the verbal statement were to specify that the increases should be linear (or some specific nonlinear form, such as monotonically increasing with a decreasing slope), then the task of translating the argument into mathematical equations would be much less ambiguous.

To return to Zetterberg's ten propositions, let us first attempt to diagram what appears to be the argument behind selecting the last four propositions as axioms. Presumably, the causal model implied is that given in Fig. 2-1, in which the number of associations per member is assumed to affect the division of labor (proposition 9), which in turn affects solidarity (proposition 7). Solidarity then affects two variables, consensus (proposition 8) and the number of rejections of deviants (proposition 10). One might suppose that a theorist would have arrived at these axioms by means of a theoretical argument that specified such more or less direct linkages. Had he inserted intervening links at various points, he might also have elected to insert additional variables into the model. But if we are given only these five

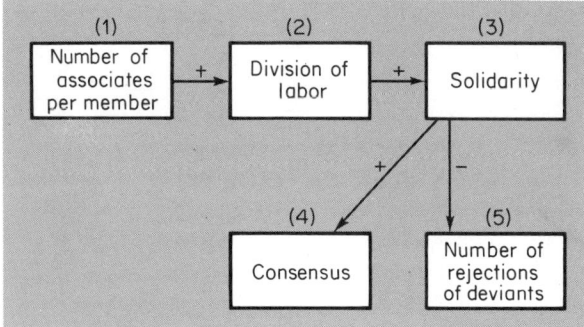

FIG. 2-1 Causal model for Zetterberg's axioms.

variables, we can assume that these particular linkages are taken as the "direct" ones, recognizing that no theoretical system can ever be complete.

The axioms might then be restated so as to make the direction of causal influence explicit:

1. An increase in the number of associates per member will produce an increase in the division of labor.
2. An increase in the division of labor will produce an increase in solidarity.
3. An increase in solidarity will produce an increase in consensus.
4. An increase in solidarity will produce a decrease in the number of rejections of deviants.

As noted previously, these axioms will need to be supplemented by a set of auxiliary assumptions in order to derive statements about covariations among the variables, unless the theoretical system is taken to be completely closed (i.e., no disturbing influences whatsoever), and unless measurement is perfect. Even with completely closed theoretical systems, it will usually be true that several plausible models will all yield identical empirical predictions. Therefore, causal assumptions such as these can never be directly tested, though they can be used to derive testable theorems stated in terms of covariations.[22]

Assuming that the proper assumptions have been made about variables left out of the system, and about measurement errors, the above four postulates can now be used to derive ten propositions or theorems concerning the

[22] For a more complete discussion of the kinds of predictions that are possible in the case of linear recursive models, see Blalock, *Causal Inferences in Nonexperimental Research*, Chap. 3.

signs of the total correlations or covariances among the five variables. These can be represented in matrix form as follows:

	(2) Division of labor	(3) Solidarity	(4) Consensus	(5) No. of rejections of deviants
Associations per member (1)	+	+	+	−
Division of labor (2)		+	+	−
Solidarity (3)			+	−
Consensus (4)				−

Each of these propositions could of course be stated verbally; for example: "There will be a positive correlation between number of associations per member and division of labor." Notice that we have not only restated Zetterberg's propositions 1–6 as theorems, but covariation statements have also been made about the variables directly linked by arrows in the four axioms (propositions 7–10).

But these are not the only deductions one can make from the theory. If one adds the assumption that all effects are linear and additive, then the model predicts that several partial correlations will also be zero. In particular, one would predict that apart from sampling error all of the following partial correlations should be zero: $r_{13.2}$, $r_{14.2}$, $r_{14.3}$, $r_{15.2}$, $r_{15.3}$, $r_{24.3}$, $r_{25.3}$, and $r_{45.3}$, where the variables have been numbered as in Fig. 2-1.[23] These predictions are based on the assumption that there are no direct links except as indicated by the arrows. For example, it is assumed that number of associates per member does not affect solidarity except through the division of labor.

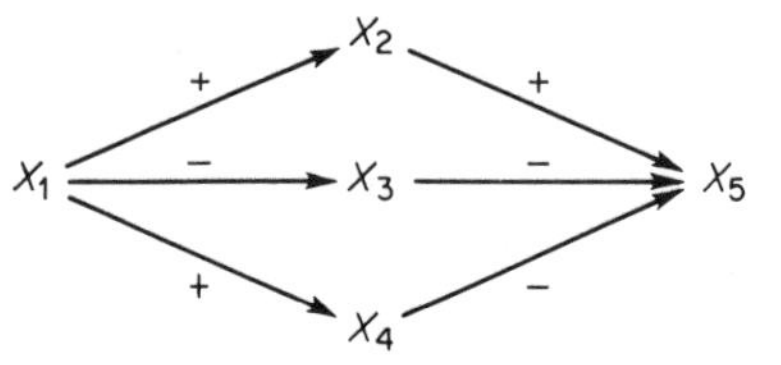

FIG. 2-2 Causal model with alternative paths from X_1 to X_5.

If the theorist has spelled out a simple causal chain, as for example in the Gibbs-Martin formulation, one might take as a first approximation a model in which there could be at most one path between any two variables. In some instances, however, an author may explicitly note that there may be several paths connecting one variable to another. If so, this can be incorporated into the causal diagram, as in Fig. 2-2. It is now more difficult to make specific predictions regarding the sign of the total correlation between the two end variables X_1 and X_5 unless, of course, the

[23] The prediction $r_{ij.k} = 0$ can of course be stated in the alternative form $r_{ij} = r_{ik}r_{jk}$.

products of the signs via each path are the same. One can predict that $r_{15.234}$ should be approximately zero, however. In general, the more complex the model the more difficult it will be to make definitive statements about total correlations. Furthermore, the task of evaluating the relative contributions via the different paths becomes more technical.[24] We shall return to a discussion of these causal chains in Chap. 3.

One additional point about causal chain models seems worth noting in the present context. If a theorist attempts a retrospective analysis of some historical sequence, he may very well reach the conclusion that the outcome was "inevitable." For example, he may conclude that a change in W (say, technology) led to a change in X (economy), which in turn affected Y (belief systems), which finally produced a change in Z (socialization patterns). He may fail to note that variations in other factors—which he has elected to ignore—might have affected the sequence at almost any point. The inevitability of such sequences seems much less obvious when one attempts to predict outcomes in advance of data collection. Likewise, an awareness of the existence of several alternative paths between variables would seem to reduce the likelihood of an analyst's using the inevitability argument.

A More Complex Example with Feedback

It is difficult to find examples of sociological theories that combine the features of being sufficiently general and complex, explicitly formulated with the direction of causal influences specified, and with a small number of well defined concepts. Certain of the propositions in *The Human Group* meet these criteria reasonably well and will be discussed in Chap. 6 in connection with dynamic models. The additional example I have selected is perhaps less well known than others, but it seems admirable for the purposes at hand.

Terence Hopkins gives an explicit theory of influence processes involving five variables and fifteen propositions.[25] The axioms have been diagrammed by Hopkins essentially as in Fig. 2-3. The propositions are as follows:

---

[24] The interested reader is referred to the literature on structural systems cited in Chap. 4, and to discussions of path analysis. See especially, C. C. Li, *Population Genetics* (Chicago: University of Chicago Press, 1955), Chap. 12; Sewall Wright, "Path Coefficients and Path Regressions: Alternative or Complementary Concepts?" *Biometrics*, 16 (June 1960), 189-202; O. Dudley Duncan, "Path Analysis: Sociological Examples," *American Journal of Sociology*, 72 (July 1966), 1-16; and *Methodology in Social Research*, ed. Hubert M. Blalock and Ann B. Blalock, Chaps. 2, 5, and 6.

[25] Terence K. Hopkins, *The Exercise of Influence in Small Groups* (Totowa, New Jersey: The Bedminster Press, 1964), pp. 51-52.

22 Axioms and Theorems

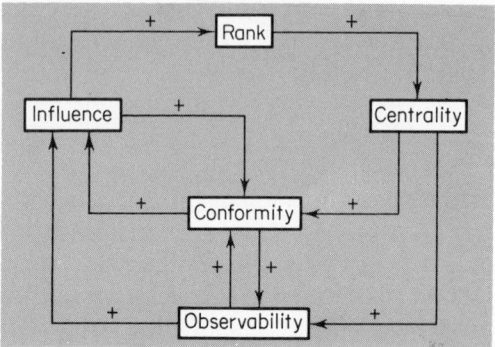

FIG. 2-3 Causal model for Hopkins' axioms. (Adapted by permission of the publisher from T. K. Hopkins, *The Exercise of Influence in Small Groups, op. cit.*, p. 52.)

For any member of a small group:

1. The higher his rank, the greater his centrality (axiom).
2. The greater his centrality, the greater his observability (axiom).
3. The higher his rank, the greater his observability (derivation).
4. The greater his centrality, the greater his conformity (axiom).
5. The higher his rank, the greater his conformity (derivation).
6. The greater his observability, the greater his conformity (axiom).
7. The greater his conformity, the greater his observability (axiom).
8. The greater his observability, the greater his influence (axiom).
9. The greater his conformity, the greater his influence (axiom).
10. The greater his centrality, the greater his influence (derivation).
11. The greater his influence, the greater his observability (derivation).
12. The greater his influence, the greater his conformity (axiom).
13. The higher his rank, the greater his influence (derivation).
14. The greater his influence, the higher his rank (axiom).
15. The greater his centrality, the higher his rank (derivation).[26]

Hopkins notes that there are 20 possible propositions connecting the five variables two at a time, if one distinguishes direction of causation and writes a different proposition for each direction of influence (e.g., propositions 6 and 7).[27] Five of these possible propositions are ignored by Hopkins as being of little theoretical interest. Notice that Hopkins has in effect applied Rule 1. He has taken as his axioms those propositions that state a direct

[26] *Ibid.*, p. 51. Quoted by permission of the publisher.
[27] *Ibid.*, p. 50.

causal link between two variables. However, both axioms and theorems have been worded in the form, "the greater the X, the greater the Y."

The concepts "rank," "influence," and "centrality" are defined in a conventional way. Conformity is defined as "the condition (or degree) of congruence between a member's profile on the relevant norms and the profile of the group-held norms."[28] (Hopkins notes that conformity is not meant to refer to the congruence between an individual's actual behavior and group norms.) Observability refers to the degree to which a group member is in a position to observe accurately the actual norms of the group.

All of the links in Hopkins' diagram are assumed to be positive. Therefore one would expect to find positive (zero-order) correlations between all pairs of variables. Hopkins discusses the nature of the data relevant to each of the associations and concludes that the model is reasonably well supported. But the Hopkins model involves a major complexity which we have not previously discussed. There are several "feedback" processes, including the major one from rank to influence (via centrality), and then from influence back to rank. In discussing the nature of the supporting evidence, Hopkins handles the relationships two or three at a time, as though some relationships can be analyzed separately while ignoring the others.[29] As we shall see in Chap. 4, this procedure is not ordinarily justified in the case of feedback models.

The problem can be seen by realizing that even though all zero-order correlations may be positive, there are large numbers of alternative models that will also predict such positive relationships. For example, how do we know that all arrows should not be reversed? Perhaps influence affects centrality via observability, with centrality having a direct impact on rank. Perhaps there is no double arrow between observability and conformity. Or maybe it runs in one direction but not the other.

In discussing the connection between centrality and influence, Hopkins deals with four possible paths as indicated in Fig. 2-4, and of course several additional alternatives can be constructed.[30] If we are in a position to ignore the rank variable, paths 1, 3, and 4 all involve one-way causation and imply specific relationships among the magnitudes of the various correlations. For example path 1 implies that the partial correlation between centrality and influence, controlling for conformity, should be approximately zero. Path 4 implies that the partial correlation between centrality and influence, con-

---

[28] *Ibid.*, p. 31.

[29] Hopkins is of course aware that such discussions of pairs of relationships are inadequate, but it is difficult to go much further than this with verbally formulated theories. Much of his discussion in Chap. 3 is concerned with the empirical evidence bearing on the relationships among the five variables, taken two at a time.

[30] *Ibid.*, pp. 83–84.

24 Axioms and Theorems

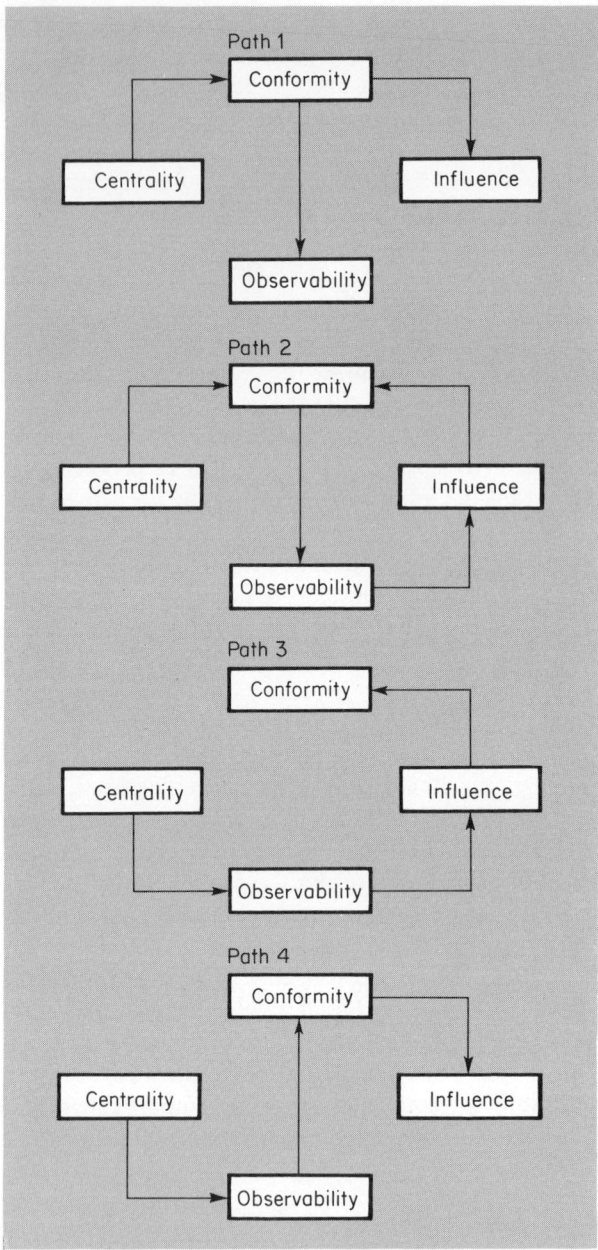

FIG. 2-4 Alternative paths from centrality to influence. (Adapted by permission of the publisher from T. K. Hopkins, *The Exercise of Influence in Small Groups, op. cit.*, pp. 83–84.)

trolling for *either* observability or conformity, should be zero. Path 2, on the other hand, involves a feedback relationship from conformity to observability, and from observability back to conformity via influence. In such a case, it would be difficult to assess empirically the relative magnitudes of the various links. How, then, would one go about sorting out these various possibilities? Hopkins implies that the answer is not simple, and he is correct in this assessment, as we shall see in Chap. 4.

This merely illustrates a very general problem that one encounters in the process of constructing really *testable* theories involving complex models. It is a relatively simple matter to draw in a double-headed arrow indicating reciprocal causation. Likewise, one may insert arrows feeding back to the original "independent" variable (e.g., rank). But it is another matter to test these theories in a definitive way. To be sure, certain models may imply that all relationships should be positive (or negative). But how does one then obtain information as to what is causing what in the process?

A simple answer would be that one merely makes use of experimental designs or collects data at a number of different points in time, noting the time sequences involved. But with values of variables changing more or less continuously, it turns out that the theory must be refined a good deal before estimates of the several components, or causal paths, can be obtained. While it is not within the scope of this short book to discuss questions of design and analysis—which become very technical in this instance—it is necessary to indicate what will be required of a theory of this sort in order to state it in testable form. This will involve a somewhat technical discussion of identification problems and dynamic theory formulation, to be treated in Chaps. 4–6.

There is an additional problem with Hopkins' explicit model, as given in Fig. 2-3. Since all causal relationships are assumed to be positive, and since there is therefore what is termed "positive feedback," one would naturally wonder whether the system could ever reach stability. Suppose, for example, that individual A starts with a high rank. Then this should increase his centrality, and therefore his observability and conformity. In turn, these should increase his influence, which will further increase his rank and therefore centrality. Presumably, then, his rank and influence might increase beyond all limits. Similarly, if individual B starts with a low rank, the positive feedback should operate to decrease his influence and therefore his rank. The group might then contain only persons with extremely high or low ranks and influences. Of course most small groups do not operate this way. Under most conditions, interaction situations tend to stabilize at some equilibrium point until there is a disturbance from an outside influence. But how can this be represented in the formal theory involving only these five variables?

Here we are concerned with the more general problem of developing theories which are truly dynamic, and which involve the time factor in some essential way. Such dynamic formulations enable the theorist to specify the conditions under which a stable equilibrium can be expected, as well as those for which instability may result. Furthermore, they provide a basis for predicting how a stable equilibrium position should shift whenever the group is exposed to "exogenous shocks" or outside influences that affect one or more of the variables.

Dynamic models virtually require mathematical formulations in order to imply definitive predictions. While it is not necessary for every theorist to be mathematically trained, it is at least advisable that he be aware of both the possibilities and limitations afforded by mathematical formulations. Such a knowledge should make it easier for persons to construct verbal theories that can be relatively easily translated into mathematical language with minimal confusion and ambiguity.

Before turning our attention to the formulation of dynamic models it is necessary to address ourselves to the question of what strategies can be used in moving from verbal to mathematical formulations (Chap. 3), and to the general problem of estimating parameters in simultaneous equations involving reciprocal causation and feedback (Chap. 4). The theory of influence proposed by Hopkins provides an excellent illustration of the complications introduced in such models.

3

Recasting Verbal Theories as Causal Models

Given the ideal of constructing a deductive theory, we must face squarely the difficult problem of specifying a set of concrete steps that may be taken in this direction. The kinds of verbal theories that now predominate in the social sciences seem much too complex to allow for mathematical formulation. Or are they simply too vague? Certainly it is not the abstractness of these verbal theories that prevents their formalization, since mathematics is the ultimate in abstract languages. Abstractness may inhibit the empirical testing of theories, but not their statement in mathematical language. More relevant, perhaps, is the complexity of existing theories, and the very large number of variables they contain.

The careful reworking of verbal theories is undoubtedly one of the most challenging tasks confronting us. The major portion of this enterprise will undoubtedly consist of clarifying concepts, eliminating or consolidating variables, translating existing verbal theories into common languages, searching the literature for propositions, and looking for implicit assumptions connecting the major propositions in important theoretical works. The final translation into formal mathematics, and the actual use of mathematical reasoning, would seem to be a relatively simpler task that can be performed by a smaller group of specialists. The more difficult prior task can be accomplished by social scientists without such technical training, provided there is an awareness of both the potentialities and limitations of mathematical formulations of different types. One of the major purposes of this book is to convey such an awareness in a nontechnical manner. But it is also necessary to consider the prior task of improving our verbal theories.

It seems much easier to discuss the formal properties of a deductive system than to provide specific guidelines that have practical value in the process of theory construction. Thus far, in sociology at least, we do not have enough good examples of reasonably systematic verbal theories to give useful insights. As more such examples are provided, it should become possible to make suggestions that are increasingly specific and therefore more useful. My own personal experiences working in a field (minority-group relations) containing very little systematic theory have been mainly based on trial-and-error methods. Since I have attempted to set forth elsewhere a rather general strategy of attack appropriate for such situations, I shall here assume that the situation is somewhat more favorable.[1]

Let us suppose that one is dealing with a substantive area in which there are several major theoretical works, though it is highly likely that these will involve different sets of concepts or variables, and quite different theoretical orientations and underlying assumptions. Also suppose that the field contains a number of empirical findings that bear reasonably directly on the validity of a series of rather disconnected theoretical propositions. If these conditions hold, the field will undoubtedly be characterized by theoretical disputes, in which the authors seem to be talking past one another, and a wide variety of attempts to develop conceptual schemes. There will also probably be a much larger number of concepts or variables than can reasonably be used in any single deductive theory. If the field is at all abstract or general, there will likely be a considerable gap between the concepts thought to be "basic" and the indicators used in empirical research. I believe that this state of affairs can be said to exist in many, if not most, of the substantive fields of sociology. I would be surprised if it did not also characterize many of the substantive fields within the other social sciences.

In a very general way, the obvious starting point under such circumstances is a careful reading of the literature, combined with a systematic listing of all important concepts or variables and theoretical propositions linking these variables. Unless this is being carried out by a large team of social scientists, it will probably not be feasible also to conduct a systematic study of the

---

[1] H. M. Blalock, *Toward a Theory of Minority-Group Relations* (New York: John Wiley & Sons, Inc., 1967).

research findings in order to evaluate the evidence for or against each of the propositions, as this will be a highly time-consuming task. Nor will it be feasible to search through every work in the field purporting to be theoretical. At this stage, comprehensiveness is obviously an impossible ideal.

As variables and propositions are collected, and as consolidation is being attempted, it should be possible to construct a causal diagram consisting of the major variables plus the presumed linkages among these variables. Such a diagram may contain additional information, such as the signs of the predicted relationships or the code number of the specific proposition that relates a given pair of variables. Certain more sophisticated kinds of predictions, such as nonlinearity, nonadditive relationships, or delayed reactions, will be somewhat more difficult to represent diagrammatically, since there is as yet no standard practice in this regard.

Sets of variables may be separated from others into theoretical "blocks," and, where relationships between or within blocks are ambiguous, this can be indicated by means of curved arrows, dashed lines, or other visual devices. As we shall see in the next chapter, such a blocking off of interrelated variables may prove to be a very useful procedure in working with causal formulations, and in making decisions about which variables can safely be ignored in a given empirical analysis. An example of such a diagram is given in Fig. 4-6 of Chap. 4.

As the process of diagramming a particular author's argument is taking place, there will undoubtedly be a number of ambiguities that will arise, some of which may not have been previously noted. Did the author intend that the implied relationship is direct or mediated through some other variable in the system? Is the direction of causality implied? Is there any indication that the predicted relationship is nonlinear? Does the effect take place quickly, or with a lengthy delay? Are other variables introduced as qualifying variables, and if so are these explicitly linked to any other variables in the system?

In asking such questions, one must allow for the possibility that an author's discussion is too vague or ambiguous to permit a definite answer. At this point, one may be tempted to make a thorough search of the author's work to obtain an answer. Such a search may very well prove fruitless, or it may be found that the author has been inconsistent or deliberately ambiguous. At the risk of being accused of professional heresy, I would suggest that in such instances one should forget what the theorist intended—even though he be a very renowned scholar—and that one insert his own theoretical linkages. Otherwise, he may become prematurely immersed in "scholarship," in the worst sense of the term. While it might seem learned to attempt an exhaustive study of Weber's or Durkheim's works in order to ascertain his position on the question, I rather suspect that one might be forced to the conclusion that the theorist had no single position, or that the question never occurred to him.

In the present chapter I would like to focus on a number of specific kinds of situations one can expect to encounter in the sociological literature in the process of attempting to formalize the work of a single author or to integrate propositions collected from diverse sources. The list of situations that follows is obviously incomplete and is based on my own limited experiences, plus those of graduate students who have been assigned this difficult task as a classroom exercise.

Typologies

Many theoretical discussions in sociology involve typologies of various kinds. Usually, although not always, one can find numerous implicit hypotheses buried among the comparisons of the several types, but it is my own observation that typology construction, for some reason, does not lend itself to an explicit focus on propositions and their interrelationships. There is no inherent reason why this must be the case, and the recent treatments of typological analysis by McKinney and Capecchi are certainly compatible with the causal orientation of the present work.[2]

It is not easy to discuss the literature on typologies in a simple manner owing to the variety of different conceptions of typology construction and of types of typologies. The reader is referred to McKinney and Capecchi for more extensive discussion. Capecchi accepts the notion of Lazarsfeld, and of Hempel and Oppenheim, that the essential characteristic of typologies is that they involve a "reduction" of what Lazarsfeld and Barton have called a "property space."[3] That is, one begins with a cross-classification of attributes (or variables), and he selects for emphasis, or as the basis for his typology, only certain of the possible category combinations. In a similar vein, McKinney defines what he calls a "constructed type" as a "purposive, planned selection, abstraction, combination, and (sometimes) accentuation of a set of criteria with empirical referents that serves as a basis for comparison of empirical cases."[4]

[2] See John C. McKinney, *Constructive Typology and Social Theory* (New York: Appleton-Century-Crofts, 1966); and Vittorio Capecchi, "Typologies in Relation to Mathematical Models," *Ikon*, supplementary number 58 (September 1966), 1–62.

[3] *Ibid.*, pp. 1–2. See also Paul F. Lazarsfeld and Allen H. Barton, "Classification, Typologies, and Indices," in *The Policy Sciences*, eds. D. Lerner and H.D. Lasswell (Stanford: Stanford University Press, 1951), pp. 155–92; and C. Hempel and P. Oppenheim, *Der Typusbegriff im Lichte der Neuen Logik* (Leiden: 1936).

[4] McKinney, *Constructive Typology*, p. 3.

This reduction aspect can be illustrated in terms of Merton's well-known typology of deviant behavior, which is as follows:[5]

Pattern	Adaptation to culture goals	Adaptation to institutionalized means
1. Conformity	+	+
2. Innovation	+	−
3. Ritualism	−	+
4. Retreatism	−	−
5. Rebellion	±	±

This typology represents a reduction or simplification in several senses. First we note the fact that there are only two variables underlying the basis for the classification, namely, adaptation to cultural goals (mainly the "success" goal) and adaptation to institutionalized means. Each of these has been dichotomized, a common practice among those who have constructed typologies in sociology. This dichotomization of course represents a gross oversimplification, since it does not recognize that there may be varying degrees of adaptation (including indifference) to both means and ends. McKinney indicates that the rationale for dichotomizing in this manner is often that the theorist wishes to pinpoint the polar types, as in the case of the folk-urban continuum of Redfield.[6] Be this as it may, the reduction of possible types resulting from this procedure may be rather extreme. For example, there are no zero values in Merton's typology.

The other instance of reduction in Merton's scheme has been noted by Capecchi as an example of reduction based neither on empirical frequency distributions nor on mathematical procedures.[7] Merton uses the symbol ± to refer to rebellion, which involves active rejection and substitution of both means and ends. But some individuals might rebel against the goals but accept the means (±, +), or simply reject the goals and rebel against the means (−, ±). There are thus four missing cells in the Merton typology, the remaining two being (+, ±) and (±, −). The question naturally arises as to the basis for this omission. Was it simply not noted, or was the selection purposeful? There may be the implicit hypothesis that certain combinations are incompatible, or at least highly unlikely. This is saying that the variables underlying the basis for the classification are empirically related in a specific

[5] Robert K. Merton, "Social Structure and Anomie," *American Sociological Review*, 2 (October 1938), 672–82.

[6] McKinney, *Constructive Typology*, Chap. 5; see also Robert Redfield, "The Folk Society," *American Journal of Sociology*, 52 (January 1947), 293–308.

[7] Capecchi, "Typologies in Relation to Mathematical Models," pp. 18–21.

manner. This could of course be stated as a theoretical proposition. Another possibility that might be inferred from the lack of zero values in the Merton typology is that neutrality is unstable, and that individuals will eventually move into one of the five (or nine) cells of the table.[8]

The essential strategy one can use in developing propositions and hypotheses from discussions of typologies is well illustrated in Udy's work with Weber's typology of the rational-legal bureaucracy.[9] Udy argues that Weber's typology represents more than a set of analytical categories. In addition it has an historical basis, being an attempt to explain the "spirit" of contemporary Western bureaucratic organizations, which combine bureaucratic features with those of rational planning. Udy suggests that the acceptance of the single "ideal-type" rational bureaucracy has been in large part responsible for the fact that organization theory has had difficulty in accounting for flexibility.

One of the principal values of "ideal types," or what McKinney refers to as "constructed types," is that they provide an abstract model, so that deviations from the extreme or ideal type can be noted and explained. Udy suggests, however, that in the case of organization theory the result has been an extensive, rather atheoretical, literature on "informal organization" to account for departures from the ideal type. Udy's alternative approach is to recast the ideal types as a model by reformulating the underlying dimensions as a set of interrelated variables to be investigated in their own right. Udy considers seven such variables, for which data were available for 150 formal work organizations in nonwestern societies. Because of inadequacies in the data, Udy found it necessary to dichotomize each of the seven variables, which were as follows: (1) hierarchical authority structure; (2) specialized administrative staff; (3) differentiated rewards by office; (4) limited objectives; (5) a performance emphasis; (6) segmental participation; and (7) compensatory rewards.[10]

The first three of these variables (coded simply as present or absent) were taken as indicators of a bureaucratic orientation, whereas the last four were indicators of a rational orientation. Udy found strong positive associations within the first set of three, and within the second set of four variables, but most of the correlations between sets were negative. The existence of a peculiar pattern of intercorrelations of course calls for a theoretical explana-

---

[8] This approach is explicitly used in Amitai Etzioni, *A Comparative Analysis of Complex Organizations* (New York: Free Press of Glencoe, 1961).

[9] Stanley H. Udy, " 'Bureaucracy' and 'Rationality' in Weber's Organization Theory: An Empirical Study," *American Sociological Review*, 24 (December 1959), 791-95.

[10] *Ibid.* Notice that whenever one conceives of relationships among variables, it will always be possible to resort to simple dichotomies if inadequacies in one's data prevent the use of more satisfactory measures.

tion linking the variables in some specific manner. In a separate article, Udy presents a causal model, involving somewhat different variables, given in Fig. 3-1.[11] There is no need to consider this model in further detail. The

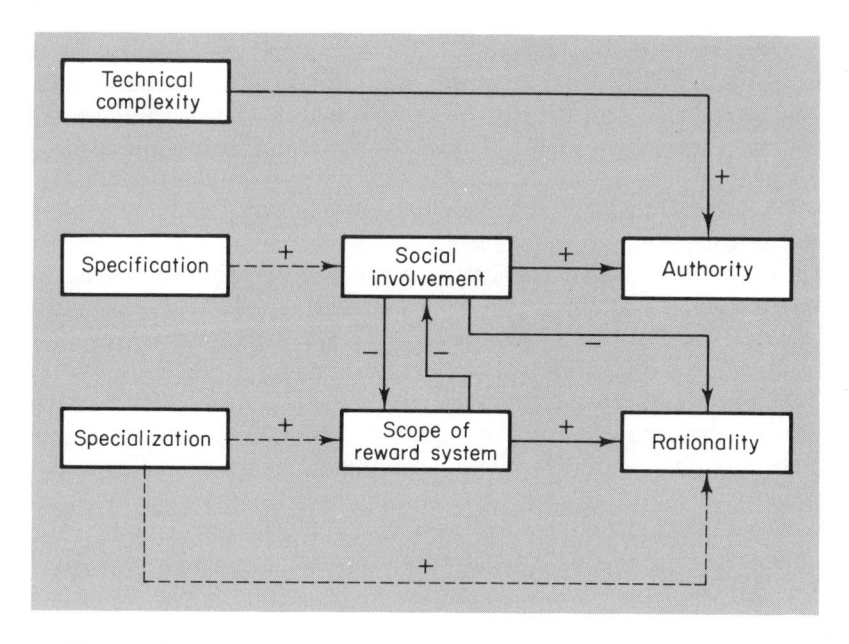

FIG. 3-1 Causal model for bureaucracy variables. (From S. H. Udy, "Technical and Institutional Factors in Production Organization," op. cit.) Note: Dotted lines represent relationships that apply only to complex organizations.

main point emphasized by Udy is that a typological theory, such as Weber's, can be reformulated by explicitly delineating the underlying variables and paying attention to how they are causally interrelated.

McKinney endorses the notion that the typologist should think in terms of continuous variables, as well as dichotomous ones.[12] As already noted, he points out that simple dichotomies are often merely polar types (e.g., folk or urban societies) used to enable the reader to visualize the end points of a continuum. He also claims that there is nothing inherently anti-quantitative in the use of typologies. He notes that historically, however, researchers skilled in the use of typologies have not been statistically or mathematically inclined, and vice versa. This may be one of the reasons for the existing gap between sociological theory and empirical research.

[11] Stanley H. Udy, "Technical and Institutional Factors in Production Organization: A Preliminary Model," *American Journal of Sociology*, 67 (November 1961), 247–54.
[12] McKinney, *Constructive Typology*, Chap. 5.

I would agree with McKinney's position regarding continuous variables and the fact that typological thinking is not at all incompatible with quantitative approaches to theory building. It seems to me that the historical lack of overlap is not mere coincidence, however. When a theorist begins the construction of a particular typology, he will soon recognize that complexities must be introduced. If his approach has been that of using cross-classifications, he will note that the number of cells increases geometrically with the addition of each new variable. Thus if one's typology involves three dichotomies, there will be eight cells. The addition of a fourth dichotomy increases this to sixteen cells, and a fifth to thirty-two possible combinations. This procedure naturally forces the theorist to simplify in two ways: (1) to confine each variable to a dichotomy, and (2) to assume a priori that certain of the combinations can be ignored. In other words, the pressures to oversimplify—prior to the collection of data—become overwhelming. And of course the accentuation of certain subtypes leads to the neglect of others.

Simplifications must of course be introduced at some point in the process of theory construction and in data analysis as well. The principle of stating an abstract "law" in terms of ideal conditions (e.g., a perfect vacuum), and then of examining real deviations of empirical cases, is common to both typological methodology and the regression approach. For example, one may examine the behavior of the residuals, or error terms, noting which cases are above or below the regression curve or surface. This strategy is of course necessary for gaining insights as to the model's inadequacies, and the nature of the variables that should be included to make the model more realistic.

The basic difference between the two approaches seems to be that typological analysis, by reducing the "property space," often *deletes* certain of the possible combinations from consideration. If this is done after an inspection of the empirical frequencies, it can be justified in terms of practical priorities, though not necessarily on theoretical grounds. Also, as already implied, the pressures to dichotomize either introduce unnecessary measurement error, or they result in ignoring intermediate categories, such as the "indifferents" missing from Merton's typology. Though it is not within the scope of the present work to consider problems of measurement error, the tendency to introduce dichotomies on the theoretical level would seem to encourage inadequate measurement, or satisfaction with simple "Yes"–"No" answers and crude categorization.

One major reason why investigators may use a typological approach is that they may suspect the existence of peculiar interaction effects, in which case the simple additive multiple regression approach would be misleading. For example, the combination of bureaucratic traits with rationalistic traits may produce strains in the system that would not be anticipated on the basis of an analysis of either set of traits taken separately. But such a situation can usually be handled by the regression approach by adding interaction terms, or by reformulating the model as multiplicative or some other specific nonadditive type.[13]

Inventories of Causes[14]

Whenever one is focusing on a particular dependent variable, or an interrelated set of dependent variables, the initial result of collecting propositions is likely to be a simple inventory of supposed causes of the dependent variable(s) under consideration. For example, one may decide to collect propositions dealing with the causes of different forms of criminal behavior. A theorist may deal with various causal factors in separate chapters of a book, or an edited volume may contain diverse points of view, with authors stressing the importance of different sets of variables. The result is likely to be an eclectic listing of possible causal factors, with little attention being given to the interrelationships among these factors themselves. The causal model appropriate for this simple situation would be as in Fig. 3-2.

Strictly speaking, this model implies zero total correlations among all of the causes of the dependent variable. If a social scientist were told that this is what his theory implied, he would undoubtedly claim that this is not what he had intended, and that in the interest of simplicity he had not attempted to spell out the relationships among the supposedly independent variables. To a certain extent, such an argument is justifiable, since one must always take certain of the variables in a system as "givens," or as unexplained. We shall later refer to such truly independent variables as "exogenous variables," though it will be necessary to allow for the possibility that exogenous variables are intercorrelated.

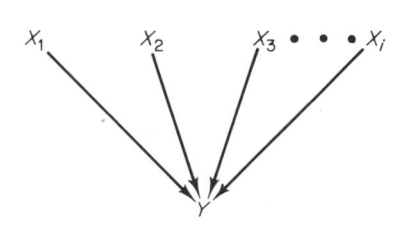

FIG. 3-2 Simple model for inventories of causes.

But the neglect of interrelationships among independent variables seems to be a major source of fruitless debates over the relative importance of one set of variables as compared with another. If one could assume no relation-

---

[13] One very simple approach to interaction is discussed in Appendix A. Admittedly, if there is a very large number of independent variables and higher-order interactions, there may be too many terms in a regression equation to lead to reasonably simple interpretations. In such instances, the kinds of approaches suggested by Capecchi may be more appropriate.

[14] The headings and organizational framework for this and the following two sections were suggested by Zetterberg, *On Theory and Verification*, Chap. 5.

ships among these variables, then relative importance could be assessed by such straightforward procedures as comparing the proportion of the variance in the dependent variable explained by one variable with that explained by a second. But as soon as one allows for the possibility that some of the "independent" variables cause the others, this reasoning breaks down and must be replaced by simultaneous-equation procedures. Therefore, the first thing one should investigate is the question of possible theoretical relationships among the independent variables. Such a practice might also help to resolve disputes in which the issue seems to involve what are sometimes referred to as different "levels" of analysis. For example, one theorist may be dealing with personality factors as explanatory variables, whereas a second may be emphasizing social structural factors.

Even so, there are likely to be a very large number of possible explanatory variables initially collected in this manner. Some must be weeded out, and highly related variables must be combined. As one attempts to conceptualize the factors, he may find that certain variables may be taken as indicators of others, being directly linked to them causally according to an explicit theory. If so, the indicator variables may either be combined into a single index or treated as belonging to a single block of variables. We shall see how these blocks can be interrelated in a meaningful way, provided that one-way causation is assumed between blocks. Such assumptions may justify the omission of specific blocks in particular empirical investigations, and they may also encourage the cumulation of empirical findings by building block upon block, as it were. Since the efficient use of such blocks involves the technical question of the identification of parameters, where there may be too many unknowns for solution, the discussion of this possibility will be deferred until the next chapter.

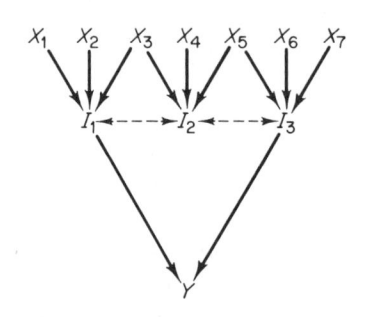

FIG. 3-3 Model with mutually exclusive and exhaustive number of intervening variables.

There appears to be an additional strategy to that of forming blocks of variables, though its implications for theory building remain to be explored. This second strategy is that of attempting to locate a relatively small number of intervening variables, through which *all* of the remaining variables are assumed to operate on the dependent variable under consideration. The general model in this case would be as illustrated in Fig. 3-3, where there are three intervening variables I_1, I_2, and I_3 assumed to be direct causes of the dependent variable Y. Each of these intervening variables might be taken as a dependent variable in its own right, and perhaps one could find an additional set of variables through which all causes of a particular intervening variable must also operate.

This strategy of theory building first came to my attention while studying motivation theory. John W. Atkinson has argued that motivated behavior can be taken as a multiplicative function of three very general kinds of variables: (1) motive strength (an internal force), (2) expectancies, or perceived probabilities of achieving goals, and (3) incentives, or external rewards.[15] Presumably all independent variables must operate through one or more of these three factors.

Several additional examples can be cited involving very different substantive problems. Cloward and Ohlin have combined Merton's emphasis on explaining deviant behavior in terms of the blockage of legitimate goals with Sutherland's stressing that many forms of deviancy require the access to illegitimate opportunities.[16] Palmore and Hammond formalized the argument of Cloward and Ohlin by taking degree of deviance as a multiplicative function of (1) blockage of legitimate opportunities, and (2) access to illegitimate opportunities.[17] They used this model to explain various nonadditive relationships among sex, race, school success, family deviance, and neighborhood deviance, arguing that each of these independent variables operated through either the legitimate or the illegitimate opportunity factor. This example, as well as Atkinson's approach to motivation, is discussed in greater detail in Appendix A.

In an attempt to account for inequalities between members of dominant and minority groups, I have suggested that most if not all independent variables should operate through one of four intervening variables as follows: (1) the resources of the dominant group, (2) minority resources, (3) the degree to which dominant-group resources are actually mobilized in a given direction, and (4) minority mobilization.[18] For example, prejudice toward the minority should affect dominant-group mobilization, but unless factors affecting the relative resources of the two groups are also considered, one cannot explain discriminatory behavior on the basis of prejudice alone.

As a more definitive and clear-cut example, population change is a simple additive function of four variables: birth rates, death rates, and rates of immigration and emigration. The major theoretical task in explaining

---

[15] See John W. Atkinson, *An Introduction to Motivation* (Princeton: D. Van Nostrand Co., Inc., 1964), Chap. 10.

[16] See Richard A. Cloward and Lloyd E. Ohlin, *Delinquency and Opportunity* (New York: Free Press of Glencoe, Inc., 1960); Merton, "Social Structure and Anomie"; and E. H. Sutherland, *White Collar Crime* (New York: The Dryden Press, 1949).

[17] Erdman Palmore and Phillip E. Hammond, "Interacting Factors in Juvenile Delinquency," *American Sociological Review*, 29 (December 1964), 848–54.

[18] H. M. Blalock, *Minority-Group Relations*, Chap. 4.

population change is that of finding the determinants of each of these intervening variables.

As a final illustration, let us consider a study by Nye, White, and Frideres, which combines the strategy of locating a small number of intervening variables with that of searching the literature for interrelated propositions.[19] These authors searched the marriage and family literature for propositions relating to family stability. They began their theoretical analysis with 68 propositions, most of which involved family stability (or similar concepts, such as divorce or separation) as a dependent variable. The authors found that the independent variables were extremely diverse and involved different levels of abstraction. They therefore reduced the number of propositions to ten (in the case of their Model A) by redefining these variables under more general labels. In effect, they thus obtained a set of more abstract independent variables, for which certain of the original variables might be considered indicators. Their list of ten propositions was as follows:

1. The greater the positive affect balance within the marriage, the greater the likelihood of marital stability.
2. The more severe the anticipated sanctions, the greater the likelihood of marital stability.
3. The greater the task interdependency, the more likely the stability of the marriage.
4. The more effective the role performances of the spouse, the more likely the positive affect balance toward the spouse.
5. The greater the congruence of values and role perceptions, the more likely the positive affect.
6. The more negative the attitudes toward divorce held by reference groups, the more severe the anticipated negative sanctions.
7. The more inadequate the alternative supports for spouse and children, the more severe the anticipated sanctions against dissolution.
8. The more effective the role performance, the more likely the task interdependency.
9. The larger the number of dependent children in the family, the more likely the task interdependency.
10. The fewer the perceived satisfactory alternative spouses, the greater the task interdependency.[20]

---

[19] F. Ivan Nye, Lynn White, and James Frideres, "A Preliminary Theory of Marital Stability: Two Models," unpublished manuscript. A revised version of this paper (involving a somewhat different model), titled "A Preliminary Theory of Marital Dissolution," was read at the annual meeting of the American Sociological Association (Boston, August 1968).

[20] *Ibid.* Quoted by permission of the authors.

Nye, White, and Frideres then argued that each of the independent variables should operate through one or more of the following three intervening variables: (1) affect balance, (2) task interdependency, and (3) severity of anticipated sanctions. Their argument was diagrammed as in Fig. 3-4.

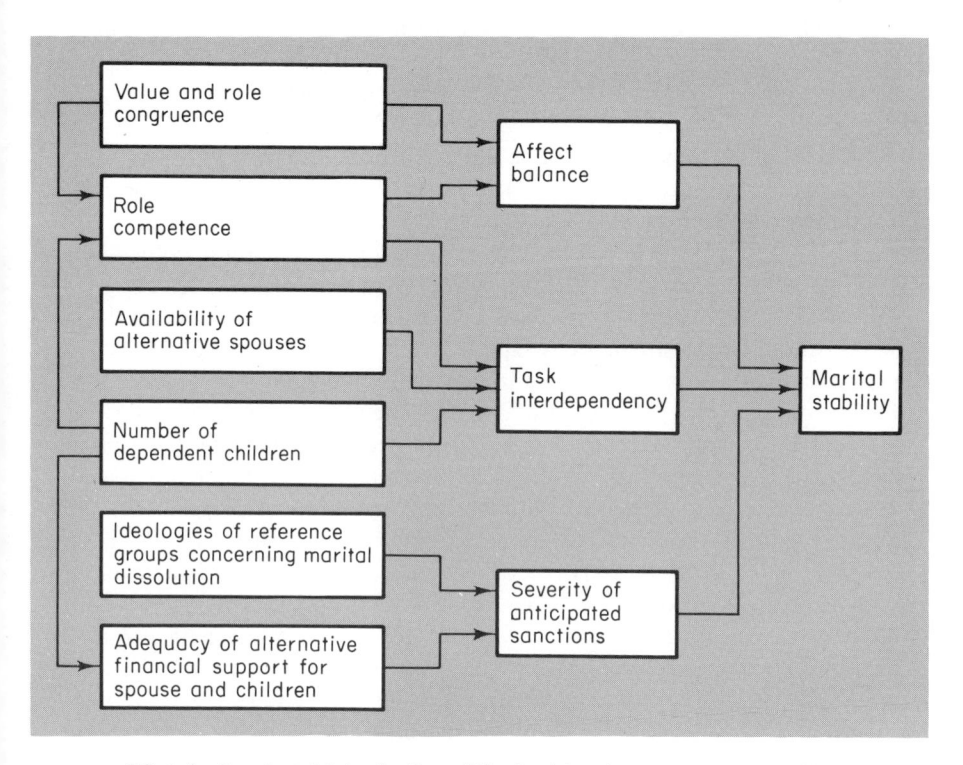

FIG. 3-4 Causal model for family stability involving three intervening variables. (From Nye, White, and Frideres, "A Preliminary Theory of Marital Stability: Two Models," op. cit. Used by permission of the authors.)

Thus the original 68 propositions were reduced to 10, and a relatively simple causal model was used to simplify what might have otherwise seemed a hopelessly miscellaneous set of propositions.

Several comments about this overall strategy are necessary. First, the procedure gives a kind of checklist against the possibility of omitting certain major variables. For example, one might tend to neglect those independent variables affecting task interdependency or, in the case of minority relations, those that could affect minority resources. Second, it provides a rationale for delimiting one's research or theoretical objectives. Thus a particular investigator might elect to study only those independent variables expected to influence task interdependency, knowing that his findings could then be integrated with those of others studying the other intervening variables.

If one expected complex interrelationships among the intervening variables, he could formulate a dynamic theory involving reciprocal causation and feedback among them. Such a theory might involve only these intervening variables plus the dependent variable, thereby simplifying the picture considerably. The various independent variables could then be taken as "exogenous" variables that could be used to help estimate the parameters of the theory in a manner that will be indicated in the following chapter. In a given piece of research, only a relatively small number of these exogenous variables might be measured.

Finally, any peculiarities in the relationships among the intervening variables, or between these variables and the dependent variable, can be used to provide indirect tests in instances where the intervening variables themselves cannot be measured. For example, if one takes degree of deviance as a multiplicative function of the two intervening opportunity variables, and if one then links each of the several independent variables with only one intervening variable, then it is possible to predict interaction effects whenever independent variables affecting different intervening variables are combined. Thus if race affects access to legitimate opportunities, while neighborhood deviance affects access to illegitimate opportunities, there should be a nonadditive effect of these two independent variables on deviance. But if school success, like race, affects access to legitimate opportunities, and if both of these variables have additive effects on this single intervening variable, then one would expect school success and race to have simple additive effects on deviance. This approach is illustrated in greater detail in Appendix A.

There is at least one major potential disadvantage of attempting to locate a small number of inclusive and yet mutually exclusive intervening variables. The variables selected may be highly abstract, or extremely general, so that the measurement of these variables becomes very indirect. The measurement of motive strength, perceived probabilities, and incentives is indeed difficult, as is the measurement of mobilization and amount of resources. If so, the tests of the resulting theoretical formulations will have to be indirect. For example, if the intervening variables cannot be directly measured, how can one determine which independent variables are linked to each? The indirect testing of these formulations may therefore have to depend on peculiarities, such as multiplicative relationships. However, as suggested in Appendix A, this theoretical strategy can at least provide useful guides in the search for additional independent variables, as well as a framework for organizing one's propositions.

Inventories of Effects

If an author is attempting to show that a particular variable has multiple consequences and therefore that it is worthy of attention as an independent variable, the result is likely to be a causal diagram that looks very much like Fig. 3-5. For example, Janowitz has pointed to various consequences of vertical mobility, and Lenski has emphasized the importance of the "religious factor" as an independent variable.[21] In such instances, the theorist is not likely to be concerned with the additional causes of each of the dependent variables or with other possible interrelationships among the dependent variables. Therefore the theory is likely to be left in a form similar to the diagram of Fig. 3-5, in which there is a simple "fanning out" from the independent variable of interest.

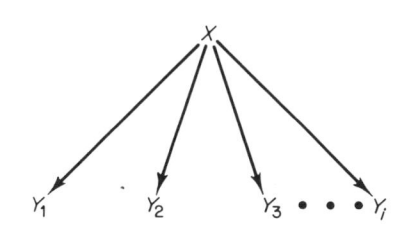

FIG. 3-5 Simple model for inventories of effects.

This approach to theory building is highly useful in pointing to neglected independent variables that need to be taken into consideration in diverse fields of investigation, but it obviously will not lead to more detailed analysis, unless it is supplemented by additional theoretical arguments linking the several dependent variables. If it can be assumed that there are, in fact, no other common sources of variation among the dependent variables, then the model of Fig. 3-5 justifies the use of factor analysis to provide a measure of the independent variable.[22] That is, the factor loadings for this single factor may be used as weights, and the dependent variables may be taken as indicators that can be combined into a single overall index. But if some of the supposedly dependent variables were taken as causes of the others, so that the network of interrelationships became much more complex, then the rationale for factor analysis would break down.[23]

---

[21] See Morris Janowitz, "Some Consequences of Social Mobility in the United States," *Transactions of the Third World Congress of Sociology*, 3 (1965), 191–201; and Gerhard E. Lenski, *The Religious Factor* (New York: Doubleday & Company, Inc., 1961).

[22] Factor analysis has been most fruitfully applied in the area of attitude measurement, where this kind of assumption seems reasonably justified. See Harry H. Harmon, *Modern Factor Analysis* (Chicago: University of Chicago Press, 1960).

[23] It will be recalled that factor analysis requires the assumption that the residual matrix can be reduced to zero with the extraction of successive factors, since all of the common variance among the dependent variables can be accounted for by these factors. But if some of the "dependent" variables cause the others, this assumption is obviously invalid. If the variables within a block are highly intercorrelated, and if no attempt is being made to sort

An interesting theoretical situation results from the combination of a simple inventory of causes with a simple inventory of effects. The resulting model would be as in Fig. 3-6. Such a double inventory might have been obtained from two separate theoretical works, one of which emphasized the causes of a given phenomenon, say urbanization, and the second its consequences. Perhaps a single author may have developed two such lists in two separate chapters. Again, if the theorists were actually confronted with such a diagram, they would probably claim that it was much too simple, and that other causal connections had been deliberately neglected. An advantage of diagramming one's arguments is, of course, that the figure immediately points to an overly simplified theory and suggests the need for elaboration.

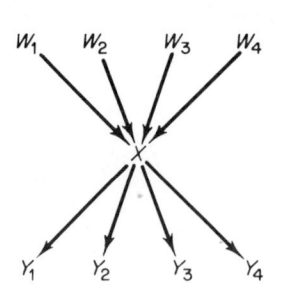

FIG. 3-6 Model combining inventory of causes with inventory of effects.

If the model of Fig. 3-6 did, in fact, seem realistic as a first approximation, then it would be possible to combine the indicators (both causes and effects) in relatively simple ways to obtain a single measure of the central variable X. The rationale for canonical correlation would appear to be appropriate for this model, though its implications remain to be explored.[24] In brief, the method of canonical correlation provides a way of weighting both the set of independent variables W_i and the dependent variables Y_i so as to maximize the ability to explain variation in the weighted Y's by means of the weighted W's. I have never been convinced of the theoretical value of canonical correlation, which on the surface seems to involve a blind empirical approach of maximizing explained variance, but the implications of this approach need to be explored in the case of models of this particular type.

It may turn out that the kind of model given in Fig. 3-6 will be most appropriate in instances where X represents either some highly abstract concept, such as "anomie," or a name given to an entire block or syndrome of highly interrelated variables, such as urbanization and industrialization. If so, then the measurement of X will be of paramount importance, and the implications of canonical correlation (or factor analysis) should be explored. Should the appropriate models turn out to be more complex, with additional

---

out their relative contributions to a set of dependent variables, then factor analysis may be used as an empirical device for combining them into a single index to represent the block.

[24] For further comments on the use of canonical correlation see Travis Hirschi and Hanan C. Selvin, *Delinquency Research* (New York: Free Press, 1967), pp. 170–71.

connections among the variables, then such a relatively simple procedure should not be used unless its implications have been fully explored. There seems to be a considerable temptation in the social sciences to employ new methodological techniques before they are adequately understood, and this temptation might be unusually strong in instances where the central variable X is a highly important but complex notion, such as urbanization or anomie.

It should be noted that in the case of linear additive relationships, one can make a simple test of the adequacy of the model of Fig. 3-6 even where X is taken as unmeasured. If we write the equation for X as follows:

$$X = a + b_1 W_1 + b_2 W_2 + \cdots + b_k W_k + u_x$$

and if each of the dependent variables Y_i is written as

$$Y_i = a_i + c_i X + u_i$$
$$= a_i + c_i(a + b_1 W_1 + b_2 W_2 + \cdots + b_k W_k) + (u_i + c_i u_x)$$

we immediately see that the coefficients for the several Y_i regressed on the W_j will be proportional. That is, the coefficients for Y_1 will be simple multiples of the coefficients for Y_2, Y_3, and so forth. If these relationships actually hold, and if there are at least three W's and three Y's, the model of Fig. 3-6 would seem highly appropriate in view of the improbability of finding simple alternative explanations for these proportional coefficients. I rather suspect, however, that a model such as that of Fig. 3-6 is more useful for heuristic purposes than as an adequate representation of the real world. Nevertheless, it could be a good starting point for more complex elaborations.

Simple Chains and Loops

As previously noted in Chap. 2, many verbal theories take the form of simple chains in which W leads to (or causes) X, which then leads to Y, and finally to Z. It will usually be found that an author will likewise attempt to identify a few additional causes of each factor. Perhaps he will also list some *conditions* under which the relationship is likely to be strengthened or weakened, thus implying the existence of statistical interaction.[25] A simple chain model can be diagrammed as in Fig. 3-7, in which the side arrows represent these additional variables.

Our previous discussion of these simple chains dealt with the fact that the

---

[25] Strictly speaking, interaction is measured in terms of differences among slopes, rather than in terms of differences among correlations or degrees of relationships. This kind of distinction is seldom made in verbal theories.

correlations will ordinarily become increasingly attenuated the further two variables are removed from each other in the causal sequence. This of course means that unless all intermediate correlations are extremely high, one cannot use simple deductive arguments about the signs of total correlations, unless one is willing to make certain assumptions regarding the behavior of the variables summarized by the side arrows. Here we shall be more concerned with the question of how one goes about elaborating such a simple chain.

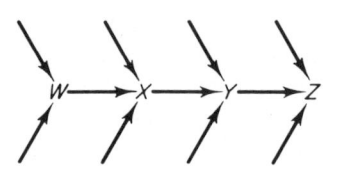

FIG. 3-7 A simple causal chain.

The first task is that of explicitly identifying the additional factors that may affect each of the variables in the causal sequence. Then one must ask whether it is realistic to assume that each of these additional factors is unrelated to variables antecedent to it in the chain. Suppose we are dealing with an additional cause of Y, which can be labeled V for convenience. Either W or X could be a direct (or indirect) cause of V, as indicated in Fig. 3-8. In this case there are two paths from W to Y, and the sign of the

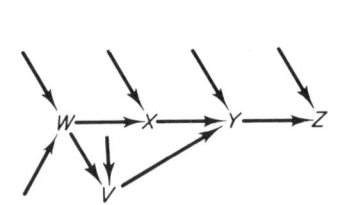

FIG. 3-8 A modified causal chain, with V an intervening variable between W and Y.

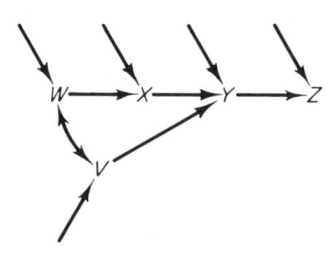

FIG. 3-9 A modified causal chain, with unspecified causal connections between W and V.

total correlation r_{wy} would depend on the signs of both paths and the relative magnitudes of the coefficients.

Another empirical possibility may be that W and V are *correlated*, but for unknown reasons. If this correlation is thought to be spurious (i.e., due to common causes of W and V), an attempt should be made to specify the variable or variables responsible for this spuriousness, bringing them into the theoretical model if possible. If this cannot be done, one can indicate that there is an unexplained association between W and V by drawing in a curved double-headed arrow, as in Fig. 3-9. The method of path coefficients (see Chap. 2, n. 24) can be used to obtain measures for the relative importance of the two separate paths from W. One may then obtain an answer to the following question: If V were to remain constant, how much of the variation in Y could be explained by W, assuming that W varied by the same amount as before?

Because of the ambiguity in the relationship between W and V, however, one cannot answer another kind of important question. For practical as well as theoretical reasons, one might like to know what change in Y would be produced by a given change in W, allowing for the fact that V might also be changed. But since we do not know whether W affects V, V affects W, both, or neither, we cannot say anything about how V would behave, given the change in W. In other words, we cannot assess the total impact of the influence of W on Y.

If a theorist has claimed that the several links in the chain will be strengthened or weakened by the operation of other variables, such as V, then he may be implying that there should be interaction or nonadditive effects that must be taken into consideration.[26] If so, one should attempt to clarify the nature of the variables involved. For example, the theorist may have merely indicated that the relationship holds only for European cultures or for the eighteenth century. If so, one would have to ask why this should be the case. Perhaps the theorist is simply being cautious, not wishing to generalize beyond the limits of his data. In this case, he is not implying interaction but merely ignorance of other contexts. But if he claims certain peculiarities of eighteenth-century Europe, then these can probably be stated in terms of specific variables, thus serving as a stimulus for further research.

Having identified the variables involved in the interaction, one can then attempt to formulate mathematical models which are reasonably simple alternatives to the kinds of additive relationships we shall study throughout the remaining portions of this book. For example, if the theorist indicates that certain geographical factors operate as necessary conditions for economic development, but that they are not sufficient, then a multiplicative model may be suggested. The essential idea is that *several* factors must be present to some degree before the phenomenon can occur. In the case of variables V and W this would suggest trying a simple function of the form $Y = kVW$, or perhaps $Y - c = kV^a W^b$, which also allows for the possibility that either a or b can be negative, and hence either V or W may be divided by the other variable. As indicated in Appendix A, such a nonadditive relationship can be tested indirectly even where measurement has been extremely crude. For example, where all variables have been dichotomized, interaction effects can be measured as a difference of differences in proportions.[27]

[26] This possibility of interaction is not conveyed in Fig. 3-8, however.
[27] See Leo Goodman, "Modifications of the Dorn-Stouffer-Tibbetts Methods for 'Testing the Significance of Comparisons in Sociological Data'," *American Journal of Sociology*, 66 (January 1961), 355–59.

Causal loops

As we saw in the case of the Hopkins theory of influence, a seemingly simple modification of the causal chain argument involves the addition of an arrow drawn from the last variable back to the first, indicating a feedback in the system. For example, an author who is arguing that changes in technology lead to a sequence of changes in other variables may recognize that technology, itself, will be affected by these other factors. He may indicate this by drawing in an arrow back to technology, or by at least suggesting that the other variables directly or indirectly feed back to technology.

The first thing to investigate in such instances is whether or not such a simple closed loop is really implied. For example, the initial formulation may be similar to that given in Fig. 3-10, in which there is no more than one (explicitly identified) cause of each variable, and where the last variable in the chain feeds back to the first. But such a simple formulation may not actually be the one that was intended by the theorist. Perhaps he wishes to imply that *each* variable feeds back directly to the first (e.g., technology). Or he may imply that there are several different feedback loops instead of just one.

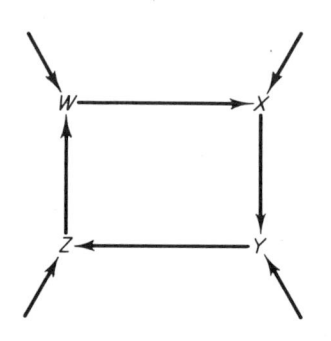

FIG. 3-10 A simple causal loop.

This apparently simple introduction of a feedback process creates a host of theoretical and empirical estimation problems, as we noted in the case of the Hopkins model. Therefore if the feedback effect is thought to be very minor, or so delayed that it can be ignored in short-run analyses, then it should undoubtedly be omitted in the interest of simplicity. The theoretical temptation is to make one's theory seem as complete as possible by drawing in arrows, or specifying relationships, even where the effects are thought to be relatively minor. As we shall see in the next chapter, however, this may produce a theoretical system in which there are too many unknowns for solution.

Nevertheless, if feedback and reciprocal causation are thought to operate in a major way, then realistic theories must incorporate these processes, even at the expense of complicating the testing and estimation procedures. As long as the model involves only one-way causation, without simultaneous feedback, so that one may use what are referred to as "recursive" systems, analysis is relatively straightforward. I say "relatively" because there will always be problems produced by imperfect measurement, nonadditivity or nonlinearity, and by the failure of omitted variables to behave as assumed. Since analysis problems in connection with one-way causation have been dealt with elsewhere, we shall not be concerned with them in the remainder of this book.[28]

The following chapter is concerned with special types of difficulties that arise whenever one wishes to estimate parameters in these causal loop models allowing for reciprocal causation and feedback. We shall see that considerable methodological sophistication is needed to formulate and test these more complex theories.

[28] See H. M. Blalock, *Causal Inferences*, and *Methodology in Social Research*, eds. Blalock and Blalock, Chap. 5.

4

Static Formulations and Identification Problems

In connection with the discussion of the possibility that the whole is greater than the sum of its parts, it was pointed out that one way in which the real world may not be "addable" is that individual equations may not be separable. In the present chapter we shall examine more carefully just what this statement means. Two questions need to be answered. First, under what special conditions is one justified in delimiting his analysis to a relatively small number of variables and a reasonable number of simultaneous equations? Second, whenever one cannot separate a given equation from a set of additional equations, what complications does this produce and how can the data be analyzed?

There are certain relatively simple models for which each equation can be analyzed separately and the results then recombined in order to give theoretical interpretations. These are what are referred to as "recursive" systems in which there is one-way causation and for which relatively simple assumptions about error terms can be made. These systems permit no feedback relationships or reciprocal causation between two or more variables.[1] That

---

[1] As we shall see in Chap. 5, an exception can be made to this statement in the case of dynamic models involving lagged variables.

is, if X_i is assumed to be a direct or indirect cause of X_j, then X_j cannot be a direct or indirect cause of X_i. By properly organizing the variables, one may write a linear additive recursive system in the form

$$X_1 = u_1$$

$$X_2 = b_{21}X_1 + u_2$$

$$X_3 = b_{31}X_1 + b_{32}X_2 + u_3$$

$$\vdots$$

$$X_k = b_{k1}X_1 + b_{k2}X_2 + \cdots + b_{k,k-1}X_{k-1} + u_k$$

(4-1)

where the u_i represent error terms. The constant terms have been omitted, without loss of generality, since one can assume that all X_i have been measured about their respective means and that the u_i also have expected values of zero.[2]

As we shall later note, even recursive systems are not simple to handle unless one can make the proper assumptions about the error terms u_i. In fact, the same sort of "identification problems" that will be discussed in the next section will also arise in recursive systems unless one puts restrictions on the behavior of the u's. In order for least-squares estimates to be unbiased estimates of the slope coefficients in the above set of equations, one must assume that the error term in any given equation is uncorrelated with all of the *independent* variables in that equation. This implies that the error terms in one equation are uncorrelated with the error terms in any other equation.[3] It is often also assumed that there is no "autocorrelation," or serial correlation among the errors for the various cases or individual X_i in any single equation. More will be said about these assumptions at a later point.

Such recursive systems might seem overly simplistic from the standpoint of building adequate theoretical models of complex reality. I am convinced, however, that most of the analysis procedures currently used in sociology and

[2] The notion of "recursiveness" is essentially that the equations can be built up and analyzed step by step. That is, one can study the second equation, then move to the third, to the fourth, and so forth. In the more general case, this will not be possible.

[3] For example: if u_3 is uncorrelated with X_1 and X_2, it must be uncorrelated with u_2 because $u_2 = X_2 - b_{21}X_1$ is an exact linear function of X_1 and X_2: $E(u_3u_2) = E[u_3(X_2 - b_{21}X_1)] = E(u_3X_2) - b_{21}E(u_3X_1) = 0$. If one starts imposing additional zero restrictions (that some of the $b_{ij} = 0$) on a recursive model, however, this particular implication may break down. For discussions of these and related assumptions see Franklin M. Fisher, *The Identification Problem in Econometrics* (New York: McGraw-Hill Book Company, 1966), pp. 93–97; and Herman Wold and Lars Jureen, *Demand Analysis* (New York: John Wiley & Sons, Inc., 1953), Chap. 2.

political science are based on such models, though this is often not explicitly realized. For example, whenever one uses statistical controls, it is presumed that he is not controlling for a dependent variable. In most experimental designs the investigator manipulates one or more independent variables and ignores the possibility of feedback. Similarly, in sample surveys one does not ordinarily stratify by dependent variables—or if he does so he is likely to reach misleading conclusions. While these questions are beyond the scope of the present work, it is nevertheless important to recognize our methodological dependence on these simple recursive models.[4]

Furthermore, in the absence of accurate measurements and carefully formulated theories, recursive models would seem to give useful first approximations to more adequate theories. In many instances it may be assumed that the amount of feedback, or reciprocal causation, is negligible. In other words, the predominant effects may run in a single direction. Likewise, certain kinds of feedbacks may be sufficiently delayed so that they can be ignored in short-run change studies. Nevertheless, it is advantageous to look ahead to the future development of theories that are less restrictive. For this reason it is essential to anticipate the complications that will arise in connection with the verification process. Fortunately, these situations have been well studied by econometricians.

For illustrative purposes we shall first turn to an example of the kinds of empirical estimation problems that have occurred in the case of supply and demand analysis. It will be seen that unless a theory involves a number of a priori restrictions there will ordinarily be too many unknowns for solution. Put another way, there will be infinitely many sets of possible parameter values that can all generate the same empirical data, making it impossible to obtain unique estimates of the true "structural parameters" that represent underlying reality.

Identification of Supply and Demand Equations

Consider a simple theory in which both quantity supplied Q_s and quantity demanded Q_d are conceived as caused by prices P according to the equations

$$Q_s = a_1 + b_1 P \qquad (4\text{-}2a)$$

$$Q_d = a_2 - b_2 P \qquad (4\text{-}2b)$$

where both b's are taken as positive and where the error term is neglected.

[4] See H. M. Blalock, *Causal Inferences*, Chaps. 3 and 4.

This means that both equations are exact, with all points lying precisely on the lines. Of course more general nonlinear functions might have been used, and under certain conditions the slope of the supply function might have also been taken as negative.[5]

Now suppose that the system settles down quickly to a stable equilibrium point, at which the quantity supplied is approximately equal to the quantity demanded. In this case one might replace Q_s and Q_d by a single value Q, and we would have the apparent paradox that Q and P would be related by *two* equations instead of one. Actually, however, there would only be a single point (Q_0, P_0) that would satisfy both equations simultaneously. This is the equilibrium point represented by the intersection of the two lines, as indicated in Fig. 4-1. If there were no other factors affecting any of the quantities in

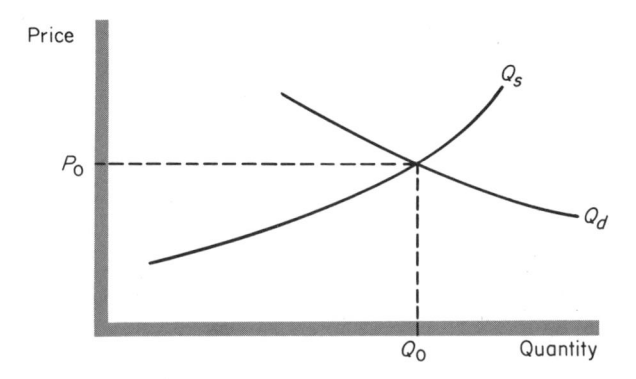

FIG. 4-1 A single equilibrium at the intersection of supply and demand functions.

these equations, one would expect that the system would settle down to this single equilibrium point and remain there indefinitely. Actually, this is not strictly implied in the above two equations, which are not formulated in dynamic terms, but we shall postpone consideration of this particular point. One could say, however, that if a stable equilibrium were attained, the equilibrium values of quantity and price would be given by the intersection of these curves.[6]

---

[5] After reading Chaps. 4 and 5, the interested reader may wish to refer to a discussion of the peculiar implications for stability produced by these downward-sloping supply functions in William J. Baumol, *Economic Dynamics* (New York: The Macmillan Company, 1959), pp. 118–22.

[6] For more detailed discussions of stability in supply and demand functions see Baumol, *op. cit.;* Carl F. Christ, *Econometric Models and Methods* (New York: John Wiley & Sons, Inc., 1966), Chaps. 5 and 6; and Paul A. Samuelson, *Foundations of Economic Analysis* (Cambridge, Mass.: Harvard University Press, 1947).

52 Static Formulations and Identification Problems

How should such curves be interpreted? We imagine a group of suppliers who determine Q_s by moving along the supply function Q_s, supplying a quantity of goods appropriate to a particular price. In other words, if we take the supply function as given, then Q_s is determined by P. The same is true for the behavior of consumers, who determine Q_d according to the price by moving along the demand curve. If there is to be an equilibrium point for which $Q_s = Q_d$, then in a free market economy this must occur where the two curves intersect.

Suppose, however, that both the supply and demand *functions* shift because of variation in other factors not represented in the above pair of equations. Then there will not only be movement along the supply and demand functions, but changes in these functions themselves. Consider three time periods t_0, t_1, and t_2. Suppose both supply and demand functions shift as indicated in Fig. 4-2. The equilibrium prices will also shift and can be

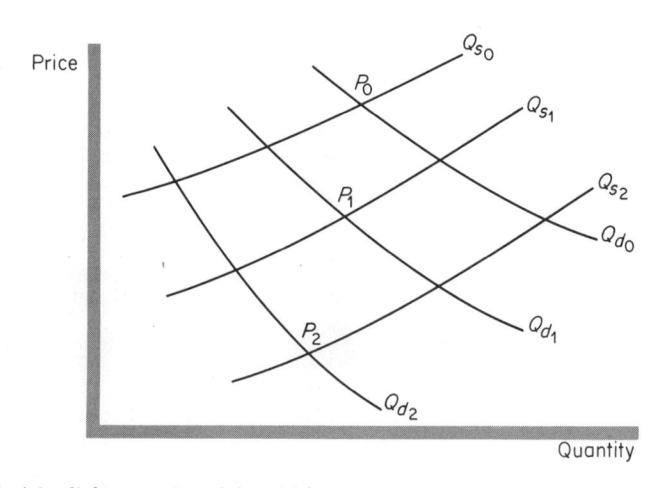

FIG. 4-2 Shifting supply and demand functions producing multiple equilibrium points.

represented as P_0, P_1, and P_2, respectively. There will of course also be three corresponding values of Q, namely Q_0, Q_1, and Q_2.

Let us imagine that time-series data on prices and quantity of goods exchanged have been obtained over a period of time. One could then plot the relationship between Q and P in an attempt to determine either the demand or supply function empirically. Actually, one would obtain a hybrid function, however, as suggested by the three intersection points in Fig. 4-2. To make the situation more clear, we might represent a large number of intersection points at times t_0, t_1, t_2, . . . , as indicated in Fig. 4-3. The general point is that empirical data will be insufficient to identify the true supply and demand functions since the data are assumed to represent a series of equilib-

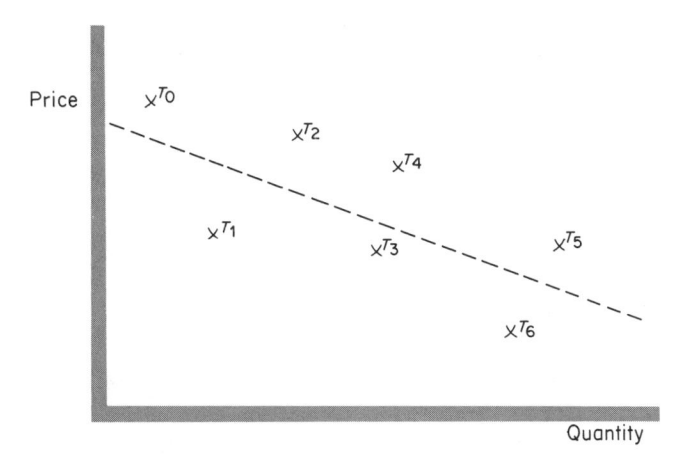

Static Formulations and Identification Problems 53

FIG. 4-3 Multiple equilibrium points producing a hybrid supply-demand function.

rium points, each of which is an *intersection* of two curves. There will thus be only a single point to represent each pair of curves. Since an infinite number of different pairs of curves can be drawn through each of these intersections, we cannot recover or estimate the underlying functions from the data.

Let us now imagine that the true demand curve does not shift but that there are large shifts in the supply function. This situation can be represented as in Fig. 4-4. Since there is a single demand function, all intersections lie

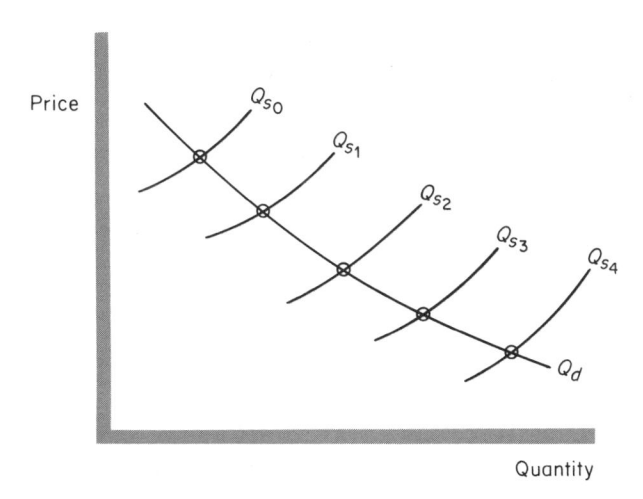

FIG. 4-4 Constant demand function and shifting supply functions enabling the identification of the demand function.

along the demand curve, and these points will trace out the true demand function. But the nature of the supply functions could not be determined by these intersection points. In other words, if one could be assured, a priori, that the demand function was not shifting but that there were major shifts in the supply function, then he would know that the demand (but not the supply) function could be identified as the intersections of the equilibrium values. The converse obviously applies to the situation where there are no shifts in the supply function.

Of course one will never know for certain that only one function is shifting. Assuming the correctness of the equilibrium model, one can only infer that one or the other, or both, functions must be shifting if the values of Q and P are observed to change over time. Usually it is most reasonable to assume that both are shifting, and it will be difficult to estimate the extent of each shift. How can one proceed to estimate the true supply and demand functions, given this apparently insurmountable difficulty?

We shall see that the situation is indeed hopeless unless one is willing to make a priori assumptions of some sort. To see what these assumptions might be, let us ask why one or the other function can be expected to shift. Here it is crucial to keep in mind the distinction between moving along a particular supply or demand function and changing the functions themselves. An individual customer or supplier takes the function at any particular time as given, and he adjusts his behavior according to the price. Shifts in the functions, on the other hand, must be accounted for by taking into consideration the behavior of other variables affecting the supply and demand functions.[7]

It has thus far been assumed that the supply and demand functions contained no error terms. That is, no other explicit or implicit factors were assumed operating. But if either or both functions contained large error terms, which varied considerably from one observation to the next, this would account for shifts in the functions. Suppose the demand function contained a very small error variance, whereas the error term for the supply function was quite large. Then the situation would be approximately the same as that indicated in Fig. 4-4, where the demand function, but not the supply function, could be identified. Such error terms could be conceived as producing the shifts in the appropriate functions.

Since the functions will in general be unknown, so will the magnitudes of the error terms. But if one were willing to assume a priori knowledge of the

---

[7] Demand functions are determined from theoretical utility functions which can rarely be determined empirically. On the other hand, supply functions can be derived from cost functions which can usually be estimated from empirical data. For a very readable discussion of the implications of this difference see Lawrence R. Klein, *An Introduction to Econometrics* (Englewood Cliffs, N.J.: Prentice-Hall, Inc., 1962), Chaps. 2 and 3.

relative magnitudes of the error variances, he could use this information to identify the true supply and demand functions.[8] We have considered only the extreme cases where one or the other error variance was assumed exactly equal to zero, but information regarding their relative magnitudes could work just as well. The major problem, of course, is that of obtaining a priori knowledge about such disturbance terms. In sociological research this would require knowledge about the variances of unknown variables acting as disturbing influences. Clearly it will be difficult if not impossible to find a priori grounds for estimating these error variances in most practical situations.

In effect, error terms summarize our ignorance, and if it is possible to reduce these error terms by bringing additional variables explicitly into an equation then this should be done. Suppose, for example, that one could explain major shifts in the supply function by adding one or two variables to the equation. Changes in supply functions may be produced by changes in production costs, including labor costs, or in the case of agricultural products by such factors as seasonal variations in rainfall. These same factors might be assumed a priori to have no effect on the demand function, at least in the short run.[9] If these were the only factors operating, then one would expect no changes in the demand function, and this information could be used to identify or trace out the demand function. Explicit knowledge of these other factors entering into the supply function would be much more useful than enlightened guesses as to the relative magnitudes of the error terms.

Let us examine the identification problem in a more systematic manner to see why the explicit introduction of independent variables, or what will be termed "exogenous" factors, enables one to identify one or both of the functions.[10] At the same time, we will be able to see the problem in a more general light. Suppose we assume a priori that an exogenous factor Z, such as production costs or rainfall, appears in the supply function but not in the demand function. This would give the (linear) equations

$$Q_s = a_1 + b_1 P + cZ + u_s \tag{4-3a}$$

$$Q_d = a_2 - b_2 P + u_d \tag{4-3b}$$

---

[8] For a more complete discussion see Fisher, *Identification Problem*, Chap. 3.

[9] This assumption that factors affecting the one function will not appreciably affect the other function(s) is most plausible when the several functions can be linked with relatively autonomous actors (e.g., suppliers and customers). See Christ, *Econometric Models*, pp. 20–21, 247; and Robert H. Strotz and Herman A. Wold, "Recursive Versus Nonrecursive Systems," *Econometrica*, 28 (April 1960), 417–27.

[10] The essential defining characteristic of an exogenous variable in this example is that it must *not* be dependent on Q_s or Q_d. I shall define the notion of an exogenous variable more carefully below.

where it is assumed that the coefficient of Z in the demand function is zero, and where error terms have been introduced in both equations.

Simultaneous equations can be written in many equivalent forms, as you will recall from elementary algebra. For example, consider the pair of equations

$$X + Y = 3 \qquad (4\text{-}4a)$$

$$X - Y = 6 \qquad (4\text{-}4b)$$

Suppose we multiply the first equation by 5 and add it to the second, thus obtaining the equation $6X + 4Y = 21$, which is mathematically consistent with the first two equations. In fact, one ordinarily "solves" for X and Y in this manner. For example, we can multiply the first equation by unity and add it to the second, getting $2X = 9$, or $X = 4.5$. This value of X may then be substituted in either equation to obtain the equation $Y = -1.5$. This new pair of equations

$$X = 4.5 \qquad (4\text{-}5a)$$

$$Y = -1.5 \qquad (4\text{-}5b)$$

is ordinarily thought of as the "solution," but it is merely a simplified version of the original pair, Eqs. (4-4), and can be referred to as a "reduced form" in which neither variable is a function of the other.

Returning to the supply-demand example, it would be possible for someone who wished to hide from us the true demand function, simply to multiply the first equation (the supply function) by some arbitrary constant λ, adding this to the true demand equation, and then to present us with this false demand function as though it were the true one. The identification problem can then be conceived in terms of whether or not we would be in a position to discover the hoax by empirical means. In real life, there may be no such persons playing tricks on us. But we will be faced with essentially the same problem since we will have available only the empirical data from which we must distinguish the true functions from an infinite set of alternatives, all of which could have produced these same results.

If we assume equilibrium conditions and replace Q_s and Q_d by the single quantity Q, and if we multiply the first equation (4-3a) by λ and add it to the true demand equation (4-3b), we shall obtain the false demand equation

$$(1 + \lambda)Q = (\lambda a_1 + a_2) + (\lambda b_1 - b_2)P + \lambda cZ + (\lambda u_s + u_d)$$

Static Formulations and Identification Problems 57

or

$$Q = \frac{\lambda a_1 + a_2}{1 + \lambda} + \frac{\lambda b_1 - b_2}{1 + \lambda} P + \frac{\lambda c}{1 + \lambda} Z + \frac{\lambda u_s + u_d}{1 + \lambda} \qquad (4\text{-}6)$$

which is of the general form

$$Q = A_1 + B_1 P + C_1 Z + U_1 \qquad (4\text{-}7)$$

But if this were presented to us as the true demand function, we would reject it because it contained Z, which we have assumed a priori does not belong in the demand equation. Only if either c or λ were zero would C_1 be zero. If λ were zero, this would in effect mean that the demand equation had not been changed at all, and we would therefore be able to identify it.[11] If c were zero it would mean that Z, say rainfall, did not actually appear in the supply function. Therefore if $c = 0$, λ could be any finite value; and since C_1 would be zero, the Z term would drop out of Eq. (4-7). The empirical data would yield estimates of A_1 and B_1, but these would not be sufficient to obtain estimates of the four quantities a_1, a_2, b_1, and b_2.

Therefore it does not help to use "exogenous" factors to identify the coefficients in one function unless they really appear in the other function. The larger the value of c, the smaller λ must be in order to keep the coefficient $\lambda c/(1 + \lambda)$ negligible enough to be indistinguishable from sampling error. In effect, the more important rainfall (Z) is as a determinant of the quantity supplied, the smaller λ must be in order for C_1 to be negligible.

Since the above argument is rather subtle, let us review briefly the steps we have taken. We have recognized that if an equilibrium model is assumed, and if one takes Q_s and Q_d as simple functions of prices, then empirical data alone will give us only the equilibrium price and quantity and cannot be used to reconstruct the entire supply and demand functions. If we knew, however, that one of the functions shifted considerably from one time period to the next, whereas the other remained constant, then the intersections would all lie along a single curve, and we could trace out or identify the coefficients in whichever function was not shifting.

One way to explain shifts in one of the functions is to postulate the existence of exogenous variables that produce variation in the one function but do not appear at all in the other. If we are willing to make the a priori assumption that some specific Z appears, say, in the supply but not the demand function, then we can distinguish the true demand function from any

---

[11] Comparing Eqs. (4-6) and (4-7) we see that if $\lambda = 0$, we would have $A_1 = a_2$ and $B_1 = -b_2$, since a_1 and b_1 would have disappeared from the equation.

linear combination of the simultaneous equations. This is true because these linear combinations will all have a nonzero coefficient for Z. There is only one pair of equations for which the second equation will have a zero coefficient for Z. By imposing the a priori restriction that Z does not appear in the demand function, we can thus distinguish the true demand function from any others that might be presented to us as possible candidates. All of these candidates, when combined with the appropriate supply function, are *mathematically* equivalent to the true equation, and will imply the same empirical results. It is only because we have assigned a zero (or other definite) value to one of the coefficients that we can obtain a unique solution.

Now suppose we wished to identify the true supply equation as well. If Z appears in this equation, but if its coefficient is unknown, then we can multiply the second (demand) equation by any λ, add it to the first (supply) equation, obtaining an equation of the form

$$Q = A_2 + B_2 P + C_2 Z + U_2 \tag{4-8}$$

But since we are assuming that Z does appear in the supply function, we cannot distinguish among all the possible candidates (having different values of λ) unless we had a priori knowledge of the numerical values of a_1, b_1, or c_1. This would indeed be almost impossible to obtain.

Suppose, however, that we are willing to assume that the demand function is affected by a different exogenous variable W that does not appear in the supply equation. Perhaps W is a variable that affects the tastes or preferences of consumers. By making the a priori assumption that the coefficient of W must be zero in the supply function, we make it impossible for someone to trick us with a false supply function, since any multiple (other than zero) of the demand function, when added to the true supply function, must contain W. In other words, if we can find two exogenous factors, one and only one of which belongs in each equation, then we can identify *both* equations. Both functions will be shifting over time, but we will be able to use this information because we have been able to locate some of the causes of these shifts. But notice that identification always involves a priori assumptions about some of the parameters.

Why not avoid all this trouble, and the necessity of making such a priori assumptions, by merely using *prediction* equations in which one simply plots the values of Q and P and uses a least-squares estimate? The answer is that this does not provide us with an adequate explanation of the relationship. As implied in Chap. 1, if we wish to build *theories* we cannot rest contented with simple empirical relationships such as this. It may be that one reason for the false dichotomy between theory construction, on the one hand, and quantitative methods, on the other, is that empirically-inclined quantitative social scientists have tended to neglect this type of model building in favor of simpler descriptions of empirical relationships.

But there is also a practical objection to the more simple estimation procedure. By extrapolation of the single curve relating Q and P, one may in fact make adequate predictions concerning the future behavior of these quantities—provided there are no basic changes in the parameters. But suppose the values of the exogenous variables Z and W were to change. One would have no idea what to expect, since the single empirical curve is a best-fitting curve to sets of intersections which would be unpredictable. Or suppose one wished to change the system in some way, as is often the ultimate goal toward which theory building is directed. In order to foresee the consequences of these changes, one must have an accurate estimate of the true structural parameters. This point should become more apparent when we later deal with the kinds of dynamic models that generate equilibrium equations of the type under present consideration.

Another way to look at the matter is to realize that whenever one wishes to translate verbal theories involving complex interdependencies into mathematical languages, he must make use of simultaneous equations. Only under special conditions will it be possible to construct realistic simultaneous equations that permit one to pull them apart and use each separate equation as a practical tool for predicting the behavior of a single dependent variable from values of several so-called "independent" variables. This should be obvious, from a common-sense standpoint, if one admits that the independent variables that appear in a single equation may themselves be dependent on each other, and perhaps on the "dependent" variable as well.

A General Linear Model

The supply-demand example involved only two simultaneous equations, and we have considered only the possibility of adding one exogenous variable to each of the equations in order to identify the other. Obviously it is necessary to consider this rather subtle question of identification much more generally. At the same time, it will be possible to define more precisely what is meant by an "exogenous" variable, and how such variables can be used to identify the coefficients. My main purpose is to show, in a nontechnical way, the implications of formulating complex verbal theories involving feedback relationships.[12]

---

[12] For a thorough but technical discussion of the general identification problem, see Fisher, *Identification Problem*. For briefer and less technical discussions, see Christ, *Econometric Models*, Chap. 8; and J. Johnston, *Econometric Methods* (New York: McGraw-Hill Book Company, 1963), Chap. 9.

60 Static Formulations and Identification Problems

Before proceeding to a rather abstract discussion of the general k-equation case, let us consider a seven-variable illustration provided by Hayward Alker and diagrammed as in Fig. 4-5.[13] Alker's model consists of four political

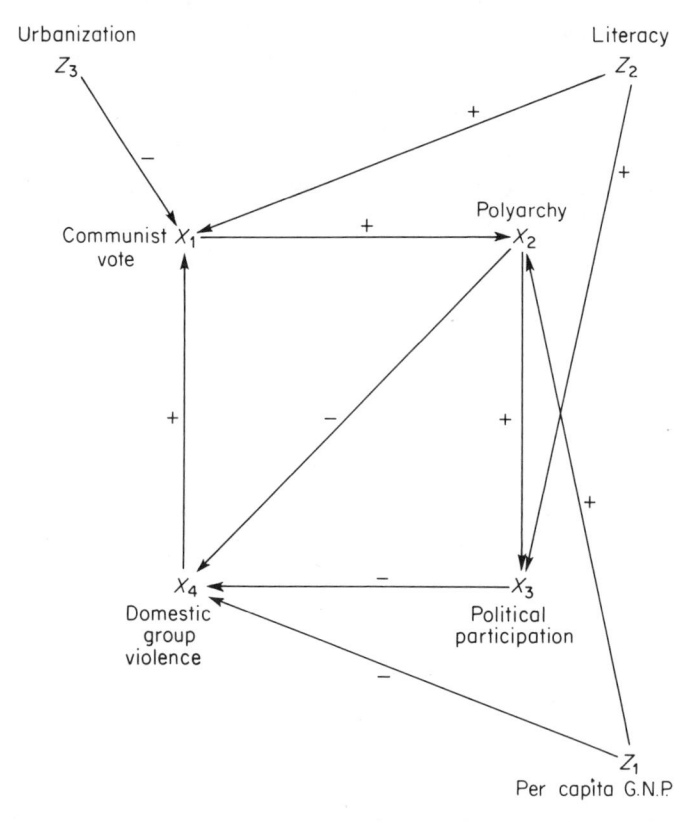

FIG. 4-5 Alker's model of political variables. (Adapted from H. R. Alker, Jr., "Causal Inference and Political Analysis," op. cit., p. 35.)

variables that are clearly reciprocally interrelated and taken as endogenous variables to be explained by the theory. These are communist vote (X_1), polyarchy (X_2), political participation (X_3), and domestic group violence (X_4). There is a major feedback loop running from communist vote to polyarchy,

[13] See Hayward R. Alker, Jr., "Causal Inference and Political Analysis," in *Mathematical Applications in Political Science, II*, ed. Joseph L. Bernd (Dallas: Southern Methodist University Press, 1966), pp. 7–43. Actually, Alker presents several alternative models, and I have taken the liberty of modifying his final model for heuristic purposes. His revised theory contains additional arrows from Z_2 to X_2 and from Z_1 to X_3, making each of the equations exactly identified.

to political participation, to domestic violence, and back to communist vote. This loop is also short-circuited by a direct path from polyarchy to violence. Unlike the Hopkins model, however, the product of the signs in both loops is negative. This means that an increase in the communist vote should set in motion a reaction, via either loop, that results in a decrease in this same vote at a later time. Similarly, a decrease in the communist vote should feed back to produce an increase in this vote. It might therefore seem as though the model automatically provides a stabilizing mechanism, though this is not necessarily the case. There might be oscillations of increasing magnitude that could ultimately produce an explosive situation. For example, a slight increase in the communist vote could produce a numerically larger decrease at the next election, followed by an even greater increase the next time, then a still larger decrease, and so forth. We shall postpone the question of stability, however, until Chap. 5.

There is another difference between the Alker and Hopkins models that is crucial from the standpoint of testability. Alker's model contains three additional variables, per capita Gross National Product (Z_1), literacy (Z_2), and urbanization (Z_3). These socioeconomic variables are taken as truly exogenous in the sense that none of them are affected by any of the political variables X_i. Nothing is said or implied in the model about the interrelations among the three exogenous variables. They may be intercorrelated, as one would naturally expect in this particular example.[14] If so, these correlations cannot be explained by the theory. In this sense the exogenous variables are the "givens" or the starting points of the theory. As we have already seen, some such "givens" will be necessary to resolve the identification problem.

In this more complex example it is not as easy to tell by inspection whether or not each of the equations can be identified. We begin by writing an equation for each of the political endogenous variables. Whenever an arrow has been drawn between two variables, we take the causal linkage to be direct, and this means that the appropriate coefficient must be taken as an unknown not equal to zero. The linear additive equations would therefore be:

$$X_1 = b_{14}X_4 + c_{12}Z_2 + c_{13}Z_3 + u_1$$

$$X_2 = b_{21}X_1 + c_{21}Z_1 + u_2$$

$$X_3 = b_{32}X_2 + c_{32}Z_2 + u_3$$

$$X_4 = b_{42}X_2 + b_{43}X_3 + c_{41}Z_1 + u_4$$

(4-9)

[14] This can be represented diagrammatically by linking the exogenous variables by means of double-headed curved arrows, as in Fig. 3.9.

where the reason for the difference between the b's and c's will be explained below.

By inspection, since the last three equations contain either X_2, X_3 or Z_1, which do not appear in the first equation, it would appear as though the first equation could be identified. Furthermore, we notice that the equations for X_2 and X_3 contain one less variable than the remaining two equations, and therefore we might expect them to be more easily identified. But we obviously need more specific guidelines if we are to tell in general which equations can possibly be identified and which cannot. We must therefore examine the general k-equation case before we can make more definite statements in this instance.

In general, there may be k variables that are assumed to be dependent on at least some other variable in the system. These are what we have been referring to as endogenous variables. Let us assume that there are n variables altogether, with $n - k$ variables being predetermined with respect to the k endogenous variables. We shall continue to refer to these predetermined variables as being exogenous variables, though some of them may be lagged endogenous variables, as we shall later see. For the time being, however, let us assume that we are dealing with n distinct variables, k of which are considered dependent. The theory for linear additive systems is well developed, but the more general case for nonlinear systems is too complex to be considered in the present context. We shall therefore confine our attention to linear models.

Let us represent the k endogenous variables as $X_1, X_2, \ldots, X_k$, and the exogenous variables as $Z_1, Z_2, \ldots, Z_{n-k}$. We then write down k simultaneous equations, one for each of the X's, as follows:

$$
\begin{aligned}
X_1 &= b_{12}X_2 + b_{13}X_3 + \cdots + b_{1k}X_k + c_{11}Z_1 + c_{12}Z_2 \\
&\qquad\qquad\qquad\qquad\qquad + \cdots + c_{1,n-k}Z_{n-k} + u_1 \\
X_2 &= b_{21}X_1 + b_{23}X_3 + \cdots + b_{2k}X_k + c_{21}Z_1 + c_{22}Z_2 \qquad (4\text{-}10)\\
&\qquad\qquad\qquad\qquad\qquad + \cdots + c_{2,n-k}Z_{n-k} + u_2 \\
&\vdots \\
X_k &= b_{k1}X_1 + b_{k2}X_2 + \cdots + b_{k,k-1}X_{k-1} + c_{k1}Z_1 + c_{k2}Z_2 \\
&\qquad\qquad\qquad\qquad\qquad + \cdots + c_{k,n-k}Z_{n-k} + u_k
\end{aligned}
$$

We have allowed for the possibility that each of the X's is caused by all of the remaining X's plus all of the exogenous variables. It should be reemphasized that we are assuming that the Z's are not caused by the X's, though we may allow for the fact that the exogenous Z's are intercorrelated with each other for unknown reasons. Some other theory could of course be constructed to allow for the possibility that the Z's, themselves, must be explained in terms of a different set of variables. The crucial point in connection with the exogenous Z's is that we are making the a priori assumption that there is no feedback from any of the X's to the Z's. This question will be considered later in connection with "block-recursive" systems.

This assumption regarding the exogenous behavior of the Z's can be stated another way by postulating that none of the error terms u_i are correlated (except for sampling error) with any of the Z_j. In causal terms, the u_i are used to represent our ignorance of additional factors affecting each of the X_i. Any factors affecting, say, X_1 will be summarized in u_1, and we must assume that none of these factors can also affect the Z's. If this assumption is violated, then the particular Z's concerned are not truly exogenous and must be treated as endogenous. This means that it will be necessary to write additional equations for each of these particular Z's. This will of course add to the number of endogenous variables and subtract from the list of exogenous variables. If one chooses to do so, this criterion of the lack of correlation between error terms and exogenous variables may be used to define what one means by an exogenous variable.[15] Any variable not meeting this criterion is, by definition, not an exogenous variable.

The coefficients of the endogenous X's have been labeled as b_{ij}, whereas those for the exogenous Z's have been distinguished as c_{ij}, in order to emphasize the different roles played by the two kinds of variables. Both sets of coefficients, however, are conceived to be the true structural coefficients that have generated the empirical data under investigation. That is, b_{ij} represents the actual change in X_i that would be produced by a unit change in X_j if all other variables in the system were held constant.

There will again be infinitely many mathematically equivalent sets of simultaneous equations, all of which can be written in this same general form with unknown coefficients, and which imply the same empirical results. The solutions to the equations will represent intersections of multidimensional surfaces in multidimensional space, and one will not be able to use the empirical information alone to identify the coefficients in each equation. In effect, there will be too many unknowns for solution. Unless a priori assumptions can be made about some of the coefficients, the situation will be mathematically hopeless. This will be true even with perfect measurement of each variable and with no error terms in the equations. In other words, the identification problem does not arise because of statistical estimation problems. It stems from the excess of unknowns over the number of pieces of information that can be obtained empirically.

Someone could transform the true structural equations into a mathematically equivalent set by multiplying each equation by a different λ_i and

---

[15] Fisher, *Identification Problem*, pp. 15–17.

then adding them to any given equation. It is convenient to examine the identification problem by looking at the coefficients of some specific equation, which can be taken as the first equation without loss of generality. If nothing whatsoever is assumed about the magnitudes or directions of the coefficients in this equation, then any linear transformation—achieved by multiplying by constants and adding linear combinations to the equation—will be indistinguishable from the true equation.

But if one were willing to assume that some of the variables do not appear in this equation, or in other words that some of the b's and c's are zero, then perhaps identification can be achieved. Those variables with assumed zero coefficients will appear with nonzero coefficients in most of the "false" equations, and these particular candidates can be ruled out as not satisfying the a priori conditions. Complete identification can not be achieved, however, unless the true equation can be distinguished from *all* of the mathematically equivalent alternatives. In practical terms this means that one must be able to distinguish the true structural parameters from all remaining sets that imply the same empirical data.

In less technical terms, whenever one is given a model which allows for many instances of reciprocal causation and feedback, it will be difficult to determine what is causing what, and to obtain accurate estimates of the relative magnitudes (and even directions) of each of the direct linkages. This problem has been recognized by most persons who have constructed complex verbal theories. The basic question, however, is whether it is possible to find mathematical procedures for disentangling the various components. The answer is "no" unless the parameters can be identified.

It is of utmost importance that we be able to specify some necessary and sufficient conditions under which the coefficients can be identified in order to determine, in advance of data analysis, whether or not a theory is inherently untestable. If necessary conditions are not met, this means that the theory must be reformulated in such a way that it at least becomes possible to obtain estimates, assuming perfect measurement and no extraneous variables. If even under such ideal conditions it can be shown that there will be too many unknown parameters, then clearly there is no point in attempting to find definitive answers. Of course the theory can be modified so as to enable one to identify the parameters. One of the important advantages of mathematical formulations is that they indicate the exact ways in which the theory must be modified.

The necessary conditions for identification of the coefficients of a given equation are relatively easy to state in the case of linear systems. One counts the number of equations or endogenous variables, k. The number of variables excluded from a given equation must then be at least equal to one less than

Static Formulations and Identification Problems   65

the number of equations, or $k - 1$.[16] This necessary condition can be stated in another equivalent way. The number of endogenous variables contained in the equation cannot be greater than one plus the number of exogenous variables excluded from the equation. Thus if there were six endogenous variables and four exogenous variables altogether, and if the first equation contained three endogenous variables, we would have to exclude at least two exogenous variables from the equation in order to identify the coefficients. This would mean that the total number of variables excluded would be three endogenous plus two exogenous variables, or five altogether. Since this is exactly one less than the total number of equations (endogenous variables), the necessary conditions would be met.

But these conditions are not also sufficient ones. The sufficient condition, stated technically, is that one must be able to form at least one determinant of order $k - 1$ from the columns of the matrix of the coefficients corresponding to the variables that have been excluded from the equation.[17] This condition is also necessary. For practical purposes, this necessary and sufficient condition requires that one find exogenous variables that can be left out of equations in such a way that no two (or more) equations are indistinguishable. For example, if the first and fifth equations each contained exactly the same combination of variables, one could not distinguish between them. One would then say that the first equation was not identified with respect to the fifth, though it might be with respect to the remaining equations. This necessary and sufficient condition is most easily discussed in connection with specific equations where one can always form the appropriate reduced matrix and see if a determinant of the proper rank can be found.[18]

---

[16] See Fisher, *Identification Problem*, pp. 39–41, for more precise statements of the necessary and sufficient conditions. The present discussion assumes that there are no additional restrictions placed on the behavior of the error terms. Later, in dealing with "block-recursive" systems, we shall assume that certain of the error covariances are zero. A more general statement of the necessary conditions is that the number of linear restrictions on the coefficients must be at least equal to $k - 1$. This allows for the possibility of other kinds of restrictions, as for example the assumption that two coefficients are equal or that they may have specified nonzero values. In practice, however, the most common assumptions are so-called "zero restrictions," that is, assumptions to the effect that certain variables do not appear in some of the equations.

[17] Determinants will be discussed briefly in Chap. 6 in connection with stability conditions for simultaneous differential equations. A determinant is of order $k - 1$ (or greater) if one can find at least one set of $k - 1$ rows and $k - 1$ columns that produces a determinant whose value is not equal to zero.

[18] Strictly speaking, these *sufficient* conditions cannot be used without making a priori assumptions, since the determinant will contain unknown parameters. Christ, *Econometric Models*, p. 322, argues that in most practical econometric models the sufficient conditions will be met whenever the necessary conditions are met.

The practical implication of these conditions is that one must bring in the exogenous variables selectively so that enough coefficients can be assumed equal to zero that the number of unknowns will be reduced to a point where identification can be achieved. This means that exogenous variables cannot be linked indiscriminately to all of the endogenous variables. For example, as the reader may easily check, all of the equations in Alker's model can be identified since the Z's in Eq. (4-9) have been brought in selectively in the proper manner. The more endogenous variables one wishes to include in a given equation, the more exogenous variables he must exclude. Thus if one believes that reality is complex, and if he wishes to model reality accurately by including a large number of endogenous variables, he must search for additional exogenous factors that can be included in some of the remaining equations. As we shall see in Chap. 5, some of these "exogenous" variables may, in fact, be values of endogenous variables at previous points in time.

The common-sense idea that complex theories are difficult to test takes on a definite meaning in this context. It means that additional variables must be found, though one must always guard against the temptation to introduce exogenous variables indiscriminately merely in order to achieve identification.

Additional Examples

We have already dealt with two illustrative examples of models where identification problems might arise, namely supply and demand analysis and Alker's model. In this section we shall briefly consider two additional examples, the Hopkins model and status-inconsistency theory.

Let us return to the five-variable feedback model proposed by Hopkins, assuming linear additive relationships as being reasonable approximations to reality. Let rank be X_1, centrality be X_2, conformity be X_3, with observability and influence being X_4 and X_5 respectively. Given the linearity assumptions, the model then implies the following equations:

$$X_1 = b_{15}X_5 + u_1$$

$$X_2 = b_{21}X_1 + u_2$$

$$X_3 = b_{32}X_2 + b_{34}X_4 + b_{35}X_5 + u_3 \qquad (4\text{-}11)$$

$$X_4 = b_{42}X_2 + b_{43}X_3 + u_4$$

$$X_5 = b_{53}X_3 + b_{54}X_4 + u_5$$

Notice several things about this set of equations. First, as was also true in the case of Alker's model, many of the possible coefficients have been set equal to zero. This is because Hopkins posits no direct links among these pairs of variables. Second, the system contains no exogenous variables since every variable in the system depends on at least one other variable. In two instances there is direct or pairwise reciprocal causation; changes in X_3 directly affect X_4, and vice versa, and the same is true for X_3 and X_5. In these two instances neither b_{ij} nor b_{ji} are equal to zero.

Third, and extremely important, one cannot legitimately use ordinary least squares to estimate any of the coefficients in the system. It will be recalled that least squares will give unbiased estimates of the b's only if it can be assumed that the error term in a given equation is uncorrelated with the independent variables in this same equation. It can be shown algebraically that this condition cannot be met in the Hopkins system, or more generally in any system with feedback. This can be seen intuitively by recognizing that factors that affect X_1, for example, are summarized in u_1. But X_1 indirectly affects X_5 via the remaining variables, and hence u_1 will be correlated with X_5. The same holds for the other equations. There are estimation procedures that can be used as alternatives to simple least squares in these feedback models, but it is beyond the scope of a short book on theory building to consider such statistical techniques.[19]

Since the necessary conditions for identifying structural parameters are not met in the above five equations (4-11), there can be no unique solution as the theory stands. In terms of the first way of stating these conditions, there must be at least $k - 1 = 4$ variables left out of each equation, which is obviously impossible since there are only five variables, at least two of which are in each equation. Alternatively, the first equation contains two (endogenous) variables, and therefore there must be at least one exogenous variable omitted. The same holds for the second equation. The third equation contains four variables, and therefore we must omit three exogenous variables. In the case of the remaining two equations, we must locate two exogenous variables that appear in one or more of the first three equations but that have been omitted from these last two. Furthermore, we shall have to be careful that exactly the same sets of variables do not appear in two or more equations. Fortunately, this last condition is easily met in the case of these particular equations, none of which contain exactly the same combinations of endogenous variables.

Thus in this model we would need to search for reasonable exogenous variables that could be added to the system so that the necessary and sufficient

---

[19] For discussions of these procedures, see Christ, *Econometric Models*, Chap. 9; and Johnston, *Econometric Methods*, Chaps. 9 and 10.

conditions could be met.[20] The minimum number of such additional variables would be three, since there must be three exogenous variables omitted from the third equation. Let us assume that Z_1 directly affects X_1 and X_2; Z_2 affects X_2 and X_5; and Z_3 affects X_1 and X_4. Thus one exogenous variable (Z_2) has been omitted from the first equation, one (Z_3) from the second, all Z's from the third, two (Z_1 and Z_2) from the fourth, and two (Z_1 and Z_3) from the fifth. It can also be shown that a determinant of at least order $k - 1$ or 4 can be constructed from the matrix of the variables omitted from each equation. The entire system (all equations) could thus be identified provided that all eight variables could be accurately measured. Needless to say, there would be numerous other combinations of three or more exogenous variables that could also be used to identify the system.

A note on overidentification and testing

In the example of the Hopkins model, we have made use of exogenous variables in such a way that exactly the right number of variables have been left out of each equation so as to make identification possible. In such a case, we say that the coefficients in each equation are "exactly identified." This means that there are just the right number of unknowns, relative to pieces of empirical information, so that each coefficient may be estimated. But under these conditions there will be no information left over with which to *test* the adequacy of the model. That is, if we are willing to *assume* the correctness of the model, estimates can be obtained. But it might be useful to have relatively more pieces of information so that additional predictions could be made that would enable us to test the adequacy of the model.

For example, in the Hopkins model we might have introduced more than three exogenous variables, or we might have assumed that Z_2 did not affect X_5, and so forth. In Alker's model the equations for X_2 and X_3 contain one less variable than the maximum number that would permit identification. In such cases we would have more empirical information than necessary to estimate the coefficients, and the equations in question would be said to be "overidentified." The advantage of overidentified models is that not all sets of data will fit the model. As we have previously noted, Hopkins' model predicts positive relationships among all variables. But this will likewise be true for many alternative feedback models linking these same variables. If we add exogenous variables so that the system is exactly identified, then we may estimate the parameters, given the model. But if it is overidentified, not all sets of data involving positive correlations will fit the model, and this fact

[20] An alternative strategy, which will be discussed in Chap. 5, would be to lag one or more variables and treat the system as dynamic.

may be used to choose among a number of alternative models in a manner analogous to tests in the case of recursive models.[21]

For example, consider the equation for X_2 in Alker's model. The coefficients for X_3, X_4, Z_2, and Z_3 have all been set equal to zero, whereas the necessary condition for identification requires that only three of these variables be omitted. In other words, had the coefficient b_{23} (or any other zero coefficient) been inserted as an "unknown" in this equation, the revised equation

$$X_2 = b_{21}X_1 + b_{23}X_3 + c_{21}Z_1 + u_2$$

would have been exactly identified. A unique estimate of the "unknown" b_{23} could therefore have been computed (provided all other equations had also been made exactly identified), and this value of b_{23} could then be compared with the hypothesized value of zero. If the original model were correct, this estimated value of b_{23} would thus be approximately zero, and if the data did not satisfy this condition the model would have to be modified or rejected. Similarly, one of the omitted coefficients in the equation for X_3 could have been replaced, estimated, and the result compared with the predicted value of zero.

The greater the number of excess pieces of information over the number of true unknowns, the larger the number of conditions the data must satisfy, and the easier it will be to reject the theory. A highly overidentified system that has successfully resisted elimination by implying numerous correct predictions can therefore be considered more adequately tested than one that is just barely overidentified.[22]

Recursive systems and status inconsistency

Let us return to simple recursive systems of the sort given by Eq. (4-1). In this particular set of equations, X_1 is obviously an exogenous variable, but the remaining X_i are endogenous. The equation for X_2 contains only one endogenous variable, and therefore can be identified. But the third contains two endogenous variables, plus X_1, and cannot be identified. The same holds for all remaining equations. Yet we have argued that least squares can be used to estimate the coefficients of each equation, and that furthermore each equation can be analyzed separately. How is this possible?

[21] For a discussion of such tests in the recursive case, see H. M. Blalock, *Causal Inferences*, Chap. 3.
[22] There are a number of alternative estimating procedures in the case of overidentified systems. In the special case where *all* equations are exactly identified, these procedures reduce to relatively simple techniques referred to as "indirect least squares" or "instrumental variables." See Christ, *Econometric Models*, Chap. 9.

The answer is that we must add some assumptions about the covariances among the error terms, and it is these assumptions plus the assumptions that half of the possible b's are zero that make identification possible. Thus if one is willing to make such assumptions about the effects of outside variables, he may use these restrictions to identify his equations. As we shall see shortly, it will always be necessary to make at least some such assumptions. In the case of recursive systems, the use of ordinary least squares requires the assumption that the expected covariances for all pairs $u_i u_j$ are zero. This means that omitted factors assumed to affect X_1 are assumed uncorrelated with omitted factors producing variation in X_2, and so forth.

Identification problems can arise even in the case of recursive systems if these assumptions regarding covariances among the error terms break down. This can be illustrated in terms of a certain class of theories in which one (or more) of the independent variables is taken as an exact function of the others. Though there are several examples of theories of this type in the sociological literature, I shall focus on only one of these, namely status-inconsistency theory.[23]

In brief, a simple form of status-inconsistency theory takes a dependent variable such as political liberalism as a function of several status variables plus the degree of inconsistency among them. For example, if there are two independent status variables, say education (X_1) and occupational prestige (X_2), then degree of inconsistency may be taken as an exact function of a difference between these two statuses. If we let this difference function be represented by $Z = f(X_1 - kX_2)$, then if this function were linear, and if Y were taken as a linear additive function of X_1, X_2, and Z we would have the two-equation system

$$Y = b_1 X_1 + b_2 X_2 + b_3 Z + u_y$$

and

$$Z = c(X_1 - kX_2)$$

where c is a constant and where there is no error term in the second equation. Here the first equation contains all of the variables in the system and cannot be identified without the aid of the covariance assumptions, which cannot be made in this instance. Therefore it will be impossible to estimate any of the b's in this equation, and this of course means that one cannot separate the inconsistency effect from the two main effects.[24]

One possible resolution would be to introduce exogenous variables, as

---

[23] See Gerhard E. Lenski, "Status Crystallization: A Non-Vertical Dimension of Social Status," *American Sociological Review*, 19 (August 1954), 405–13; and H. M. Blalock, "Status Inconsistency, Social Mobility, Status Integration, and Structural Effects, "*American Sociological Review*, 32 (October 1967), 790–801.

[24] This argument is spelled out in greater detail in H. M. Blalock, "Status Inconsistency."

has been done in the previous illustrations. In this particular instance, however, there is an alternative approach that is more compatible with the original formulation of inconsistency theory by Lenski and others. The inconsistency effect may be taken as a specific nonlinear function. For example, degree of inconsistency can be defined as the square of the difference between statuses, thus disregarding the direction of inconsistency. In other words, the inconsistency effect would be taken as the same regardless of whether education was higher than occupation, or vice versa. If the direction as well as the degree of inconsistency were thought to affect Y, then additional terms could be added to the equation to represent these directional components. While the exact procedure is somewhat technical, the main point in this connection is that by specifying a nonlinear form for the relationship, one can circumvent the identification problem that arises in the case of the linear model. Fisher points out that the introduction of nonlinearity into simultaneous systems often aids and seldom hinders identification.[25] However, a greater burden is placed on the theorist to specify the form of nonlinear relationship that is to be used.

This status-inconsistency example also illustrates another important point. We are dealing in this instance with a limiting case in which one independent variable is an exact linear function of some of the others. In many practical situations some of the independent variables will be highly intercorrelated, though not perfectly related through an exact equation. In these instances, the necessary conditions for identification may technically be met, but the gain will be more apparent than real. The higher the intercorrelations among independent variables relative to their correlations with the dependent variable(s), the greater the *sampling* error.[26] Thus, although the slope estimates may be unbiased, they may have very large standard errors, and one may get a false sense of security if his results are based on a single sample. Therefore one should attempt to find a set of exogenous or independent variables that are not highly interrelated.

Block-Recursive Systems[27]

Suppose we wished to combine the very simple features of recursive systems with more complex feedback models. In other words, suppose we wished to

---

[25] Fisher, *Identification Problem*, pp. 148–51.

[26] For discussions of this problem of "multicollinearity" see Christ, *Econometric Models*, pp. 387–90, 478–80; Johnston, *Econometric Methods*, pp. 201–7; and Robert A. Gordon, "Issues in Multiple Regression," *American Journal of Sociology*, 73 (March 1968), 592–616.

[27] For a more complete discussion of block-recursive systems see Fisher, *Identification Problem*, pp. 99–102, 121–26.

72 Static Formulations and Identification Problems

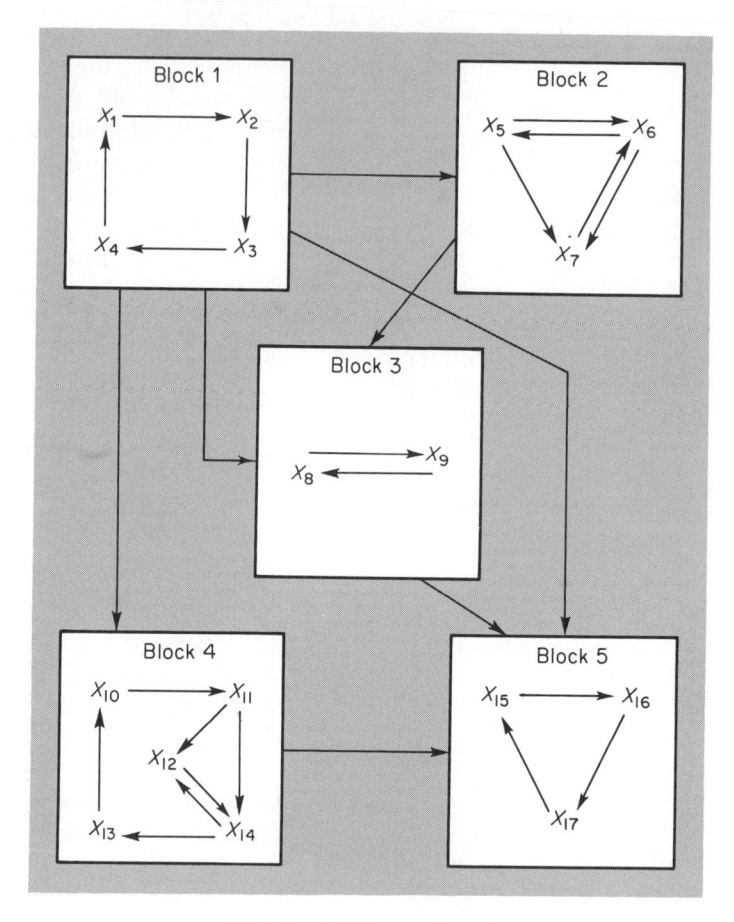

FIG. 4-6 A block-recursive system.

allow for feedback within only part of the total system. We might construct what have been termed "block-recursive" systems, an example of which is given in Fig. 4-6. *Within* each of the blocks there may be feedback or reciprocal causation. But the relationships *among* blocks are recursive. In fact, one might attempt to obtain a single measure for all of the variables in Block 1, and similarly for the remaining blocks. If so, he would be able to relabel his "block variables" as X_1 through X_5 and then work with a recursive model involving these five very general "variables." We shall return to this strategy later.

Let us focus on Block 3 for purposes of illustration. Variables X_1 through X_7 contained in the lower-numbered blocks would be considered exogenous with respect to the Block 3 variables X_8 and X_9. The error terms for these latter two variables, u_8 and u_9, would be assumed uncorrelated with each of these exogenous variables, as previously discussed. But this means that the error terms for Block 3 will be uncorrelated with the error terms u_1 through u_7. In other words, some of the covariances among u_i and u_j will be assumed equal to zero. But u_8 and u_9 *will* be intercorrelated, since there is feedback within Block 3.

If the focus of attention is to be on the interrelationships among the variables in Block 3, then higher-numbered blocks (here Blocks 4 and 5) can be ignored, since by assumption none of the variables in these blocks affect the relationships in Block 3. But someone studying Block 5 might wish to use all or some of the variables in Blocks 1-4 as exogenous variables. If so, then the error terms for variables X_{15} through X_{17} would be assumed uncorrelated with those for X_1 through X_{14}.

A little thought should convince one that whenever a theorist decides to delimit the number of variables that he will consider—and of course this will always be necessary—he is basically assuming that the world is block-recursive. More correctly, he is assuming that a block-recursive model can give a reasonably accurate representation of reality. First, he must assume that variables in higher-numbered blocks can safely be ignored. Thus he cannot allow for the possibility of feedback from every variable to every other variable. In effect, his blocks must be hierarchically arranged. But he must also take some variables as exogenous, or as "givens" which his theory cannot explain. As we have seen, he must assume negligible feedback to these exogenous variables.

This does not mean that particular variables cannot be shifted about from one block to another according to the nature of one's theory. For example, an alternative theory might be proposed to the model of Fig. 4-6 in which there might be feedback from Block 3 to Block 2. A reconceptualization might therefore combine X_5 through X_9 into a single block within which feedback has been allowed. The variables in Block 1 might remain as exogenous variables, or perhaps another set might be used. As theories become more and more complex, the sizes of the blocks may thus increase. Nevertheless, at some point one must stop with a finite number of variables in each block. He must then commit himself on the nature of the relationships between blocks, and in order to derive definitive results he must use a block-recursive model. This is what I meant by the earlier statement that *some* of the error terms must be assumed uncorrelated with each other.

This kind of explicit formulation would seem to help clarify relationships among different theories and to specify how a division of labor can be carried out. Perhaps a group of social scientists would find it possible to formulate preliminary "grand theories" involving large numbers of variables separated into several blocks. Investigators could then concentrate on different blocks in a carefully worked-out division of labor. Reformulations would of course be found necessary, with shifts between blocks resulting. Some investigators might work entirely within blocks, using variables from lower-numbered blocks as exogenous variables. Others might wish to treat relationships between blocks. Presumably, if research were carefully planned in such a manner, the task of fitting the whole theory together would be tremendously simplified.

One further remark is necessary concerning such a hypothetical division of labor. Sometimes an investigator may recognize that there is a complex relationship among the variables within a given block, but he may not wish to focus on this problem. Instead, he may merely obtain one or two measures to summarize the entire set of variables in this block. Suppose, for example, that one wishes to focus on Block 5. He may find that the three variables in Block 2 are highly correlated, so much so that he cannot hope to disentangle their separate effects. He may then treat them as a "syndrome" and give a general label to the block (e.g., *industrialization*). The same condition may apply in Blocks 3 and 4. But perhaps the investigator wants to focus on the effects of Block 1 on Block 5, and suppose he finds that the variables of Block 1 are not so highly interrelated that their individual effects cannot be distinguished. The variables X_1 through X_4 may therefore be taken as (correlated) exogenous variables. Three other exogenous "variables" may also be constructed, one for each of the Blocks 2, 3, and 4. The resulting theoretical simplifications may be sufficient to obtain definitive results even where each of the separate variables cannot be directly measured.

If one wants to focus primarily on the feedback relationships within a single block, then whenever possible, data should be collected at several points in time. As we shall see in the following chapter, it then becomes possible to test dynamic formulations, which offer an alternative way of resolving the identification problem.

Concluding Remarks

It has been emphasized that the use of exogenous variables requires simplifying assumptions. Most often these will take the form of "zero assumptions" to the effect that certain variables do not directly affect some of the others. Of course if one were willing to commit himself a priori on specific non-zero values (e.g., $b_{21} = 11.56$), then identification could be achieved in a similar fashion. Such specific assumptions would seem highly unlikely, however, if we keep in mind that these values could not be determined from the data. Conceivably, they might be obtained from data collected by very different means, e.g., by combining cross-sectional and time-series data, though this will often lead to additional methodological problems.[28] Another alternative is to specify that certain pairs of coefficients should be approximately equal, or that their ratio should equal a known constant. A final alternative, which will be explored in the next two chapters, is to use dynamic formulations in which lagged endogenous variables play the role of exogenous variables.

Thus the use of exogenous variables presupposes that the theorist is willing to make a priori assumptions of a restrictive nature. Perhaps many social scientists would not be prepared to play this game, but they must then ask themselves about the possible alternatives. Are they willing to assume *any* truly exogenous variables, to which there is no feedback from the endogenous variables under consideration? Can they find some for which the feedback is minimal, or sufficiently delayed that it can be ignored in the short run? If the answer is "no," then they may be in serious trouble. Theories can, of course, be stated in full generality; but when they are so stated, it may not be possible either to test them or to estimate their structural parameters.

Presumably, theories can be generated and accumulated by some process such as this: A theorist may settle on a relatively small number of variables or blocks that he hopes to interrelate. He should formulate relatively simple models, being careful to distinguish between endogenous and exogenous variables, and to satisfy at least the necessary conditions for identification of the parameters. Estimates will have to be obtained on the basis of the a priori assumptions made in the theory. Someone else may then choose to modify these assumptions or add new variables. Variables originally taken as exogenous may later be incorporated as endogenous variables, with additional exogenous variables being added in order to achieve identification. In such a manner, simple theories can be made more and more complex.

It might be thought that such an ideal practice is impossible or at least impractical, given the present state of our knowledge. How can one justify making particular a priori assumptions rather than others? If we were to examine our actual practices, however, we would soon discover that such assumptions are in fact being made, though they are made more often than not only implicitly. Consider estimates based on a single equation. The "independent" variables in many such equations will be intercorrelated, and yet the investigator may take the (partial) slopes as estimates of the "effects" of each variable. But what if some are causes of the others? Likewise, if the "dependent" variable feeds back to influence the other variables, part of the association with each independent variable will be produced by this feedback. The single-equation approach involves the implicit assumption that there are no such feedbacks.

[28] For a discussion of problems involved in combining time-series and cross-sectional data, see Klein, *Introduction to Econometrics*, pp. 73–74.

5

Single-Equation Dynamic Models

Everyone knows that a "dynamic" theory is a good one, whereas a mere "static" formulation is inadequate. Therefore if one wishes to belittle a particular man's theory, he can claim that it is static and incapable of accounting for change. In sociology we have had numerous discussions concerning the static nature of so-called functionalism and equilibrium analyses, without much light having been thrown on the dispute. Exactly what does one mean by a dynamic theoretical formulation as contrasted with a static one, and under what circumstances can each be used? And what are the advantages of dynamic formulations?

Problems of stability and change are of considerable importance in the social as well as the natural sciences. There has recently been an upsurge of interest in "systems analysis" and various kinds of feedback mechanisms that seem analogous to servomechanisms operating in self-guidance systems.[1]

---

[1] See especially Walter Buckley, *Sociology and Modern Systems Theory* (Englewood Cliffs, N.J.: Prentice-Hall, Inc., 1967); Karl W. Deutsch, *The Nerves of Government* (New York: The Free Press, 1963); David Easton, *A Systems Analysis of Political Life* (New York: John Wiley & Sons, Inc., 1965); and Herbert Simon, *Models of Man* (New York: John Wiley & Sons, Inc., 1957), Chap. 13.

In these systems a certain portion of the energy is utilized to obtain information regarding system outputs, so that these outputs may be automatically adjusted to the demands of the environment. But aside from this rather recent development within the social sciences, there has been a continuing interest in cyclical phenomena such as economic booms and busts, periodic revolutions, or circulations of elites. The so-called vicious circle of poverty is just one example of an equilibrating process in which each variable in the system seems to reinforce the others to maintain a constant level of all variables. Students of economic development have recognized that at some point there may be a "takeoff" from an equilibrium level of development, and that once this point has been reached there may be an accelerating rate of change until, perhaps, a new equilibrium is attained at a much higher economic level. Human populations seem to have been relatively stable over long periods of time only to explode at accelerating rates during other epochs.

While most of these phenomena of change and stability can be described rather dramatically, an adequate theoretical explanation in causal terms requires an understanding of what are referred to as "stability conditions." Provided the theoretical system can be stated in relatively simple terms, these stability conditions can be rigorously studied with the aid of dynamic mathematical formulations of the type that will be discussed in this chapter and the next.

The Nature of Dynamic Models

Consider a simple equation such as $Y = a + bX$. If this is used to represent a structural equation, then one may say that a change in X of one unit should produce a change in Y of b units. Similarly, one may write a system of simultaneous algebraic equations containing slope coefficients with comparable interpretations. One can then trace out the direct and indirect changes in all of the remaining variables produced by a change in X_1. Is such a formulation "dynamic"? In a very loose sense it is, since one can use it to predict changes throughout the system, provided one is willing to assume that changes in the one variable are followed almost immediately by changes in the others. But suppose one wished to study the *process* of change and to trace out the time paths followed by each of the variables. For example, suppose one were to assume that X_1 affects X_2 but only with a specific time lag. Or suppose one were interested in whether the change in X_2 could be traced by a smooth curve that always increased (or decreased) monotonically, or whether it oscillated prior to reaching an equilibrium value. Perhaps the system would not reach an equilibrium at all, since a positive change in X_1 might bring about a sequence of changes that further increased its own value, and so on indefinitely. How can these and other possibilities be handled?

I shall adopt the usage of economists such as Baumol and Samuelson to the effect that a dynamic formulation is one in which the time factor enters into the theory in an essential way.[2] One could, for example, merely insert the subscript t into all terms of an equation, e.g., $Y_t = a + b_1 X_t + b_2 Z_t + u_{yt}$. This would remind the reader that one is dealing with time-series data. Thus one might have X, Y, and Z scores for a business firm, or small group, at a number of different points in time, and these values might be used to estimate the regression coefficients using ordinary least squares. But this is no different, in principle, from the use of least squares with cross-sectional data. The time factor is used merely to enable one to keep track of which scores go together to represent a single observation.

Suppose, however, that one's theory specifies that the impact of X on Y is almost immediate, that a change in Z produces a change in Y only after the lapse of one time period, and that a change in W will produce both an immediate change in Y, and also a delayed reaction after two time periods. Then the equation for Y might be written as follows:

$$Y_t = a + b_1 X_t + b_2 Z_{t-1} + (b_3 W_t + b_4 W_{t-2}) + u_{yt} \qquad (5\text{-}1)$$

where for simplicity we again assume linear and additive effects and an error term u_{yt} summarizing the immediate effects of outside or unmeasured variables. Now the temporal subscripts play a more important role in the formulation since they are not all alike, and since they specify the relative times it takes for each change to take effect on Y. Presumably an equation with a different set of subscripts would imply very different results. It is in this sense that we say that time enters into the formulation in an "essential" way. Let us see how dynamic models of this type can be used to resolve the identification problem.

Lagged Endogenous Variables and Difference Equations

Recall the general (static) model discussed in the previous chapter. It was pointed out that the selective use of exogenous variables Z_i, assumed to be unrelated to the error terms, can be used to help identify the structural parameters. But the successful use of exogenous variables depends on our being able to locate exogenous variables which both explain a major portion of the variation in a given endogenous variable and which can be assumed

---

[2] For discussions of the distinction between static and dynamic systems, see Baumol, *Economic Dynamics*, Chap. 1; and Samuelson, *Foundations of Economic Analysis*, pp. 314–17.

not to appear in some of the equations. What if we are unable to find such variables? Or suppose our theories are not sufficiently well established that we are willing to make the a priori assumption that some of the coefficients are zero? As a conjecture, it may turn out that most sociologists and other social scientists are unwilling to admit that any truly exogenous variables exist! There may of course be some variables for which feedback can for all practical purposes be assumed negligible (e.g., environmental factors such as rainfall), but these factors may not be sufficiently important contributors to the unexplained variance. If so, what can be done?

One apparently attractive alternative is to formulate dynamic models involving lagged endogenous variables treated as though they were exogenous. This can be illustrated in terms of a simplified version of Hopkins' theory. Suppose we deal only with rank, centrality, and influence as in Fig. 5-1. The omitted variables observability and conformity were assumed to be influenced by centrality; likewise, these two omitted variables affected influence, and in the original Hopkins formulation there was a feedback assumed from influence to conformity, as well as a reciprocal link between observability and conformity. Thus there was no "direct" arrow running from influence back to centrality (except via rank, which we are retaining in the simplified system). Because we have gotten rid of conformity and observability, we can draw in an arrow from centrality to influence, taking this relationship to be "direct" in the simplified version.

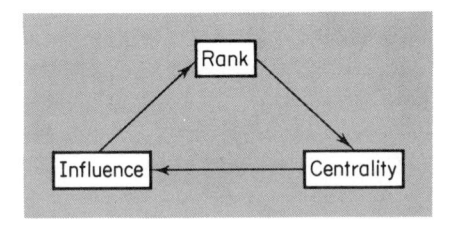

FIG. 5-1 A simplified version of the Hopkins model.

This gives an example of what I shall term a *simple closed loop* (or *simple loop*) characterized by single arrows running either clockwise or counterclockwise and ending at the starting point. We shall later examine conditions for stability in such simple loops, but for the time being it is sufficient to emphasize that, as the theory stands, there is an identification problem and the assumptions required for least squares cannot be met.

Suppose, however, that the theory specifies that there will be a delayed reaction in the relationship between influence and rank, but that elsewhere the changes will take place almost immediately. It is not necessary that such a theory hold in all instances. Let us assume that we are dealing with a bureaucratic organization in which promotions take place once a year, or in some other specified interval. Influence will ultimately be translated into rank, but this takes time; whereas we might assume that a change in rank will automatically produce an immediate change in centrality. Similarly, we might assume that a change in centrality will produce an almost immediate change in influence, which in the following year may again affect one's rank.

Needless to say, this model represents an idealization of real processes. But if one were to observe the organization at yearly intervals, the time periods for consummating changes in centrality due to rank, or influence due to centrality, might be so brief relative to the observation interval that for all practical purposes they might be taken as instantaneous. Obviously, in other kinds of groups this particular dynamic formulation might have to be replaced, perhaps by one in which influence had an immediate impact on rank but where the effect of centrality on influence was delayed.

Writing rank at time t as X_{1t}, centrality at t as X_{2t}, and influence at t and $t-1$ as X_{3t} and $X_{3,t-1}$, respectively, we could express the dynamic formulation as follows:

$$X_{1t} = a_1 + b_{13} X_{3,t-1} + u_{1t} \tag{5-2a}$$

$$X_{2t} = a_2 + b_{21} X_{1t} + u_{2t} \tag{5-2b}$$

$$X_{3t} = a_3 + b_{32} X_{2t} + u_{3t} \tag{5-2c}$$

Notice that it is only the first equation that contains both the subscripts t and $t-1$. This is one form of what is referred to as a *difference equation*. One may make substitutions from the algebraic equations (5-2b) and (5-2c) in order to rewrite the difference equation (5-2a) in terms of rank X_1 at the two successive time periods $t-1$ and t. Let us see what insights this gives.

From Eqs. (5-2b) and (5-2c) we have

$$\begin{aligned} X_{3t} &= a_3 + b_{32}[a_2 + b_{21} X_{1t} + u_{2t}] + u_{3t} \\ &= (a_3 + b_{32} a_2) + b_{32} b_{21} X_{1t} + (b_{32} u_{2t} + u_{3t}) \end{aligned} \tag{5-3}$$

Since this is true for the arbitrary time t, we assume it is also true at $t-1$, and therefore we may substitute $t-1$ for t wherever the latter subscript appears.[3] This gives

$$X_{3,t-1} = (a_3 + b_{32} a_2) + b_{32} b_{21} X_{1,t-1} + (b_{32} u_{2,t-1} + u_{3,t-1})$$

---

[3] This kind of assumption is characteristic of "causal" systems, as contrasted with "historical" ones. See Samuelson, *op. cit.*, pp. 317–35. It amounts to assuming that values depend only on initial values and the amount of time that has elapsed, regardless of the actual (historical) time which t_0 represents.

which may be substituted in Eq. (5-2a), yielding:

$$X_{1t} = a_1 + b_{13}[(a_3 + b_{32}a_2) + b_{32}b_{21}X_{1,t-1} + (b_{32}u_{2,t-1} + u_{3,t-1})] + u_{1t}$$

$$= (a_1 + b_{13}a_3 + b_{13}b_{32}a_2) + b_{13}b_{32}b_{21}X_{1,t-1} + (b_{13}b_{32}u_{2,t-1} + b_{13}u_{3,t-1} + u_{1t})$$

or

$$X_{1t} = A_1 + b_{13}b_{32}b_{21}X_{1,t-1} + (U_{1t} + U_{2,t-1} + U_{3,t-1}) \tag{5-4}$$

Thus we have expressed X_1 at time t as a function of itself at $t-1$ and various error terms. This simply means that we have completed the loop, and that a change in X_1 feeds back to influence itself at a later period in time.

A simple inspection of the coefficient $b_{13}b_{32}b_{21}$ which appears in front of $X_{1,t-1}$ will in this case enable us to determine what should happen over time, provided that we can ignore the disturbance terms. If all three b's are positive (or if one is positive and two are negative), then an increase in X_1 will bring about further increases at successive time periods. If the numerical value of the product $b_{13}b_{32}b_{21}$ is greater than unity, then an initial change of one unit will produce a greater than unit change in the next interval, and this will be followed by successively greater changes until the system explodes, or until changes in other variables are such that the model is no longer appropriate. [See Fig. 5-2(a).] On the other hand, if the value of the product is less than unity, then the successive changes in X_1 will become smaller and smaller, and the system will stabilize. [See Fig. 5-2(b).] How rapidly this occurs will depend on how much less than unity the product is.

This is the case of positive feedback implied by Hopkins' original formulation. If one or all three of the b's were negative, as was the case in Alker's model, then an increase in X_1 at time 1 would produce a decrease at time 2, followed by an increase at time 3, a decrease at time 4, and so forth. If the absolute value of the product were greater than unity, these oscillations would increase in amplitude until the system exploded. [See Fig. 5-2(c).] If the magnitude were less than unity, the oscillations would dampen to zero as time progressed. [See Fig. 5-2(d).] Thus in the case of this very simple system, with a single difference equation, we can very readily see the implications over time.

If we think of the system as given at any particular moment, and not subject to disturbing influences, we would be in a position to predict its path at all later moments in time. If these movements approach a fixed limiting value, as in the case where the magnitude of the product of the slopes is less than unity, then we refer to this limiting position as a stable equilibrium

82 Single-Equation Dynamic Models

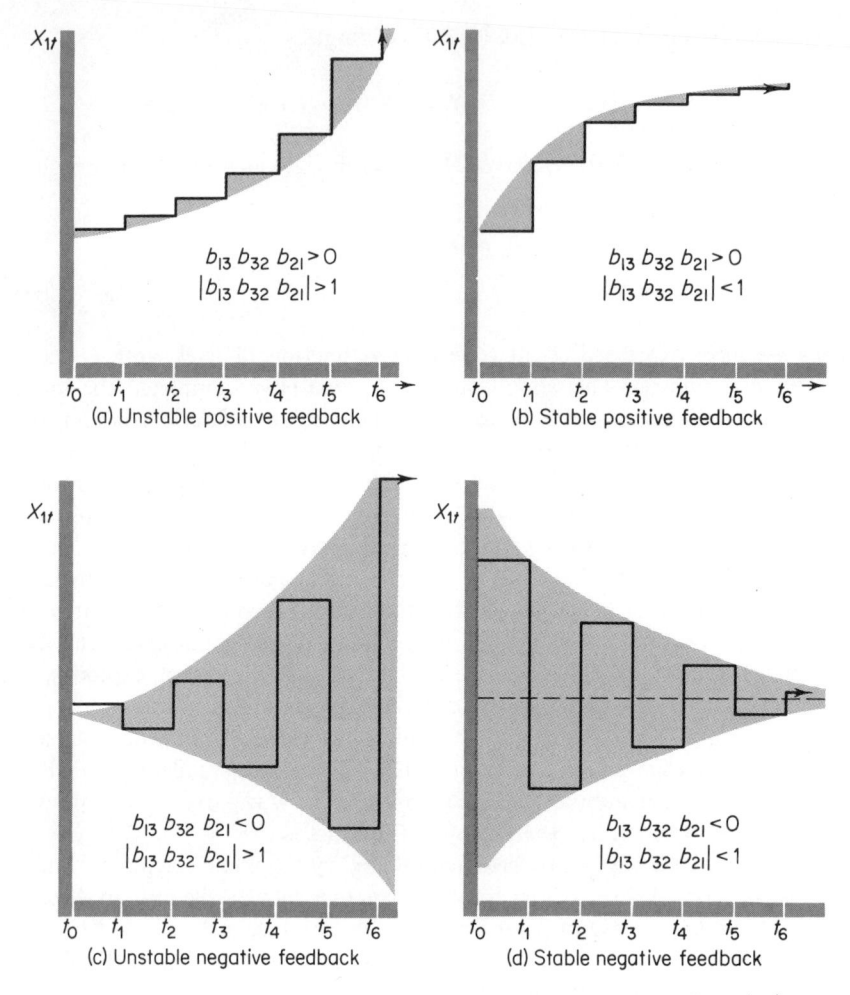

FIG. 5-2 Types of feedback situations for the difference equation $X_{1t} = A_1 + b_{13}b_{32}b_{21}X_{1,t-1}$.

(a) Unstable positive feedback: $b_{13}\,b_{32}\,b_{21} > 0$, $|b_{13}\,b_{32}\,b_{21}| > 1$

(b) Stable positive feedback: $b_{13}\,b_{32}\,b_{21} > 0$, $|b_{13}\,b_{32}\,b_{21}| < 1$

(c) Unstable negative feedback: $b_{13}\,b_{32}\,b_{21} < 0$, $|b_{13}\,b_{32}\,b_{21}| > 1$

(d) Stable negative feedback: $b_{13}\,b_{32}\,b_{21} < 0$, $|b_{13}\,b_{32}\,b_{21}| < 1$

point.[4] As we noted in the case of supply and demand functions, real-life systems will always be subject to outside disturbances, or "random shocks," and therefore the equilibrium points will never remain fixed. But our theoretical formulation can be very much simplified if we learn to think in terms of closed systems not subject to such disturbances. It is another matter with respect to empirical tests and estimating procedures, however.

[4] See Samuelson, *op. cit.*, pp. 260–65 and Chap. 11, for discussions of various types of stability.

From the standpoint of estimation, note that the system of equations (5-2) is recursive, provided we think of X_3 at times t and $t-1$ as distinct variables. Suppose that we are concerned with a particular time t and that we treat the lagged endogenous variable $X_{3,t-1}$ as though it were an exogenous variable Z. The equations (5-2) could then be written as

$$X_1 = a_1 + b_{13}Z + u_1 \tag{5-5a}$$

$$X_2 = a_2 + b_{21}X_1 + u_2 \tag{5-5b}$$

$$X_3 = a_3 + b_{32}X_2 + u_3 \tag{5-5c}$$

where I have dropped the subscript t in order to emphasize the similarity with recursive systems as discussed in Chap. 4. Thus by this simple device we seem to have gotten around the identification problem.

Herman Wold has argued that the use of dynamic formulations involving lagged endogenous variables not only resolves the identification problem, but it also affords relatively simple interpretations of reality in terms of stimulus and response interactions in which definite lags must occur.[5] This is especially true whenever each equation can be linked to an autonomous actor, as in the case of suppliers and their customers. The immediate concern, however, is that of whether the identification problem can be so simply resolved in this manner. Of course the resolution requires that data be collected at two or more points in time, but this would seem a small price to pay for the advantages.

The difficulty involves the behavior of the error terms, which, as we have seen, can be quite elusive and troublesome. Let us examine Eq. (5-5a) containing the "exogenous" variable Z, which is really X_3 at an earlier point in time. The fundamental defining property of an exogenous variable, as previously discussed, is that it must be independent of the disturbance term u_{1t}. But Z, or $X_{3,t-1}$, depends on $X_{2,t-1}$ which, in turn, depends on $X_{1,t-1}$. Thus Z depends on the disturbance term for X_1 at the earlier time $t-1$. Call this disturbance $u_{1,t-1}$. Hence u_{1t} must be independent of $u_{1,t-1}$ if the assumptions are to be met. Whatever factors that affect X_1 at time t must operate in such a way that they are uncorrelated with factors affecting this same variable at $t-1$.

Clearly, this is a very strong assumption that is likely to be violated in real systems. It would hold true if there were very brief random shocks producing once-and-for-all changes in X_1. But suppose there were an

---

[5] See especially, Wold and Jureen, *Demand Analysis*, Chap. 2; and Strotz and Wold, "Recursive versus Nonrecursive Systems."

unknown variable influencing X_1 that retained its values over a reasonably long period of time. Perhaps it would take on relatively high values over the first five time periods, gradually shifting to low values over another series of intervals. If this factor were positively related to X_1, then we would expect X_1 to have higher than average values during the first five periods, followed by unusually low ones over some other interval of time. If so, the values of successive error terms would be correlated, contrary to assumption. This is the problem of "autocorrelation," or self-correlation, frequently encountered with time-series data.

In general, autocorrelations are apt to be most serious for short intervals because of the fact that the error terms are more likely to be dominated by disturbances that act continuously throughout a brief interval. As the time between observations is increased, errors are more likely to behave randomly unless there are a few major disturbances of prolonged duration. Thus the investigator is faced with a dilemma. Frequent observations at short intervals give more information and are often necessary to check on the adequacy of a difference equation involving discrete time intervals. But one cannot simply double or triple the effective number of "cases" by reducing the observation intervals. The replications will not be independent, owing to autocorrelation.

Questions of possible bias due to autocorrelation, as well as significance tests, are treated in most econometrics texts and need not be discussed in the present context.[6] It should be emphasized, however, that this is not a trivial statistical artifact that can be passed off as having minor significance. The problems of autocorrelation and measurement error are two of the most crucial difficulties that are likely to be encountered in attempts to test dynamic theories and estimate the structural parameters of change. Since our principal concern is with theory *construction*, however, I shall not deal extensively with these particular problems except to introduce caveats at various points in the discussion.

Cobweb models

As a further illustration of the use of difference equations in constructing dynamic models of the recursive form, let us consider a type of supply and demand situation involving a lag in the supply function. In the case of certain types of agricultural or manufactured products, it is not too unrealistic to assume that producers make their production decisions early during a given time period, and that it is difficult for them to gradually

---

[6] See Christ, *Econometric Models*, pp. 481–88; Fisher, *Identification Problem*, pp. 168–75; and Klein, *An Introduction to Econometrics*, pp. 168–75.

modify these decisions during this time interval. For example, farmers may decide on their wheat or corn acreage early during the growing season, and this may be a major determinant of the total yield at the end of the season. Assuming the entire supply is placed on the market, rather than being stored or otherwise withheld, it seems reasonable to assume that the supply at time t depends on market conditions at $t - 1$, and perhaps earlier time periods as well. The consumer demand, however, can be adjusted much more rapidly to present prices. These considerations suggest a simplified linear model of the following form:

$$S_t = a_1 + b_1 P_{t-1} + u_s \qquad (5\text{-}6a)$$

$$D_t = a_2 - b_2 P_t + u_d \qquad (5\text{-}6b)$$

$$S_t = D_t + \epsilon \qquad (5\text{-}6c)$$

where the symbols S, D, and P represent supply, demand and prices respectively, and where Eq. (5-6c) says that at equilibrium supply and demand should be approximately equal.[7]

This system is recursive and can be identified. If someone were to multiply the second (demand) equation by some constant and add it to the first, the resultant hybrid equation would contain a term involving prices at time t, as well as at time $t - 1$. Since by assumption supply is not determined by present prices, the hoax could be discovered.

Let us examine how supply and demand can be expected to change over time, given this model. A difference-equation model of this type does not necessarily imply that the system will actually reach a stable equilibrium. Suppose that prices at a given point are high. This will encourage farmers to produce more goods, which will be placed on the market in the next time period. But a large supply will lower prices (without a lag), and these reduced prices will motivate farmers to produce less during the next period. But this reduced supply will again raise prices for the next interval, which will increase production and again lower prices. We see that it is possible for producers to "overshoot the mark" each time, so that there is a theoretical possibility that the amplitudes (peaks and troughs) will get greater and greater, rather than dampening to zero.

The conditions for stability in this simple model can be seen with the aid of several diagrams, though they can also be deduced more rigorously from the equations. Compare Figs. 5-3 and 5-4. In Fig. 5-3, the supply curve is

---

[7] See Baumol, *Economic Dynamics*, pp. 111–15; and Wold and Jureen, *Demand Analysis*, Chap. 3.

FIG. 5-3 A stable cobweb model.   FIG. 5-4 An unstable cobweb model.

steeper than the demand curve, whereas the reverse is true in the case of Fig. 5-4. Let us first consider what happens over time in the case of Fig. 5-3. Prices at time₁ are represented by P_1, and these (partly) determine the quantity supplied at time₂. This quantity supplied at time₂, represented by Q_2, can be found by moving across horizontally until the supply function S is intersected. But this very large supply at time₂ lowers the price at time₂ (represented as P_2), given the demand curve D. P_2 can be determined by moving down from Q_2 to the demand curve. But this price P_2 affects Q_3, the supply at time 3, which can be obtained by again moving horizontally until the supply function is intersected. We obtain the price P_3 corresponding to Q_3 by moving vertically to the demand curve. Moving horizontally and then vertically we next obtain Q_4 and P_4, and so forth. Because of the fact that the supply function is steeper than the demand function, the resulting path spirals inward to the equilibrium point represented by the intersection of the two functions.

In the case of Fig. 5-4, however, the demand function is steeper than the supply function, and the "cobweb" pattern spirals outward away from the intersection point. In this instance, the suppliers are each time overcorrecting by an increasing amount, so that they continually overshoot the mark, creating greater and greater peaks and troughs. Obviously, such a situation could not go on indefinitely, but the model is at least suggestive. A more realistic model could be constructed by using nonlinear supply and demand functions, as in Fig. 5-5. You should convince yourself that in such a case it is possible to obtain cycles or oscillations which have stable amplitudes (e.g., the path continues around a single loop).[8]

In this case the stability conditions can be simply stated and inferred by

---

[8] For a more detailed discussion of such nonlinear models applied to cobweb models, see Baumol, *Economic Dynamics*, Chap. 13.

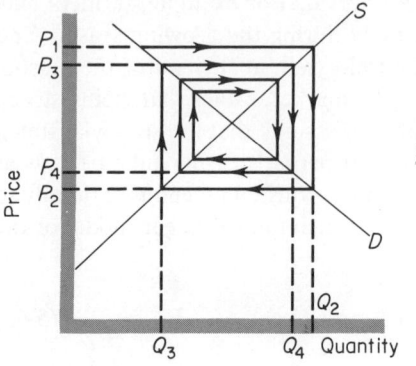

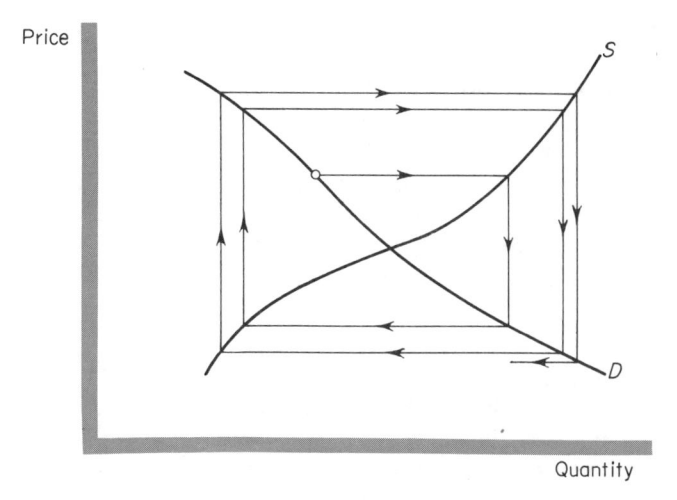

FIG. 5-5 A cobweb model involving nonlinear supply and demand functions.

reference to a diagram. In the case of simultaneous difference equations, where more than one equation contains subscripts referring to several different time periods, the stability conditions are not so obvious. The main point this example illustrates is that whether or not a given equilibrium point (e.g., the intersection point) is stable depends on a set of conditions that must be specified. In most sociological research and theory building we are not in a position to determine exact values for the equilibrium points or structural parameters. Nevertheless, certain qualitative statements can be made. For example in the case of the cobweb model, one could argue that any factors operating to increase the slope of the supply function, relative to that of the demand function, should aid in stabilizing the system. This is by no means a trivial observation, nor would it be suggested by common sense.

If one can ascertain the nature of the necessary stability conditions, and if he then observes that a given empirical system is relatively stable over a reasonable period of time, he may argue that the stability conditions must have been met. If so, these conditions will place restrictions on the model which may be theoretically useful. This is essentially the observation made by Homans in connection with equilibrium in small groups.[9] After examining the use of differential equations in some detail, we shall return in Chap. 6 to a formalization of Homans' theory of human groups in which Herbert Simon makes effective use of such stability conditions in deducing certain relationships predicted to hold in the case of equilibrium.[10]

[9] Homans, *The Human Group*, pp. 305–8.
[10] Simon, *Models of Man*, Chap. 6.

Differential Equations

In making use of difference equations, I have been assuming that there are discrete time periods and that jumps occur from one time period to the next, rather than continuously. This makes sense in a few special instances, such as in the case of farm products, political elections, or small groups that meet at regular intervals in a laboratory setting. But in most situations changes occur more or less continuously through time.

Some processes take place more rapidly than others. It is often convenient to think in terms of three categories of time changes relative to the intervals of observation.[11] First, there are changes that occur so rapidly that they must for all practical purposes be considered instantaneous. As we have seen, algebraic equations are appropriate for describing these changes, since the actual process of change cannot be studied. Second, certain change processes will take place at a rate that is appropriate for study during the observation period. If these occur continuously through time, differential equations will be appropriate; if time can be treated in terms of discrete intervals, then difference equations will be preferable. Third, there will be changes that occur so gradually that for all practical purposes the "variables" involved can be treated as fixed parameters. In longer-run formulations, models can be complicated by taking these latter parameters as variables.

What are differential equations and how do they differ from difference equations? As already implied, differential equations permit one to construct continuous time models appropriate for analyzing those changes that occur during the interval of observation. The basic idea underlying the calculus and differential equations is that of imagining indefinitely short time intervals Δt during which small changes ΔX occur in the variable X. One can then express a *rate* of change by considering the ratio $\Delta X/\Delta t$. Of course empirical data must be collected at points in time that are separated by finite intervals. But we imagine these periods getting shorter and shorter until some sort of limit is approached. As the time period Δt becomes infinitesimal, the amount of change ΔX in that time period also becomes very small. But although both quantities approach zero, their *ratio* may be a finite number which we can represent by the symbol dX/dt. This symbol dX/dt is referred to as the *derivative* of X with respect to t; and it is formally defined as *the limit of $\Delta X/\Delta t$, as Δt approaches zero*.

In this and the following chapter we shall only be concerned with very simple kinds of differential equations in which there is a single differential expression, such as dX/dt, taken as a function of various algebraic quantities.

---

[11] See Samuelson, *Foundations of Economic Analysis*, pp. 330–31; and Herbert Simon, *Models of Man*, pp. 143–44.

For example, we may have $dX/dt = k$, where k is a constant. As is pointed out in Appendix B, this is the equation of a straight line, which of course has the property that the slope is the same everywhere, or a constant. Or dX/dt may be taken as a function of t, indicating that the rate of change in X can be described in terms of time itself. Of greater theoretical interest, dX/dt may be a function of the level of X or the levels of other variables assumed to be causally related to X. For example, we might have the equation $dX/dt = k_1 X + k_2 Y$, where Y is assumed to be exogenous. In Chap. 6 we shall deal with simultaneous differential equations in which a separate equation might be written for dY/dt as a function of X and Y. In both instances, we shall be primarily interested in considering causal interpretations for these equations, studying their implications, and analyzing various stability conditions.

Let us briefly consider two specific substantive examples, the second of which will be elaborated in Chap. 6. Demographers are obviously interested in predicting and explaining population growth, which as we have already indicated may be taken as a function of birth, death, and migration rates. Models of varying complexity can be constructed and their implications for stability made explicit.[12] Taking an extremely simple model in which migration is assumed to be negligible, we may write the rate of change in population dP/dt as an exact function of the number of births less the number of deaths. If the birth and death *rates* were both constant, this would imply that the change in population would be a simple function of the size of the population itself. Thus we could begin with the equation $dP/dt = kP$. If the birth rate exceeded the death rate, then the larger the population the more rapid the growth rate, and in fact the population would increase exponentially. The reason for this exponential growth is explained in Appendix B. But if the death rate exceeded the birth rate, the population would decline at a decelerating rate until it eventually reached zero.

Human and animal populations are obviously limited by environmental factors that, in effect, produce changes in the birth and death rates, so that the above assumption of constancy is unrealistic. If there were some absolute limit N to the size of the population because of a constant but limited food supply, then as P approached N the rate of growth would slow down to zero. There are of course a number of possible equations that could represent this fact, but one of the simplest is

$$\frac{dP}{dt} = kP(N - P), \quad \text{where } P \leq N \tag{5-7}$$

[12] See A. J. Lotka, *Elements of Physical Biology* (Baltimore: Williams & Wilkins Co., 1925); and Nathan Keyfitz, *Introduction to the Mathematics of Population* (Reading, Mass.: Addison-Wesley Publishing Co., Inc., 1968).

Still more complex equations could be developed that took into consideration migration, which might be a function of food supply, and also changes in the food supply. If there were predator and prey populations, the sizes of which were each a function of the other, this could be represented by a pair of differential equations, one each for P_1 and P_2. Questions might then be asked concerning the conditions under which stability might be reached, or whether cyclical growth and decline patterns might develop.

As a second example, it has frequently been noted that armament levels in one nation affect those in another nation, with the result that an uncontrolled arms race may develop. If there were k such nations it would be necessary to deal simultaneously with k differential equations, one for each of the nations concerned. This particular kind of situation will be discussed in Chap. 6 in connection with Richardson's theory of arms races.[13] Here let us assume that we are dealing with a single nation reacting to the armament level of a second nation, the behavior of which is taken to be exogenous. (Perhaps this second nation is so large that it need not be concerned with what goes on in the first.)

Let X_1 be the level of armaments in the first nation, and let X_2 be that of the second. Then as a first approximation we might use the equation

$$\frac{dX_1}{dt} = a + b_1 X_1 + b_2 X_2 \tag{5-8}$$

where b_1 is ordinarily negative and b_2 positive. This would indicate that the greater the level of armaments X_2 in the second nation, the greater the rate of increase in the first nation's arms. But with each increase in X_1 there might be a diminishing returns or "fatigue" effect, in Richardson's terms. That is, the level of X_1 may affect the rate of growth dX_1/dt because of its indirect effects via cuts in nonmilitary spending and other factors. Finally, the rate of increase in armaments might depend on more or less constant factors summarized by a. As will be indicated in greater detail in Chap. 6, such constant "grievance" factors (Richardson's term) turn out not to affect the stability of arms races, though they may affect the *levels* at which arms races ultimately stabilize.

These two examples should be sufficient to indicate the potential utility of differential equations. However, we cannot consider the "solutions" to either single equations or simultaneous systems without discussing a few very elementary principles of calculus. A brief introduction to the subject is given in Appendix B, and this should be enough for an understanding of the

[13] See Lewis F. Richardson, *Arms and Insecurity* (Pittsburgh: Boxwood Press, 1960).

remainder of this chapter and the next. Obviously, a true working knowledge will require much more background in mathematics.

Assuming that the reader is familiar with these elementary principles, I shall next examine several different kinds of differential equations that are most likely to be useful in sociological theories.

Change in X as a function of time

Perhaps the most simple kinds of differential equations are those that express a change in X as a polynomial or other function of time alone, or as a constant. If $X = X_0$ at time zero, we might have the following differential equations and their solutions:

Differential equations   *Solutions*

$$\frac{dX}{dt} = b \qquad\qquad X = X_0 + bt \qquad\qquad (5\text{-}9a)$$

$$\frac{dX}{dt} = b_1 + 2b_2 t \qquad\qquad X = X_0 + b_1 t + b_2 t^2 \qquad\qquad (5\text{-}9b)$$

$$\frac{dX}{dt} = b_1 + 2b_2 t + 3b_3 t^2 \qquad\qquad X = X_0 + b_1 t + b_2 t^2 + b_3 t^3 \qquad\qquad (5\text{-}9c)$$

$$\frac{dX}{dt} = \frac{b}{t}, \quad t \neq 0 \qquad\qquad X = b \log_e t + C, \quad t \neq 0 \qquad\qquad (5\text{-}9d)$$

Equations of this type of course cannot be used to explain *why* X changes over time, but they can be used to describe the time path of X. Sometimes it is useful to add terms that are functions of time t onto differential equations involving other variables in order to approximate known time-series trends in real data. In one sense, expressing a change in X as a function of time is an admission of one's ignorance as to the causal dynamics. But the equation may serve as a challenge to explain why the path should follow one particular temporal sequence rather than another.

Change in X as a Function of X and Other Variables [14]

As indicated in Appendix B, the differential equation $dX/dt = bX$ has the particular solution $X = X_0 e^{bt}$, where X_0 represents the initial value of X

---

[14] For a more technical discussion of the materials in this section see James S. Coleman, "The Mathematical Study of Change," in *Methodology in Social Research*, eds. Blalock and Blalock, Chap. 11.

at time zero. Let us next examine an equation in which dX/dt is taken as an additive function of some constant a and X. It can be shown that the particular solution to the equation

$$\frac{dX}{dt} = a + bX$$

is

$$X = \frac{a}{b}(e^{bt} - 1) + X_0 e^{bt}, \qquad \text{for } b \neq 0 \qquad (5\text{-}10)$$

This more complex result may be checked by differentiating X with respect to t.[15]

We can examine the behavior of X as time passes, or as t becomes large. First consider the case where b is negative. The expression e^{bt} will decrease to zero, since we are raising a quantity greater than one to a negative power. The speed with which this occurs will depend on the magnitude of b. If the (negative) slope is large, terms involving e^{bt} will dampen to zero very rapidly and can be ignored as time passes. Hence X will approach the quantity $-a/b$ in the limit, as indicated in Fig. 5-6. If X begins above the equilibrium level, the curve will approach the asymptote $-a/b$ from above, whereas the asymptote will be approached from below if X starts out below the equilibrium value. Thus as time passes, the initial or starting point becomes less and less relevant. Notice that if the constant a is positive, the equilibrium value $-a/b$ will also be positive, since b is negative. If $a = 0$, then the equilibrium level will of course be zero, meaning that X will approach zero as time passes. Finally, note that the equilibrium value could also have been found by setting dX/dt equal to zero, giving $0 = a + bX$, or $X = -a/b$.

If b is positive, however, the expression e^{bt} increases at an accelerating rate, and X will either increase or decrease indefinitely, according to whether the initial value X_0 is greater or less than $-a/b$. This result, shown in Fig. 5-7, can be seen by rewriting Eq. (5-10) as

---

[15] Differentiating Eq. (5-10) gives

$$\frac{dX}{dt} = b\left(\frac{a}{b}\right)e^{bt} - 0 + bX_0 e^{bt} = a e^{bt} + bX_0 e^{bt}$$

But

$$a + bX = a + b\left[\left(\frac{a}{b}\right)(e^{bt} - 1) + X_0 e^{bt}\right] = a + a(e^{bt} - 1) + bX_0 e^{bt}$$

$$= a e^{bt} + bX_0 e^{bt} = \frac{dX}{dt}$$

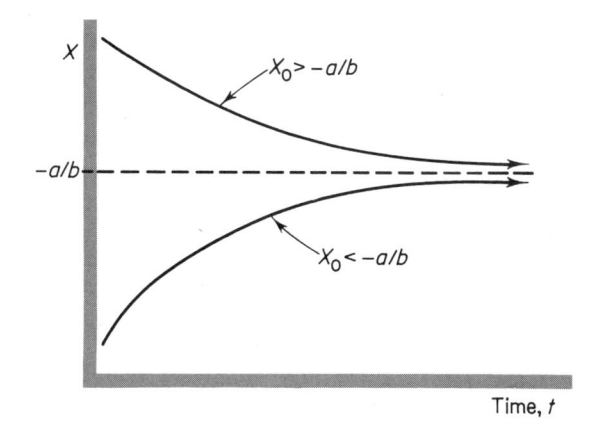

FIG. 5-6 The stable condition ($b < 0$) for the differential equation $dX/dt = a + bX$.

$$X = -\frac{a}{b} + \left(\frac{a}{b} + X_0\right) e^{bt}$$

The first term $-a/b$ is just a constant and will be completely dominated by the exponential term. We see that if $X_0 > -a/b$, the coefficient of the exponential will be positive, whereas if it is less than $-a/b$, this coefficient will be negative and the function will decrease at an accelerating rate. In the

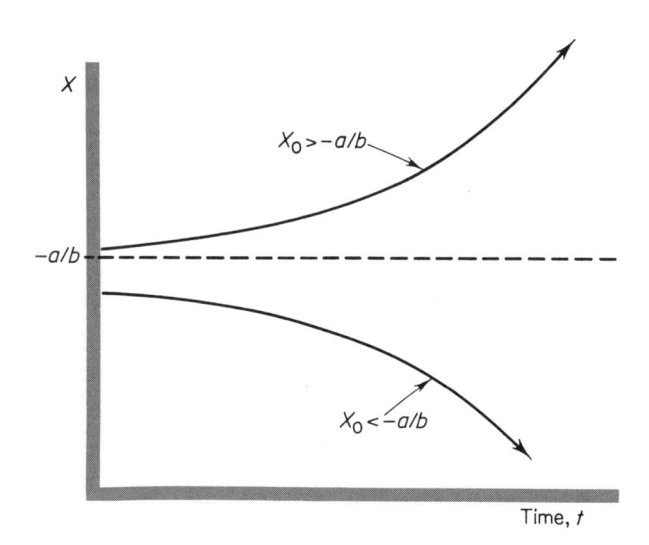

FIG. 5-7 The unstable condition ($b > 0$) for the differential equation $dX/dt = a + bX$.

special case where X_0 is exactly equal to $-a/b$, the exponential term will drop out and we will have $X = -a/b$. This is sometimes referred to as an *unstable* equilibrium. As long as there are no exogenous shocks, X will remain constant. But a slight push in either direction will begin an accelerated movement away from the value $-a/b$.[16]

Before discussing the substantive implications and interpretations of these results, I shall introduce one further complication. Suppose we wish to write dX/dt as a function not only of a constant and X itself, but of other variables as well. A slight change of notation will be necessary. Let us refer to several different X_i, focusing on dX_1/dt without loss of generality. Since the general linear model represents a straightforward extension of the two-variable case, we can confine our attention to the equation:

$$\frac{dX_1}{dt} = a + b_1 X_1 + b_2 X_2 \tag{5-11}$$

which has the following solution:

$$X_{1t} = \frac{a}{b_1}(e^{b_1 t} - 1) + e^{b_1 t} X_{10} + \frac{b_2}{b_1}(e^{b_1 t} - 1) X_2 \tag{5-12}$$

This solution can again be checked by differentiating X_1 with respect to time.

The various terms can be interpreted as follows. The first two terms on the right-hand side are the same as before, except for the subscripts. This portion of the equation says that the value of X_1 at any particular time t (written X_{1t}) is a function of X_1 at time zero (written X_{10}), which was previously labeled X_0. The new term on the right-hand side of the equation involves X_2.[17] We see that the coefficient of this term has exactly the same form as the first term, with the exception that b_2 replaces a. Note that stability depends only on b_1, the coefficient of X_1 in the differential equation. If $b_1 < 0$, then as time passes $e^{b_1 t}$ approaches zero, and X_{1t} approaches the limiting value $-(a/b_1) - (b_2/b_1)X_2$, which could also have been obtained by setting dX_1/dt equal to zero and solving Eq. (5-11) for X_1. It can easily be seen that the addition of terms involving X_3, X_4, and so forth, will create no special problems.

---

[16] In the special case where $b = 0$, $dX/dt = a$, and we have a "neutral" equilibrium in which X increases or decreases at a constant rate.

[17] It should be noted that the solution (5-12) may be modified if X_2 is not constant over time. See Coleman, "The Mathematical Study of Change," pp. 441–43.

Interpretations of the slopes

In order to interpret these results, let us focus first on the feedback term involving b_1, which as we have seen must be negative if the system is to approach a stable equilibrium value. Of course if b_1 is a very small positive number, the rate of change dX_1/dt may be virtually constant over a rather long period of time, though if the model remains appropriate over the long run we know that the system will eventually explode. What does it mean, substantively, to say that the rate of change in X_1 depends on the *level* of X_1? If interpreted causally, this might sound like extreme mysticism. The slope b_1 may serve to describe what actually occurs over time, but how can we explain why this should be? What substantive interpretation can be given to the coefficient b_1?

Coleman notes that in a sense b_1 summarizes our ignorance of the details of the feedback process, and that the term b_1X_1 stands as a surrogate for other terms that should be brought into the equation explicitly in order to explain the feedback process.[18] He argues that the notion "X_1 causes X_1" might be used to substitute for a causal argument involving one or more feedback loops, as for example, $X_1 \rightarrow X_2 \rightarrow X_3 \rightarrow X_4 \rightarrow X_1$. If there is an odd number of negative signs, then b_1 will be negative; if they are all positive, or if there is an even number of minuses, then the feedback will be positive, as in the case of the Hopkins model. If all of these variables could be brought into the system explicitly, then the b_1 term would not be needed unless there were additional feedback loops. But because this will be difficult if not impossible practically, it is necessary to introduce feedback terms so that one may at least allow for the possibility that the theoretical system is incomplete. Our aim, however, is to handle feedback explicitly through the introduction of explanatory links, rather than treating it implicitly through the b_1X_1 term.

It will be recalled that in the example of the Hopkins model we made use of a single difference equation to handle the positive feedback implied by the original formulation. It turned out that stability required that the coefficient $b_{13}b_{32}b_{21}$ be less than unity in magnitude, whereas we have just seen that in the case of differential equations stability requires a negative coefficient. This difference is due to the way the two kinds of equations were set up. In the case of the simple difference equation $X_t = KX_{t-1}$, stability requires that $|K| < 1$. If K is negative the system will oscillate. These oscillations will increase in amplitude if $K < -1$ and will dampen if $-1 < K < 0$. In the case of the equation system (5-2) used to represent the Hopkins model, the

---

[18] *Ibid.*, pp. 438–41.

difference equation combined with the two algebraic equations produced a value of $K = b_{13}b_{32}b_{21}$.

To see more clearly the relationship between K and b, we can rewrite the difference equation in terms of a *change* in X. Subtracting X_{t-1} from both sides of the equation we would have

$$\Delta X = X_t - X_{t-1} = (K - 1)X_{t-1} \tag{5-13}$$

Thus it is $K - 1$ that is roughly analogous to b, whenever K is positive. If $0 < K < 1$ then $K - 1$ will be negative, and this is the situation in which the path of X approaches equilibrium without oscillating. If $K > 1$, then $K - 1$ will be positive and the values of X will increase (or decrease) without limit, but without oscillating. In instances where K is negative, however, the oscillations have no counterpart in the case of simple linear first-order differential equations. In this sense the difference-equation formulation is "richer" than its differential-equation counterpart, provided, of course, that it is realistic to allow for the possibility of overshooting the mark (e.g., as in the cobweb model).[19]

As a final interpretive comment, we have already noted that stability in Eq. (5-12) depends only on b_1 and not on b_2. It might seem peculiar that the form of this last term resembles the first term more than the second term involving X_1. It must be remembered, however, that we are dealing with a single equation in which X_2 is taken as exogenous. There is no equation specifying the behavior of X_2 over time, and therefore X_2 must be conceived as producing only a constant effect. When we consider simultaneous equations, which may permit a study of how X_2 changes over time as a result of changes in X_1, we shall see that coefficients such as b_2 play a role in determining whether or not the system will be stable. Here, however, we conceive of X_2 as an explicit cause of X_1, but one that produces a once-and-for-all effect that has no bearing on the stability of the system. This value of X_2 does, however, affect the equilibrium level $-(a/b_1) - (b_2/b_1)X_2$, which is approached asymptotically if b_1 is negative.

These points may be illustrated in terms of the arms race example involving the reactions of the first nation to the arms level of the second nation, the behavior of which for the present is being taken as exogenous. As just noted, the level of arms in the second nation does not affect whether or not the system will stabilize. Stability depends only on whether the "fatigue" coefficient is in fact negative. The larger the negative value of b_1, the more rapidly

---

[19] See Baumol, *Economic Dynamics*, pp. 282, 301–2; and Samuelson, *Foundations of Economic Analysis*, pp. 265ff.

the exponential $e^{b_1 t}$ will approach zero, and therefore the more rapidly a stable equilibrium will be reached.

It is instructive to examine the effects of the various parameters on the level of armaments in the first nation when stability has been reached. This equilibrium level $-(a/b_1) - (b_2/b_1)X_2$ will of course be positive if b_1 is negative, provided a and b_2 are positive. We see that the level of armaments will be increased by (a) an increase in the "grievance" constant a; (b) an increase in the level of arms in nation 2, as represented by the value of X_2; (c) an increase in the (positive) value of b_2, which can be interpreted as measuring the sensitivity in the first nation to the arms level of the second nation; and (d) a decrease in the magnitude or absolute value of the fatigue coefficient b_1.

These conclusions are of course consistent with what one would expect on a common-sense basis, though often such common sense does not prove as systematic in spelling out all of the implications of a given model. Beyond this, we see that this particular linear formulation implies that the fatigue coefficient plays a more important role than either the constant term or b_2. If b_1 turned out to be nearly zero, not only would this mean a very slow approach to equilibrium, but it would also imply a very high level of armaments in the first nation once stability had been reached. We shall see in the case of two nations engaged in a simultaneous arms race, in which the second nation also reacts to the arms level of the first nation, that stability will require rather large negative fatigue coefficients in *both* nations. Given this importance of the negative feedback term b_1, it becomes virtually necessary to attempt to explain its magnitude by inserting specific variables in the feedback loop. In this example, this would involve replacing the coefficient b_1 with variables that could be used to explain this fatigue effect.

Estimation with Least Squares

If we are given data at two or more points in time, least-squares procedures can be used to estimate the parameters a, b_1, and b_2, provided there is no major autocorrelation effect. Details of this procedure have been discussed by Coleman and can be summarized briefly to show the connection between theory building and empirical estimation procedures.[20]

Consider a panel study involving only two points in time, represented as 0 and t. Notice that the solution

$$X_{1t} = \frac{a}{b_1}(e^{b_1 t} - 1) + e^{b_1 t} X_{10} + \frac{b_2}{b_1}(e^{b_1 t} - 1)X_2$$

[20] Coleman, "The Mathematical Study of Change," pp. 435–37, 441.

can be thought of as involving three "variables," X_1 at times 0 and t, and X_2. We are dealing with only two points in time, and therefore for any given interval, t (or really $t - 0$) is fixed. Thus the equation could be rewritten as

$$X_{1t} = A + B_1 X_{10} + B_2 X_2 + u_{1t} \tag{5-14}$$

where an error term u_{1t} represents the effects of all omitted variables on the value of X_1 at time t, and where

$$A = \frac{a}{b_1}(e^{b_1 t} - 1)$$

$$B_1 = e^{b_1 t} \tag{5-15}$$

$$B_2 = \frac{b_2}{b_1}(e^{b_1 t} - 1)$$

Coleman shows that the coefficients A, B_1, and B_2 can be found by simple least squares, and that the parameters of the differential equation can then be estimated by converting back to a, b_1, and b_2 using the formulas:

$$a = \frac{A}{t}\left(\frac{\log_e B_1}{B_1 - 1}\right)$$

$$b_1 = \frac{\log_e B_1}{t} \qquad b_2 = \frac{B_2}{t}\left(\frac{\log_e B_1}{B_1 - 1}\right) \tag{5-16}$$

As previously noted, there is one major complication in this process, namely the possibility of autocorrelation. Least-squares procedures require the assumption that the error term u_{1t} must be uncorrelated with both "independent" variables in the system. If X_2 is truly exogenous there is no difficulty with respect to the X_2 term, though of course if X_2 is involved in a feedback relationship with X_1 we shall be in trouble. But we can ordinarily expect that factors affecting X_1 at time t (and summarized in u_{1t}) will be correlated with the causes of X_1 at the first period of time. The longer the interval between the first and second observations, the more reasonable it would be to assume no autocorrelation, though a test for this possibility should always be made.[21]

It may turn out that it will be preferable to obtain estimates directly from the differential equation itself, by assuming that the differential expression

---

[21] See Christ, *Econometric Models*, pp. 522–30.

can be approximated by a difference term for which the error terms may be more plausibly assumed to be non-autocorrelated. This seems to be the approach that is more frequently used by econometricians, though it remains to be seen how serious this autocorrelation problem will be in panel and longitudinal studies of major interest to sociologists and political scientists.

An additional caveat is also needed. We are assuming that there is no measurement error in any of the variables. It is well known that slope estimates are attenuated by random measurement error in independent variables, and that the seriousness of the distortion is positively related to the size of the measurement error variances relative to the variances of the independent variables. If the time period is short, it is likely that real changes between X_1 at time 0 and X_1 at time t will be relatively small, and hence real changes may be masked by measurement error. Coleman has suggested a method for taking out the random measurement error component, assuming no autocorrelation effect. His procedure requires observations at least three points in time, however.[22]

[22] Coleman, "The Mathematical Study of Change," pp. 453–56.

6

Simultaneous-Equation Dynamic Models

Most realistic models of real world processes will have to involve simultaneous equations. We have seen that simple recursive algebraic systems present no special estimation problems, provided the assumptions required for ordinary least squares are reasonably justified. Somewhat more complex in nature are the more general algebraic systems that allow for reciprocal causation, and that ordinarily involve identification problems unless there are the proper number of exogenous variables. By lagging some of the variables, we may in effect treat what are really difference equations as though they were algebraic systems. We noted, however, that the use of lagged endogenous variables ordinarily introduces autocorrelation among the error terms, making estimation more difficult.

The use of differential equations does not enable one to get around such estimation problems, as already indicated in the case of a single differential equation. In discussing Coleman's suggested estimation procedure, we noted that one must inevitably estimate the coefficients by collecting data at two or more points in time, and that autocorrelation effects may invalidate simple least-squares procedures. Needless to say, the introduction of simultaneous differential equations will not resolve this problem, and it will still be necessary to make simplifying assumptions about disturbing influences and the way they operate.[1] Since our concern is primarily with theory construction, rather than testing or estimation, we shall ignore the error terms in the discussion to follow. If it turns out that really useful dynamic theoretical formulations can be developed, we shall ultimately have to face up to these estimation problems before adequate empirical tests can be made.

In the previous chapter we studied the behavior of single difference and differential equations, though we also allowed for the possibility that there might be one or more algebraic equations holding simultaneously. For example, we assumed that only one of the relationships in the Hopkins theory of influence might operate more slowly than the rest. But what if we wish to allow for the possibility that several of the relationships operate slowly? Perhaps they all take place at approximately the same speed.

It is theoretically possible to write out a differential equation for each of the endogenous variables, to solve the resulting simultaneous equations, and to obtain the stability conditions appropriate for the entire system of equations. However, in many instances the general mathematical solutions are not known. In the case of linear differential equations with constant coefficients, the necessary conditions for stability can be stated in the general k-equation case. These conditions will be discussed later in the chapter. If one wishes to use nonlinear equations, however, he will find that there are at present no known general solutions. Provided one is willing to confine the system to two nonlinear differential equations, plus any number of algebraic ones, certain graphic methods can be used to provide qualitative insights concerning the stability conditions. These nonlinear methods will not be discussed in the present context because of their rather technical nature.[2]

Let us again consider the simplified version of the Hopkins model involving just the three variables rank, centrality, and influence, labeled X_1, X_2, and X_3 respectively. The general linear system (with constant coefficients) can be represented as follows:

$$\frac{dX_1}{dt} = b_{11}X_1 + b_{12}X_2 + b_{13}X_3$$

$$\frac{dX_2}{dt} = b_{21}X_1 + b_{22}X_2 + b_{23}X_3 \quad\quad (6\text{-}1)$$

$$\frac{dX_3}{dt} = b_{31}X_1 + b_{32}X_2 + b_{33}X_3$$

---

[1] I shall not discuss simultaneous *difference* equations in this chapter since the basic principles are similar to those for differential equations. See Baumol, *Economic Dynamics*, Part V.

[2] For discussions of nonlinear systems, see Baumol, *op. cit.*, Chaps. 13 and 14; Coleman, "The Mathematical Study of Change"; and Simon, *Models of Man*, Chaps. 7 and 8.

In the case of the Hopkins system, we are assuming no direct arrow from centrality to rank, from influence to centrality, or from rank to influence. Therefore b_{12}, b_{23}, and b_{31} are all zero. However, we are allowing for the possibility that all three feedback terms b_{ii} may be nonzero. In the case of a single differential equation we saw that stability depended only on the sign of the (single) feedback term. The b_{ij} terms, with $i \neq j$, did not affect stability one way or the other.

A number of questions naturally arise when we attempt to extend the system to include more than one differential equation. For stability, must *all* of the feedback terms b_{ii} be negative? How are the signs of the b_{ij} terms related to stability, as for example where we assume a positive major loop from rank to centrality to influence, and back to rank? Can we neglect the magnitudes of the b_{ij} terms, or must we consider their sizes relative to those of the b_{ii} or feedback terms? If they cannot be neglected, how should the relative magnitudes be compared? Suppose one adds a set of truly exogenous variables, or perhaps a set of factors that are completely dependent on these three variables. How will the stability of the system be affected? Or suppose one wished to elaborate on the theory by specifying additional variables in one or more of the feedback loops. How could this be done, and how might this affect the stability conditions?

Theoretical Specification of Feedback Relationships

Before turning to the abstract nature of the stability conditions in a system of simultaneous differential equations, let us first examine the kind of overall strategy one may employ in moving from verbal theories to dynamic mathematical formulations. Consider the Hopkins theory. We saw that the initial formulation involved all positive terms, so that one might expect that individuals beginning with high ranks would continue to become more and more influential and prestigious, whereas those beginning with below-average positions might experience a continued downward fall. Obviously, most groups do not operate in this manner. Or if they do, they are soon subject to disruptive mechanisms that make the theoretical formulation inappropriate. Our task, then, is to specify the nature of the processes that may operate to counteract this kind of positive feedback.

As we have seen, one may handle negative feedback mathematically by simply introducing a feedback term summarizing our ignorance of the exact processes. One can then state the mathematical relationships that must obtain in order for the entire system to stabilize. This will be done in the next section. But if one stopped here, the exercise would be a fruitless one from the standpoint of theory construction. It is necessary to substitute real variables for the abstract b_{ii} terms. Once the variables in the feedback loop have been named or identified, presumably they can be measured and explicitly brought into the theoretical system as additional variables. But are there any general principles that can be used to help one identify such variables? This is an extremely important question that deserves considerable study. I can only outline some approaches that may turn out to have reasonably general applicability.

Consider each of the feedback terms b_{11}, b_{22}, and b_{33} in the Hopkins example. In the case of an individual's rank or prestige in the group, one possible feedback mechanism involves the resistances posed by rival candidates. As a person gains in rank or prestige, others may become envious. They may gossip or attempt by other means to undermine his position. It may also require an increasing proportion of his time and energy to raise his position by a given amount. In the case of centrality, we recognize that centrality produces increasing time demands. The result may be that the individual attempts to insulate himself from others who may demand his time, and this, in turn, may decrease his centrality. Or the resentment engendered may tend to isolate an otherwise centrally located individual. With respect to the feedback of influence on itself, we recognize that attempts to increase one's influence may produce resentment, and they may also take time away from other activities. Rival parties who wish to increase their influence may form coalitions against any individual who is becoming too influential. If there is an actual power struggle there may be a circulation of the elite phenomenon.

These feedback mechanisms, and there are undoubtedly many others, are all specific to the Hopkins example. Presumably factors such as resentment levels and limitations on time and energy could be measured and explicitly incorporated into the theory. In the case of any particular theory, one should systematically examine each of the feedback terms and attempt to list the variables that could be operative, recognizing of course that in many instances these might be of only minor importance. In other words, one should not make the mistake of assuming that stability is inevitable, or that stabilizing mechanisms will be sufficiently potent to prevent an explosion or accelerating rate of change.

There would appear to be at least three kinds of negative feedback mechanisms that can be expected to apply more generally than in the case of the Hopkins example. Samuelson observes that the rationale underlying many, if not most, dynamic theories in economics involves some maximizing or minimizing principle.[3] For example, every individual is assumed to have

---

[3] Samuelson, *Foundations of Economic Analysis*, Chap. 3.

a set of "utilities" or preferences for various goods and services. But each of these goods or services involves a certain cost, and his resources are necessarily limited. It might be assumed, however, that the individual can be described in terms of a utility function, in which the utility of each good or service is weighted by its cost. The individual is then assumed to behave in such a way that he maximizes his expected utility, subject to the limitations imposed by his resources in time and money. Similarly, a producer is assumed to attempt to minimize a cost function, subject to certain restraints. Mathematically, one may write down such functions, take derivatives and set them equal to zero, and then use the signs of the second derivatives to impose additional conditions to obtain maximum rather than minimum values (or vice versa).

Simon has objected that in most complex situations persons are unable to operate in such a manner.[4] Seldom will they possess the knowledge, or time, to express exact functions and locate the maximum (or minimum) positions of these functions. This does not mean that we should not assume "rational" behavior. Instead, their rationality is bounded by their lack of knowledge of the important parameters. In place of maximizing behavior, Simon prefers to think in terms of "adjustive" behavior. The essential idea is that the individual may recognize or attempt to predict whether a given course of action will improve or worsen his position. He may then select those courses of action that are expected to improve his position, even though he may not be in a position to select that single course that would actually maximize his position. Having taken this course, he gradually modifies his behavior so as to attempt to move continuously in the right direction. We might imagine a popcorn peddler at a county fair who is not in a position to view the entire panorama. But he can push his cart in the direction of the largest visible crowd. Having moved there, he can continually adjust his position so as to move with the crowd, though he may not be in a position to select the truly optimal locations.

In either case it may prove reasonable to assume, as a general rule, that individuals will attempt to improve their positions, subject to certain restraints which may vary from person to person. For example, we might assume that each individual will attempt to improve his rank and influence, subject to the limitations imposed by his resources. One type of limitation will involve the time factor. Each individual will be willing to devote only so much time and energy to the group. As one's centrality and influence increase, there may be increasing expectations placed upon him. As a result, he may find it necessary to delegate responsibilities or withdraw from certain activities, thereby reducing his influence. Furthermore, as his rank increases,

[4] Simon, *Models of Man*, pp. 165–68, 196–206.

other goals may become more important. Once he has become a club officer, having a high rank may lose its appeal, and he may elect to devote his time to other organizations. In other words, there may be a "saturation" effect similar in nature to the notion of diminishing returns in economics.[5]

A second type of general mechanism, also apparent in the case of the Hopkins example, involves limitations imposed by the fact that there will ordinarily be competition among individuals or groups, whose rival claims and actions will serve as restraints or limiting factors. For example, when a number of persons compete for influential positions, each individual will be limited both by his own resources and the behavior of rivals. Coalitions may be formed, as already noted. Various mechanisms of social control may be brought to bear on persons who are becoming too influential, or who may be attempting to exploit their superior status.

It may of course be unrealistic to assume that all individuals are attempting, subject to certain restraints, to improve their positions. Some may elect to leave the group, or for masochistic or other reasons may try to lower their positions. But many such apparent exceptions may be handled by recognizing that the restraining or limiting conditions may vary considerably from one individual to the next. Even the laziest student attempts to do as well as possible on an examination, subject to the restraint that he may limit his study to one-half hour immediately before the exam, or that he cannot make his cheating too obvious. Similarly, each individual may try to improve his rank, though some persons may devote much less time or energy to this objective than others.

Recognizing that the restraining factors may take on different values for the various individuals, one may expect to find differences in rank, centrality, and influence at any given point in time. If one's data are confined to a single point in time, and if he is willing to assume that the negative feedback terms are sufficiently large to produce stability, then he may carry out a static analysis by interrelating the variables at this fixed point in time. But if he is unwilling to assume that the system has reached approximate stability, it will be desirable to collect data at several points in time.

A third kind of feedback mechanism that may be operative in many kinds of social systems is analogous to "servomechanisms" in mechanical or electrical systems. These systems may contain built-in, self-regulatory devices capable of adjusting the system's output regardless of changes that may occur in the system's environment. A simple thermostat system can be used to illustrate the process. In effect, some of the system's output is fed back to

---

[5] Herbert Simon makes effective use of this "saturation" effect to construct *nonlinear* differential equations that are somewhat more realistic than the linear models discussed in the present chapter. See his *Models of Man*, Chaps. 5–7.

an information control center (e.g., the thermostat), which checks this output against some standard (e.g., the temperature setting), and either increases or decreases this output accordingly. There are obvious parallels with output controls operative in business firms and other large-scale organizations and perhaps even in small groups. In fact, the processes involved appear to be extremely general, though careful attention will have to be given to the specifics of these feedback processes before really useful theories can be developed in the social sciences. The interested reader is referred to the growing body of literature on this subject, as cited and discussed by Buckley and Deutsch.[6]

As a theoretical tool in the study of feedback processes, and as an aid in the search for those feedbacks that are most likely to have the greatest stabilizing influences, it would seem useful to have available a general strategy or method for specifying the stability conditions appropriate for any given model. Since the number of possibilities increases geometrically with the addition of each new variable, it will be necessary to show how these stability conditions can be obtained for the general linear model. Fortunately, this can be done with the use of simple algebra, though in order to understand the rationale behind these conditions one would need a knowledge of the theory of differential equations.[7] After studying these abstract conditions we shall discuss two substantive illustrations in some detail.

Stability Conditions

As we have seen, stability depends only on the sign of the feedback term in the case of a single linear differential equation. Though we shall later deal with illustrations involving only two or three simultaneous differential equations, it will be useful to state the general stability conditions for the k-equation case, though restricting ourselves to linear differential equations with constant coefficients. It can be shown that most nonlinear systems of practical interest give results similar to those for linear equations.[8]

It is helpful to write the equations in a standard form so that one may express the stability conditions in terms of coefficients that have simple intuitive meanings. It turns out that the constant terms may be ignored in considering the question of stability, though they would of course affect the

[6] See Buckley, *Sociology and Modern Systems Theory*, and Deutsch, *The Nerves of Government*.
[7] A very readable text on differential equations is Shepley L. Ross, *Differential Equations* (New York: Blaisdell Publishing Company, 1964). See also, Baumol, *Economic Dynamics*.
[8] See Ross, *Differential Equations*, pp. 480–83.

position at which equilibrium would occur under stable conditions. Therefore, without loss of generality, we may consider the following equation system:

$$\frac{dX_1}{dt} = b_{11}X_1 + b_{12}X_2 + \cdots + b_{1k}X_k$$

$$\frac{dX_2}{dt} = b_{21}X_1 + b_{22}X_2 + \cdots + b_{2k}X_k \qquad (6\text{-}2)$$

$$\vdots$$

$$\frac{dX_k}{dt} = b_{k1}X_1 + b_{k2}X_2 + \cdots + b_{kk}X_k$$

where $b_{11}, b_{22}, \ldots, b_{kk}$ are the feedback terms. We will be interested primarily in cases where the b_{ii} terms are negative and most of the remaining b_{ij} are positive, but it will not be necessary to restrict ourselves to such special cases.

It is possible to state stability conditions that are both necessary and sufficient, but these will involve what are referred to as the latent roots of the characteristic equation of the above system.[9] It is more convenient, however, to state the necessary (though not sufficient) conditions in such a way that they can be interpreted intuitively in terms of the b coefficients. In the case of necessary conditions, we are assured that if stability is observed then these conditions must hold, though the converse is not necessarily true. That is, we are not assured of stability merely because these conditions are met, since they are not simultaneously sufficient.

Since our primary purpose in examining such conditions is to obtain qualitative insights regarding stability, rather than precise quantities that can be empirically measured, the lack of sufficiency will not be of great concern. In the event that all variables can be accurately measured, the necessary and sufficient conditions can be applied to the characteristic equation, which will be a polynomial equation of degree k.

The two necessary conditions can be stated as follows:

I. $$\sum_{i=1}^{k} b_{ii} < 0$$

II. $$|b_{ij}| > 0, \quad \text{if } k \text{ is even, and}$$
$$|b_{ij}| < 0, \quad \text{if } k \text{ is odd,}$$

[9] See Baumol, *Economic Dynamics*, pp. 303–4, 365–66.

where **b**$|_{ij}|$ represents the determinant[10] of the slope matrix

$$(b_{ij}) = \begin{pmatrix} b_{11} & b_{12} & \cdots & b_{1k} \\ b_{21} & b_{22} & & b_{2k} \\ \vdots & \vdots & & \vdots \\ b_{k1} & b_{k2} & & b_{kk} \end{pmatrix}$$

The first of these conditions states that the sum of the feedback terms must be negative. If all feedbacks are negative, this condition is of course automatically met. But it will also be met if some of the feedbacks are positive, as long as these are counterbalanced by larger negative feedbacks. We must remember, however, that it may not be sufficient if we have a large number of small positive feedbacks. Also, we are interested practically in those situations in which the damping is sufficiently pronounced that stability occurs within a reasonable length of time, however this may be defined in terms of the period of observation. Therefore, for all practical purposes, we shall require that the sum of the feedback terms be considerably less than zero. Those readers familiar with matrix algebra will note that Condition I states that the sum of the elements in the main diagonal (or the *trace* of the matrix) must be negative.

Turning to Condition II, it may be necessary to call your attention to the fact that although a matrix of the b's is simply a representation or array of many quantities, the determinant of this matrix is a scalar quantity that will have a definite numerical value. We shall see how to compute these values in the context of specific examples illustrating the implications of this second condition, which has thus far been stated too abstractly to have much intuitive appeal.

The two-equation case

In the case of two equations

$$\frac{dX_1}{dt} = b_{11}X_1 + b_{12}X_2$$

$$\frac{dX_2}{dt} = b_{21}X_1 + b_{22}X_2$$

(6-3)

we have just two feedback terms, b_{11} and b_{22}, plus the two terms b_{12} and b_{21}

---

[10] Since both determinants and absolute values are represented by a pair of vertical lines, I shall distinguish between the two by using boldface type to indicate a determinant and ordinary type to indicate an absolute value.

representing the influence of the one variable on the other. The determinant for Condition II is

$$\begin{vmatrix} b_{11} & b_{12} \\ b_{21} & b_{22} \end{vmatrix} = b_{11}b_{22} - b_{12}b_{21} \tag{6-4}$$

which must be positive, since $k = 2$. (Recall that a 2-by-2 determinant is equal to the product of the terms b_{11} and b_{22} in the "main diagonal"—upper left to lower right—minus the product of the terms b_{12} and b_{21} in the other diagonal.) Thus the two necessary conditions in the case of two equations are (I) $b_{11} + b_{22} < 0$, and (II) $b_{11}b_{22} > b_{12}b_{21}$.

If the effects of X_1 on X_2, and vice versa, are both positive or both negative, then for stability the product $b_{11}b_{22}$ must also be positive (from II), which means that both feedback terms must be negative in order to satisfy Condition I as well. Since the product of the feedback terms must be larger than $b_{12}b_{21}$, this means that ordinarily both negative feedbacks must be reasonably large. In particular, if $b_{22} = 0$ we cannot rely on a large negative feedback b_{11} to assure stability.

Notice that whereas stability in the single-equation case depended only on the sign of the feedback term, we must now be concerned with the relative magnitudes of all four coefficients. The reason that b_{12} and b_{21} are now relevant for stability is that neither variable can be considered as exogenous; values of each are affected by changes in the other. The general simultaneous-equation system (6-2) does not contain any exogenous variables, though by setting enough of the parameters and derivatives equal to zero we could handle exogenous variables as special cases, as will be done below. Of course for $k = 1$, Condition II requires that $|b_{11}| = b_{11} < 0$, which we have noted is also the condition for stability in the more general case of the single equation (5-11) involving an exogenous variable.

These stability conditions for two-equation systems will be illustrated later in terms of Richardson's model for arms races and Simon's representation of propositions taken from Homans' *The Human Group*. Before considering these particular applications, however, let us turn to more complex equation systems.[11]

The three-equation case

In the case of three simultaneous linear differential equations with constant coefficients it will be necessary to evaluate the determinant of a 3-by-3 matrix as follows:

---

[11] The reader may easily visualize the extension of the Richardson model to three or more nations if he finds this helpful in illustrating the rather abstract discussion that follows.

$$\begin{vmatrix} b_{11} & b_{12} & b_{13} \\ b_{21} & b_{22} & b_{23} \\ b_{31} & b_{32} & b_{33} \end{vmatrix} \quad\quad (6\text{-}5)$$
$$= b_{11}b_{22}b_{33} + b_{12}b_{23}b_{31} + b_{13}b_{21}b_{32} - b_{13}b_{22}b_{31} - b_{11}b_{23}b_{32} - b_{12}b_{21}b_{33}$$

Notice that the right-hand side consists of six terms, each of which is a product of three b's. It is obtained as follows. First we take the product in the main diagonal ($b_{11}b_{22}b_{33}$). We next move one column to the right and form the product of the terms that would constitute the main diagonal in a new determinant in which the second and third columns of the original determinant are each moved one position to the left, and the first column of the original determinant becomes column 3 of the new determinant. The third term, which is added to the first two terms, is obtained by a similar process. The remaining three terms, which are all *subtracted* from the sum of the first three terms, are obtained by working with the minor or secondary diagonals (from top right to bottom left).

The various terms can be written down almost by inspection if one simply recopies the first and second columns to the right of the original three columns. Diagonal lines (here numbered to correspond with the six terms) can be drawn in to help keep track of the various components:

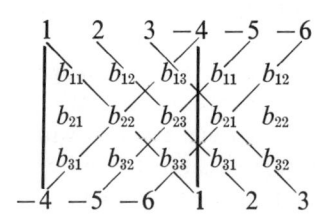

$$\begin{array}{ccccccc} 1 & 2 & 3 & -4 & -5 & -6 & \\ b_{11} & b_{12} & b_{13} & b_{11} & b_{12} & \\ b_{21} & b_{22} & b_{23} & b_{21} & b_{22} & \\ b_{31} & b_{32} & b_{33} & b_{31} & b_{32} & \\ -4 & -5 & -6 & 1 & 2 & 3 \end{array}$$

Condition I of course states that $b_{11} + b_{22} + b_{33}$ must be negative, and Condition II requires that the value of the determinant must also be negative, since k is odd. But the determinant's expansion consists of six terms, too many perhaps to have much intuitive appeal. Of course if we were actually given the numerical values of the b's, or if they could be accurately estimated, then we could determine whether or not the necessary conditions had been met. Here we are more concerned with qualitative statements that have implications for theory construction. It will therefore be helpful to consider a series of interesting special cases, for which many of the terms will drop out. Before doing so, however, several more general observations can be made.

Consider each of the six terms in the expansion of the determinant. The first consists of the product of the three feedback terms $b_{11}b_{22}b_{33}$. If all three feedbacks are negative, the product will of course be negative. It can also be negative if two feedbacks are positive, and one negative, though Condition I requires that the sum of the b_{ii} be negative. Therefore in this case the single negative feedback term must be very much greater than the two positive feedbacks.

Intuitive meaning can also be given the second and third terms by examining Fig. 6-1. The product $b_{12}b_{23}b_{31}$ represents the product of the slopes of the loop going in the counterclockwise direction from X_1 to X_3 to X_2 and finally back to X_1. Similarly the third term $b_{13}b_{21}b_{32}$ represents the clockwise loop from X_1 to X_2 to X_3 and back to X_1. If either of these loops is broken, this will be represented by setting one (or more) of the b's equal to zero, and the corresponding term of the determinant will disappear.

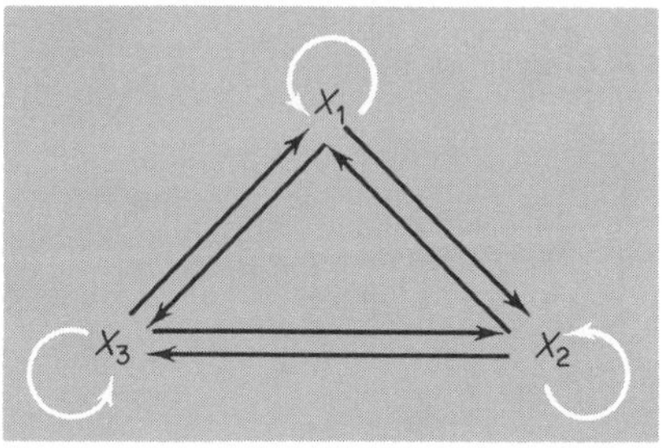

The remaining three terms, which are all subtracted from the rest, have similar forms but do not seem to have as much intuitive appeal. Each involves the product of a single feedback term times the product of the b's relating the remaining two variables. For example, the fourth term is $b_{22}(b_{13}b_{31})$, with the term in parentheses representing the product of the reciprocal relationship between X_1 and X_3. Unless there is a double arrow connecting these variables, this term will of course drop out.

FIG. 6-1   The general three-variable model.

If all the b_{ij} (with $i \neq j$) are positive, and if all the b_{ii} are negative, then the first term will be negative; but all of the remaining five will be positive, since each of the last three terms will involve subtracting a negative sum from the total. Since a necessary condition for stability is that the entire sum be negative, it will clearly be necessary that all three feedback terms be numerically large relative to the rest. Thus, although Condition I would not rule out the possibility that two of the feedback terms could be small but positive, the two conditions combined virtually require that all three be rather large negative numbers. However, if one of the b_{ij} were also negative, thereby producing a negative feedback loop in either the clockwise or counterclockwise direction, three out of the six terms would be negative, and it would not be necessary for the first term to be as large a negative quantity. In fact, if all three feedback terms b_{ii} were zero, then only the second and third terms of Eq. (6-5) would remain. Since one of these would be positive and the other negative, the relative magnitudes of these two loops would determine whether or not stability would be possible. Of course in this very special case, we would have $\Sigma b_{ii} = 0$ and, strictly speaking, Condition I would not be met. Let us next consider some more interesting and perhaps more general special cases.

Simple loops, with feedbacks. Suppose we are dealing with a model such as indicated in Fig. 6-2 (and in the Hopkins illustration) in which we have what can be called a "simple loop" that does not involve any instances of reciprocal causation between pairs of variables, but that is such that a simple causal chain (e.g., $X_1 \rightarrow X_2 \rightarrow X_3$) is combined with a feedback from the last variable to the first. We allow for feedbacks from each variable to itself. In this particular model all of the arrows directed counterclockwise have been erased, so that $b_{12} = b_{23} = b_{31} = 0$. This means that the determinant of the b's reduces to:

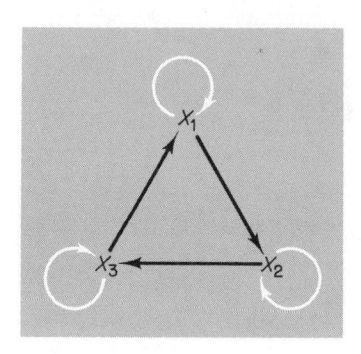

FIG. 6-2 A simple three-variable loop.

$$\begin{vmatrix} b_{11} & 0 & b_{13} \\ b_{21} & b_{22} & 0 \\ 0 & b_{32} & b_{33} \end{vmatrix} = b_{11}b_{22}b_{33} + b_{13}b_{21}b_{32} \qquad (6\text{-}6)$$

Condition II therefore requires that if all nonzero b_{ij} are positive and all b_{ii} negative, then we must have $|b_{11}b_{22}b_{33}| > |b_{13}b_{21}b_{32}|$. This is of course a straightforward extension of the two-equation case where we saw that the stability condition required that $b_{11}b_{22}$ be greater than the product $b_{12}b_{21}$. If all b_{ii} are negative, and if one of the b_{ij} is also negative, Condition II (as well as Condition I) will automatically be satisfied, as we would expect intuitively. Conceivably, two of the b_{ii} could be positive as long as their sum was less in absolute value than that of the remaining b_{ii}. But if the two positive feedback terms were numerically small, and if all of the b_{ij} were positive, it would be difficult to satisfy Condition II. We shall see that these results generalize readily to longer loops involving more variables, provided that we confine ourselves to simple loops of the sort represented in Fig. 6-2. The two-equation case involving just X_1 and X_2 can of course be considered a very short "loop" from X_1 to X_2 and back to X_1.

Pairwise reciprocal causation, no loops. Suppose that X_2 and X_3 are related through reciprocal causation, but that X_1 is related to these two variables in such a way that there are no complete loops through X_1 (except through itself as represented by b_{11}). Consider any of the models (a)–(d) in

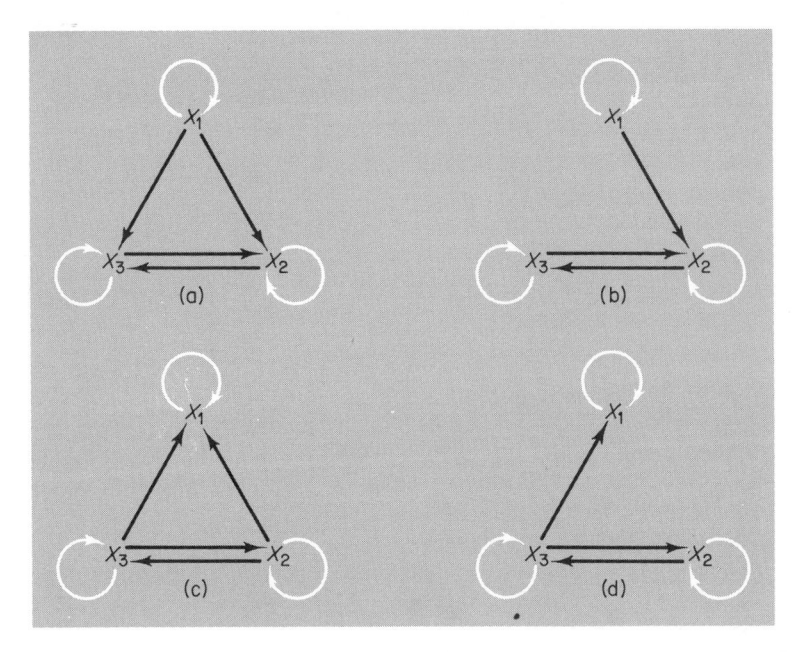

FIG. 6-3 Pairwise reciprocal causation, no loops.

Fig. 6-3. It can be seen that each of these models involves exactly the same stability conditions. Condition I is of course that $b_{11} + b_{22} + b_{33} < 0$. In the case of Condition II, different sets of b_{ij} are set equal to zero, but always in such a way that either the first row or the first column of the determinant contains two zeros. The results are as follows:

$$\text{(a)} \quad b_{12} = b_{13} = 0 \qquad \begin{vmatrix} b_{11} & 0 & 0 \\ b_{21} & b_{22} & b_{23} \\ b_{31} & b_{32} & b_{33} \end{vmatrix} = b_{11}(b_{22}b_{33} - b_{23}b_{32}) \tag{6-7a}$$

$$\text{(b)} \quad b_{12} = b_{13} = b_{31} = 0 \qquad \begin{vmatrix} b_{11} & 0 & 0 \\ b_{21} & b_{22} & b_{23} \\ 0 & b_{32} & b_{33} \end{vmatrix} = b_{11}(b_{22}b_{33} - b_{23}b_{32}) \tag{6-7b}$$

$$\text{(c)} \quad b_{21} = b_{31} = 0 \qquad \begin{vmatrix} b_{11} & b_{12} & b_{13} \\ 0 & b_{22} & b_{23} \\ 0 & b_{32} & b_{33} \end{vmatrix} = b_{11}(b_{22}b_{33} - b_{23}b_{32}) \tag{6-7c}$$

$$\text{(d)} \quad b_{21} = b_{12} = b_{31} = 0 \qquad \begin{vmatrix} b_{11} & 0 & b_{13} \\ 0 & b_{22} & b_{23} \\ 0 & b_{32} & b_{33} \end{vmatrix} = b_{11}(b_{22}b_{33} - b_{23}b_{32}) \tag{6-7d}$$

Several interesting things can be noted regarding the common stability conditions for these models. First, since b_{12}, b_{21}, b_{13}, and b_{31} do not enter into these stability conditions, we conclude that the links between X_1 and the pair of variables X_2 and X_3 can be ignored in considering stability. This is as expected, though interestingly enough we cannot ignore the feedback term b_{11}, which is necessary to assure the stability of X_1, apart from the behavior of X_2 and X_3. In situations (a) and (b) X_1 is an exogenous variable, there being no feedback from either X_2 or X_3. In (c) and (d), however, X_1 is a dependent variable, and it seems somewhat surprising that exactly the same stability conditions apply to relations with exogenous and dependent variables. As we shall see, this result readily generalizes to more complex models and is consistent with notions regarding block-recursive models. In situations (a) and (c), X_1 is directly linked to both X_2 and X_3, whereas in (b) and (d) it is linked to only one variable in the pair. Again, this makes no difference in considering stability.

If b_{11} is negative, then Condition II requires that the quantity $(b_{22}b_{33} - b_{23}b_{32})$ must be positive, since the entire expression must be negative. This is of course just the condition required in the two-equation case. In particular, if b_{23} and b_{32} are both positive, then b_{22} and b_{33} must both have the same sign and be relatively large. Conceivably, both could be positive, if their sum were less than the magnitude of b_{11} (Condition I). We must remember, however, that Conditions I and II are not sufficient, and it seems doubtful that in most instances the sufficiency conditions would also be met in this case. In the more usual situation in which all three b_{ii} are negative, we see that we can ignore X_1 altogether in considering the stability of X_2 and X_3.

Suppose b_{11} happened to be exactly zero, so that strictly speaking Condition II would not be met. In the case of situations (a) and (b), the first equation for dX_1/dt would contain all zero coefficients. Since we are assuming that the constant term in this equation is also zero, this would mean that $dX_1/dt = 0$, or that X_1 would be a constant. If so, the three equations would be reduced to two, and constant terms would be inserted into the second and third equations in place of the X_1 term. This would therefore be a degenerate case that should be analyzed in terms of the two-equation stability conditions.

In the cases of (c) and (d) we note that X_1 does not appear in the equations for X_2 and X_3, since it is a dependent variable. Suppose that $b_{11} = 0$, and that the values of the other coefficients are such that stability is attained in the relationship between X_2 and X_3. These two variables will then eventually take on constant values which will ordinarily not be zero. If so, then with no negative feedback term in the equation for X_1, we will have $dX_1/dt = K$, and X_1 will continue to increase or decrease indefinitely according to the sign of K. We thus see that a negative value of b_{11} would ordinarily be necessary to guarantee the stability of X_1.

Suppose b_{11} were positive. Condition II could conceivably be met if the expression $(b_{22}b_{33} - b_{23}b_{32})$ were negative. This could occur if b_{23} and b_{32} were both very large and of the same sign, even if both b_{22} and b_{33} were negative. However, the sum of the latter two feedback terms would have to be negative and numerically larger than b_{11} if Condition I were also to be satisfied. This kind of situation seems not to have a very simple intuitive interpretation, would probably not be encountered often in practice, and also might not satisfy the sufficient conditions for stability. One advantage of an explicit mathematical statement of stability conditions, however, is that it calls our attention to unusual possibilities of this sort that would not otherwise be suggested by common-sense reasoning.

Loop plus pairwise reciprocal causation. Consider next a model, such as indicated in Fig. 6-4, in which the features of the previous two situations are combined. We have a clockwise loop from X_1 to X_2 to X_3 and back to X_1, combined with reciprocal causation between X_2 and X_3. In this model only b_{12} and b_{31} are zero, and the determinant for Condition II becomes:

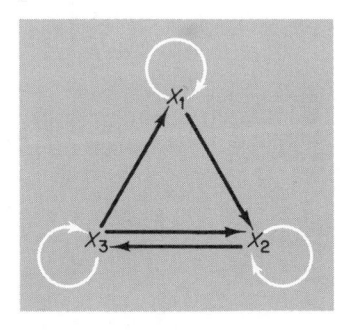

FIG. 6-4 Loop plus pairwise reciprocal causation.

$$\begin{vmatrix} b_{11} & 0 & b_{13} \\ b_{21} & b_{22} & b_{23} \\ 0 & b_{32} & b_{33} \end{vmatrix} = b_{11}b_{22}b_{33} + b_{13}b_{21}b_{32} - b_{11}b_{23}b_{32} \\ = b_{11}(b_{22}b_{33} - b_{23}b_{32}) + b_{13}b_{21}b_{32} \quad (6\text{-}8)$$

If all nonzero b_{ij} are positive and all feedback terms b_{ii} negative, then only the $b_{11}b_{22}b_{33}$ term will be negative, and stability will depend on this term being numerically large as compared with the others. Contrasting this model with the one in which there was only a simple loop (Fig. 6-2), we see that the addition of a positive reciprocal relationship between X_2 and X_3 makes it more difficult to attain stability since it requires larger negative feedback terms. This is of course as expected. Looking at it in terms of the second way of writing the right-hand side of Eq. (6-8), if all nonzero b_{ij} are positive, and if b_{11} is negative, then $b_{22}b_{33}$ must be considerably larger than $b_{23}b_{32}$ in order for the first term to be both negative and numerically larger than the product $b_{13}b_{21}b_{32}$ representing the clockwise loop. Of course if one of the terms involving X_1 in this loop is negative (say b_{13}), then the latter product will be negative, and this will aid stability. If b_{32} is negative, with the remaining nonzero b_{ij} positive and the b_{ii} all negative, then the necessary conditions will automatically be met.

Double pairwise reciprocal causation. As our final three-equation model, suppose there is reciprocal causation between X_2 and each of the other variables, with no direct links between X_1 and X_3. Then $b_{13} = b_{31} = 0$, and the model would be represented as in Fig. 6-5, with the determinant being:

$$\begin{vmatrix} b_{11} & b_{12} & 0 \\ b_{21} & b_{22} & b_{23} \\ 0 & b_{32} & b_{33} \end{vmatrix} = b_{11}b_{22}b_{33} - b_{11}b_{23}b_{32} - b_{33}b_{12}b_{21} \qquad (6\text{-}9)$$

If all nonzero b_{ij} are positive and all b_{ii} negative, then only the first term will be negative. Furthermore, the second and third terms contain the feedback coefficients b_{11} and b_{33}, respectively. In order for the first term to dominate, b_{22} must therefore be numerically large relative to b_{11}, b_{33}, and the b_{ij}. Thus in this situation it is essential that the "middle" variable, connected to the other two by reciprocal relationships, have a large negative feedback term. If one of the four b_{ij} were also negative this would aid stability. Again, the results are consistent with common sense, though of course much more refined.

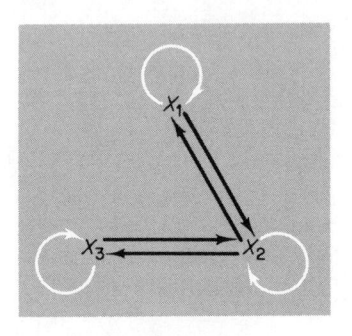

FIG. 6-5 Double pairwise reciprocal causation.

The k-equation case

In the more general case of k equations there are obviously numerous possibilities, only a few of which can be examined. It is not as simple to expand a determinant, and the number of terms multiplies rapidly with the addition of each new variable. Again, however, we can study the implications of important special cases for which many of the terms will drop out because of zero values.

We first need to review the rule for expanding higher-order determinants. Given a k-by-k determinant, we can always write this as a function of a number of determinants having $k - 1$ rows and columns. These, in turn, can be written in terms of determinants with $k - 2$ rows and columns, and so forth until we reach 3-by-3 determinants that can be expanded directly. We do this by selecting a convenient row or column. We then multiply each element in this row or column by what is referred to as its "minor." In doing so, we alternate signs and add. The minor is obtained by striking out both the row and the column corresponding to a given element, giving a determinant with $k - 1$ rows and columns.

The procedure can be illustrated in terms of a 4-by-4 determinant as follows:

$$\begin{vmatrix} b_{11} & b_{12} & b_{13} & b_{14} \\ b_{21} & b_{22} & b_{23} & b_{24} \\ b_{31} & b_{32} & b_{33} & b_{34} \\ b_{41} & b_{42} & b_{43} & b_{44} \end{vmatrix} = b_{11} \begin{vmatrix} b_{22} & b_{23} & b_{24} \\ b_{32} & b_{33} & b_{34} \\ b_{42} & b_{43} & b_{44} \end{vmatrix} - b_{12} \begin{vmatrix} b_{21} & b_{23} & b_{24} \\ b_{31} & b_{33} & b_{34} \\ b_{41} & b_{43} & b_{44} \end{vmatrix}$$

$$+ b_{13} \begin{vmatrix} b_{21} & b_{22} & b_{24} \\ b_{31} & b_{32} & b_{34} \\ b_{41} & b_{42} & b_{44} \end{vmatrix} - b_{14} \begin{vmatrix} b_{21} & b_{22} & b_{23} \\ b_{31} & b_{32} & b_{33} \\ b_{41} & b_{42} & b_{43} \end{vmatrix}$$

(6-10)

Here we have expanded in terms of the elements of the first *row*. We multiply the first element in this row, b_{11}, by the determinant obtained by striking out the first row and column. We then move to the next element b_{12}, reversing the sign and striking out the first row and the second column.[12] When we again reverse signs in the case of the third element, we obtain a positive sign. This term involves b_{13} multiplied by the 3-by-3 determinant obtained by striking out the first row and the third column. The procedure is repeated until we come to the end of the row. Since each of the new determinants is a 3-by-3 determinant, which when expanded will contain six terms, the expanded 4-by-4 determinant will contain 24 terms. A 5-by-5 determinant can be expanded in terms of five 4-by-4 determinants and will therefore involve 5(24) = 120 terms. Obviously, we shall have difficulty giving simple intuitive interpretations for Condition II in the most general case. We therefore turn to some of the more interesting special cases.

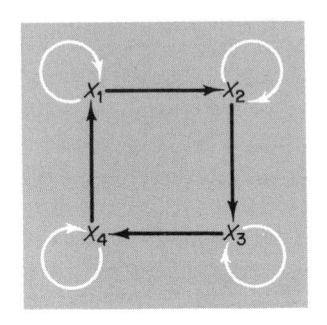

FIG. 6-6 A simple four-variable loop.

---

[12] We may determine the sign to be placed in front of any particular element b_{ij} by simply counting down from the top left-hand element b_{11} to the appropriate row and then across to the appropriate column, changing the sign with each move. If the b_{ij} are labeled as in the above 4-by-4 determinant, it can be seen that the sign will be positive if $i + j$ is even, and negative if $i + j$ is odd.

Simple loops, with feedbacks. First consider the four-equation case represented in Fig. 6-6. Since this involves a clockwise loop, all of the coefficients corresponding to the counterclockwise direction will be zero, as will those connecting X_1 with X_3 and X_2 with X_4. In expanding the resulting 4-by-4 determinant it is convenient to select a row or column containing as many zeros as possible. In this case they all contain two zeros, and so one might as well expand in terms of the first row. The result is as follows:

$$\begin{vmatrix} b_{11} & 0 & 0 & b_{14} \\ b_{21} & b_{22} & 0 & 0 \\ 0 & b_{32} & b_{33} & 0 \\ 0 & 0 & b_{43} & b_{44} \end{vmatrix} = b_{11} \begin{vmatrix} b_{22} & 0 & 0 \\ b_{32} & b_{33} & 0 \\ 0 & b_{43} & b_{44} \end{vmatrix} - 0 + 0 - b_{14} \begin{vmatrix} b_{21} & b_{22} & 0 \\ 0 & b_{32} & b_{33} \\ 0 & 0 & b_{43} \end{vmatrix} \quad (6\text{-}11)$$

$$= b_{11}b_{22}b_{33}b_{44} - b_{14}b_{21}b_{32}b_{43}$$

Since k is even, Condition II requires that this expression be positive for stability, and again we see that the product of the feedback terms must be numerically greater than the loop product $b_{14}b_{21}b_{32}b_{43}$ if all nonzero b_{ij} are positive and all b_{ii} negative. Of course two of the b_{ii} could be positive, provided that their sum were numerically less than the sum of the two negative feedback terms. Once more it should be recalled, however, that we are dealing with necessary but not sufficient conditions.

We can see how the pattern develops by examining a five-equation loop as diagrammed in Fig. 6-7. The resulting determinant now has zeros in all but the first and last positions of the first row. Therefore we have

$$\begin{vmatrix} b_{11} & 0 & 0 & 0 & b_{15} \\ b_{21} & b_{22} & 0 & 0 & 0 \\ 0 & b_{32} & b_{33} & 0 & 0 \\ 0 & 0 & b_{43} & b_{44} & 0 \\ 0 & 0 & 0 & b_{54} & b_{55} \end{vmatrix} = b_{11} \begin{vmatrix} b_{22} & 0 & 0 & 0 \\ b_{32} & b_{33} & 0 & 0 \\ 0 & b_{43} & b_{44} & 0 \\ 0 & 0 & b_{54} & b_{55} \end{vmatrix} + b_{15} \begin{vmatrix} b_{21} & b_{22} & 0 & 0 \\ 0 & b_{32} & b_{33} & 0 \\ 0 & 0 & b_{43} & b_{44} \\ 0 & 0 & 0 & b_{54} \end{vmatrix}$$

Expanding the first of these 4-by-4 determinants by the first row, and the second by the first column, we get

$$b_{11}b_{22} \begin{vmatrix} b_{33} & 0 & 0 \\ b_{43} & b_{44} & 0 \\ 0 & b_{54} & b_{55} \end{vmatrix} + b_{15}b_{21} \begin{vmatrix} b_{32} & b_{33} & 0 \\ 0 & b_{43} & b_{44} \\ 0 & 0 & b_{54} \end{vmatrix} \quad (6\text{-}12)$$

$$= b_{11}b_{22}b_{33}b_{44}b_{55} + b_{15}b_{21}b_{32}b_{43}b_{54}$$

The result is again familiar. Notice that the signs of the "loop" product alternate as k increases, as does the sign required under Condition II. Where

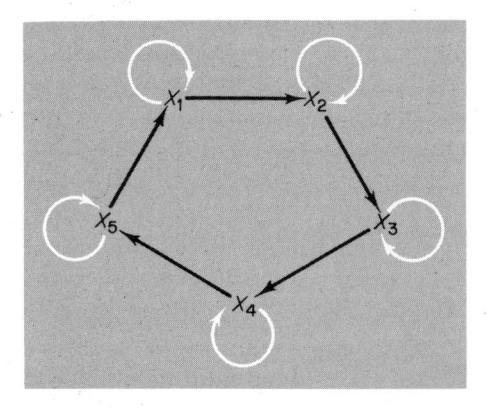

FIG. 6-7 A simple five-variable loop.

all nonzero b_{ij} are positive and all b_{ii} negative, the requirement is once more that the product of the b_{ii} be numerically greater than that for the b_{ij} representing the loop.

It should now be clear that in the case of simple loops, the k-equation situation involves a straightforward extension. The first row of the k-by-k determinant will contain all zeros except for the first and last elements. This will result in only two terms in the first expansion. The reduced determinants can likewise be simplified, until the 3-by-3 determinants can be expanded. The general result will be

$$b_{11}b_{22}b_{33} \cdots b_{kk} + (-1)^{k-1}b_{21}b_{32}b_{43} \ldots b_{k,k-1}b_{1k} \tag{6-13}$$

where the alternating signs have been taken care of by the expression $(-1)^{k-1}$, and where we label the variables in such a way that the loop proceeds from X_1 to X_2 to X_3 to ... X_k, and then from X_k to X_1.

We might note, incidentally, that it will be possible to shortcut such simple loops by deleting certain of the variables and replacing the arrows by direct ones. For example, in the case of Fig. 6-7 we could delete X_4 and X_5 and draw in a direct arrow between X_3 and X_1, giving us the model of Fig. 6-2. By comparing the equations for the stability conditions for these two models we see that the quantity $b_{33}b_{44}b_{55}$ has been replaced by a new b_{33}, and that $b_{43}b_{54}b_{15}$ has been replaced by a new b_{13}.

Addition of recursive exogenous variables. In our earlier discussion of general systems of algebraic equations, it was pointed out that one way to resolve the identification problem was to introduce exogenous variables into the theoretical system. It was also emphasized that the theorist must make the fundamental assumption that the real world can be approximated by a block-recursive model, in which the total set of variables can be partitioned into blocks in such a way that there is no feedback between blocks. This makes it possible to take certain variables as clearly dependent, and to make simplifying assumptions regarding error terms. The selective use of exogenous variables also aids identification.

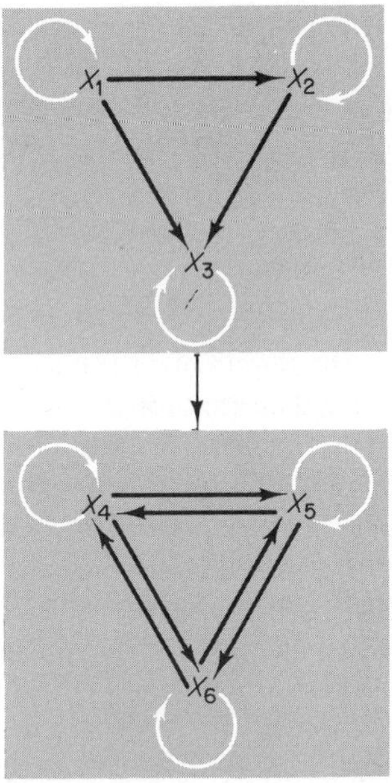

Here we shall be concerned only with the question of stability conditions. Suppose we were to add a set of exogenous variables to the system of reciprocally related variables. Furthermore, suppose that the exogenous variables are recursively interrelated. Of course, as a special case we might also consider the possibility that the exogenous variables are completely unrelated to each other, but it is more convenient to allow for the possibility that they are recursively related. To be specific, suppose there are three exogenous variables, X_1, X_2, and X_3, and three additional variables X_4, X_5, X_6, taken to be reciprocally interrelated and simultaneously dependent on the exogenous variables as well. This model has been diagrammed in Fig. 6-8, in which the single arrow from the upper to the lower block indicates that each of the variables in the lower block could be directly affected by each variable in the upper block.

FIG. 6-8 Recursive exogenous variables plus general three-variable model.

Because of the recursive relationships among X_1, X_2, and X_3, plus the lack of feedback from variables X_4, X_5, and X_6, a large number of the coefficients can be set equal to zero. In particular, the first row of the determinant will consist of b_{11} and five zeros. This permits a simple expansion of the determinant in terms of this first row. The "minor" determinant will have a first row consisting of b_{22} and four zeros, permitting another simple expansion by the new first row. This situation will, in general, continue through the last of the exogenous variables, as long as we are dealing with a recursive situation with the exogenous variables ordered according to their causal priority. Thus the matrix for Condition II is as follows:

$$\begin{vmatrix} b_{11} & 0 & 0 & 0 & 0 & 0 \\ b_{21} & b_{22} & 0 & 0 & 0 & 0 \\ b_{31} & b_{32} & b_{33} & 0 & 0 & 0 \\ b_{41} & b_{42} & b_{43} & b_{44} & b_{45} & b_{46} \\ b_{51} & b_{52} & b_{53} & b_{54} & b_{55} & b_{56} \\ b_{61} & b_{62} & b_{63} & b_{64} & b_{65} & b_{66} \end{vmatrix} = b_{11}b_{22}b_{33} \begin{vmatrix} b_{44} & b_{45} & b_{46} \\ b_{54} & b_{55} & b_{56} \\ b_{64} & b_{65} & b_{66} \end{vmatrix} \quad (6\text{-}14)$$

Since the 3-by-3 determinant involves only X_4, X_5, and X_6 we may ignore the exogenous variables in considering the stability of the lower-block variables, provided we assume that the product $b_{11}b_{22}b_{33}$ is negative.[13] Again we encounter some interesting possibilities if two of the three feedback terms b_{11}, b_{22}, and b_{33} are positive, or if one or more of them is zero. Let us therefore examine the behavior of the exogenous variables, this being possible since X_4 through X_6 do not appear in any of their equations. The recursive system's equations are of course as follows:

$$\frac{dX_1}{dt} = b_{11}X_1 \quad (6\text{-}15a)$$

$$\frac{dX_2}{dt} = b_{21}X_1 + b_{22}X_2 \quad (6\text{-}15b)$$

$$\frac{dX_3}{dt} = b_{31}X_1 + b_{32}X_2 + b_{33}X_3 \quad (6\text{-}15c)$$

and the determinant for Condition II is

$$\begin{vmatrix} b_{11} & 0 & 0 \\ b_{21} & b_{22} & 0 \\ b_{31} & b_{32} & b_{33} \end{vmatrix} = b_{11}b_{22}b_{33}$$

The determinant for Condition II is triangular (i.e., with all zeros above the main diagonal), with the result that all of the b_{ij} terms drop out, leaving us with the very simple condition that $b_{11}b_{22}b_{33}$ must be negative. Since there is no constant term in the equation for dX_1/dt, if $b_{11} = 0$, X_1 will be a constant (except for random shocks, which have not been explicitly incorporated in the model). If b_{22} were also zero, this would mean that dX_2/dt would be a

---

[13] Note that although $k = 6$ for the model of Fig. 6-8, k becomes odd ($k = 3$) when the exogenous variables are ignored, and therefore Condition II involves a change of signs in this instance.

constant, so that X_2 would increase or decrease indefinitely according to the sign of this constant. Therefore X_3 would also increase or decrease indefinitely, if $b_{33} = 0$. The negative feedback terms are thus needed to assure the stability of the recursive system. When we make use of algebraic equations, for which the dX_i/dt are all zero, we implicitly assume that such stabilizing forces are operative.

The essential point is that, provided the stability of the system of recursively related exogenous variables is assured, we need only examine the question of the stability of the variables that are reciprocally related.[14] This of course justifies our breaking off the set of exogenous variables, either to study this system in its own right, or to ignore it in studying the stability of systems of variables dependent on it. An analogous property holds in the case of variables that are totally dependent on a given set of variables. As an exercise, you might wish to verify this fact in the case of six variables, the first three of which are reciprocally interrelated, and the last three recursively related but dependent (with no feedback) on the first three.

Replacing feedback terms with loops. It has been emphasized that a feedback term such as b_{ii} merely summarizes our ignorance, though it may be necessary in order to assure stability. If one is to avoid the mystical or even teleological position that there must always be feedback mechanisms in social systems, he must attempt to explain such feedbacks by introducing specific variables wherever possible. In other words, one should attempt to replace the b_{ii} with specific loops involving additional variables that can be measured and explicitly brought into the theoretical system. As Coleman has noted, it may remain necessary to retain additional b_{ii} terms, but to the degree that we have been successful in explaining the feedback mechanisms, these "residual" terms should get smaller and smaller.[15] The strategy is to use the stability conditions to see where feedback terms would be necessary in order to obtain stability. If it appears that, in reality, systems of a given type do in fact tend toward stability, we are then told where to look. The searching procedure in effect consists of trying to replace the unexplained b_{ii} by more specific loops.

The procedure can be illustrated in terms of a simple model, as in Fig. 6-9. Suppose the model originally consisted of variables X_1, X_4, and X_5 plus the three feedback terms. Suppose, also, that we suspect that a large proportion of the feedback term b_{11} can be explained by introducing the loop from X_1 to X_2 to X_3 and back to X_1. We retain a residual b_{11} term just in

[14] This statement also holds for exogenous variables that are reciprocally interrelated. For example, if all possible arrows are drawn connecting X_1, X_2, and X_3, Condition II reduces to the product of the 3-by-3 determinant involving X_4, X_5, and X_6 times each of the terms of Eq. (6-5).

[15] See Coleman, "The Mathematical Study of Change," pp. 440–41.

case there are additional mechanisms, and we also allow for additional feedback terms b_{22} and b_{33} which, hopefully, can be small. The resulting determinant for Condition II can easily be expanded in terms of the elements of the second row as follows:

$$\begin{vmatrix} b_{11} & 0 & b_{13} & b_{14} & b_{15} \\ b_{21} & b_{22} & 0 & 0 & 0 \\ 0 & b_{32} & b_{33} & 0 & 0 \\ b_{41} & 0 & 0 & b_{44} & b_{45} \\ b_{51} & 0 & 0 & b_{54} & b_{55} \end{vmatrix} = -b_{21} \begin{vmatrix} 0 & b_{13} & b_{14} & b_{15} \\ b_{32} & b_{33} & 0 & 0 \\ 0 & 0 & b_{44} & b_{45} \\ 0 & 0 & b_{54} & b_{55} \end{vmatrix} + b_{22} \begin{vmatrix} b_{11} & b_{13} & b_{14} & b_{15} \\ 0 & b_{33} & 0 & 0 \\ b_{41} & 0 & b_{44} & b_{45} \\ b_{51} & 0 & b_{54} & b_{55} \end{vmatrix}$$

$$= (-b_{21})(-b_{32}) \begin{vmatrix} b_{13} & b_{14} & b_{15} \\ 0 & b_{44} & b_{45} \\ 0 & b_{54} & b_{55} \end{vmatrix} + b_{22}b_{33} \begin{vmatrix} b_{11} & b_{14} & b_{15} \\ b_{41} & b_{44} & b_{45} \\ b_{51} & b_{54} & b_{55} \end{vmatrix} \quad (6.16)$$

$$= b_{21}b_{32}b_{13}(b_{44}b_{55} - b_{45}b_{54}) + b_{22}b_{33} \begin{vmatrix} b_{11} & b_{14} & b_{15} \\ b_{41} & b_{44} & b_{45} \\ b_{51} & b_{54} & b_{55} \end{vmatrix}$$

While this result is perhaps too general to provide intuitive insights, we can note the general structure of the equations. The expression $b_{21}b_{32}b_{13}$ to the left of the parentheses in the first term represents the loop which was introduced to partially replace the feedback term b_{11}, which now appears as only one element of the determinant in the second term. This "loop" product is multiplied by the factor $(b_{44}b_{55} - b_{45}b_{54})$ representing only variables X_4 and X_5.

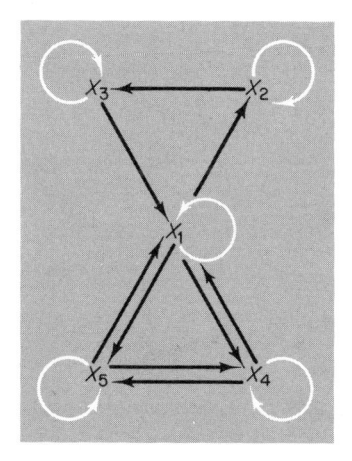

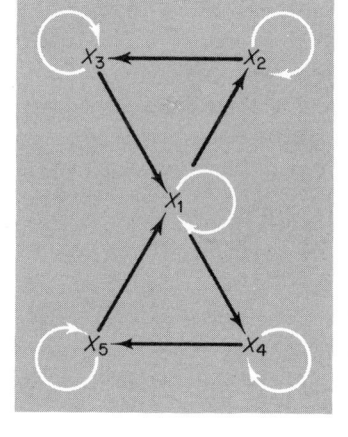

FIG. 6-9 Simple loop plus general three-variable model.

FIG. 6-10 Two loops through a single variable.

The second term involves multiplying the two feedbacks of the "loop" variables X_2 and X_3 by a determinant involving the "original" variables X_1, X_4, and X_5. We see that if either b_{22} or b_{33} is zero, the second term vanishes. If in addition the loop replacing b_{11} is negative (say, because b_{32} is negative), then Condition II requires that $(b_{44}b_{55} - b_{45}b_{54})$ must be positive. We might also note that the second term in Eq. (6-16) is just the stability expression in the case where X_2 and X_3 operate as exogenous variables. For example, if one were to reverse the arrow from X_1 to X_2, then there would be no feedback loop involving X_1, X_2, and X_3, and the latter two variables would be exogenous.

Now consider the simplified case represented in Fig. 6-10, in which the counterclockwise loop from X_1 to X_5 to X_4 to X_1 has been removed. This means that $b_{14} = b_{45} = b_{51} = 0$, and the expression for Condition II becomes

$$b_{11}b_{22}b_{33}b_{44}b_{55} + b_{22}b_{33}(b_{41}b_{54}b_{15}) + b_{44}b_{55}(b_{21}b_{32}b_{13})$$

which of course must be negative in order for stability to be achieved. Suppose b_{11} is zero (or very small) and that $b_{21}b_{32}b_{13}$ is negative and $b_{41}b_{54}b_{15}$ positive. Then if the remaining b_{ii} are negative, the sign of the total expression will depend on the relative magnitudes of the second and third terms. If $b_{44}b_{55}$ were very large relative to $b_{22}b_{33}$, or if the links in the negative feedback loop were large compared to the "original" loop involving X_4 and X_5, then stability could be achieved. As already noted, if either b_{22} or b_{33} were close to zero, this would aid stability in the case of a positive loop through X_4 and X_5.

Multiple loops. As a final example, suppose one's theory predicts a direct causal link from X_1 to X_2, but that it is also expected that there are various indirect feedbacks via other variables to X_1. Rather than simply drawing in a single arrow from X_2 to X_1, it would be insightful to attempt to specify the nature of these loops by identifying and measuring the variables involved. For illustrative purposes let us consider the cases where there are two and three such loops, as indicated in Figs. 6-11 and 6-12.

In the case of two such loops and four variables, the expression for Condition II reduces to

$$b_{11}b_{22}b_{33}b_{44} + b_{21}(b_{33}b_{14}b_{42} + b_{44}b_{13}b_{32})$$

whereas the expression in the case of three loops and five variables is

$$b_{11}b_{22}b_{33}b_{44}b_{55} + b_{21}(b_{33}b_{44}b_{15}b_{52} + b_{33}b_{55}b_{14}b_{42} + b_{44}b_{55}b_{13}b_{32})$$

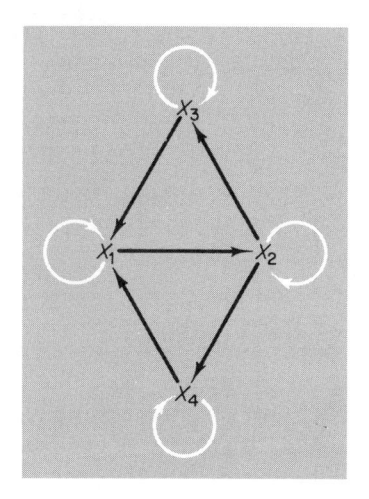

FIG. 6-11 Two loops connecting a pair of variables.

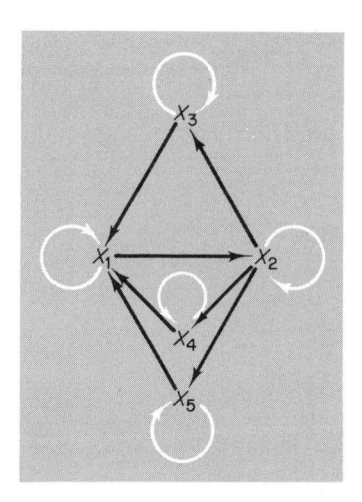

FIG. 6-12 Three loops connecting a pair of variables.

From these results we can see the general pattern. The first term consists of the usual product of feedbacks. The second involves multiplying the direct link b_{21} by a series of terms. Each of the latter terms consists of the product of the coefficients in one of the loops (e.g., $b_{13}b_{32}$) multiplied by the feedback terms that do *not* appear in this loop (e.g., $b_{44}b_{55}$). In the case of four variables, Condition II indicates that the expression must be positive for stability, whereas in the case of five variables it must be negative. If all b_{ii} are negative, the first term will aid stability. But stability will also depend on the signs and magnitudes of the coefficients in the various loops. For example in the case of five variables, if the loop through X_3 is negative, then a large $b_{44}b_{55}$ term will aid stability, assuming that all b_{ii} are negative and that b_{21} is positive. If, say, b_{33} is zero, both the four and five variable expressions will be reduced to only one term, the sign of which will determine stability. Notice that in this case, the nonvanishing term involves the loop (i.e., $b_{21}b_{13}b_{32}$) for which the b_{ii} term (i.e., b_{33}) is zero. If $b_{11} = 0$, or if $b_{22} = 0$, only the first term will drop out. Given that we are attempting to reduce these terms to approximately zero by specifying additional loops, this result is not at all surprising.

General remarks

The various examples of this section should be sufficient to illustrate the general strategy of working with stability conditions. We have seen that it is possible to write down the stability conditions with the aid of only simple algebra, and to study their implications in abstract situations. The insights obtained in this manner must of course be supplemented by those gained through working with actual substantive theories, and it is as yet too early to foresee the nature of specific problems that may arise, or the potential utility of this general approach. The two substantive examples that will be discussed in the next section should be suggestive in this respect.

One feature of these stability conditions, which is especially apparent in the case of the k-equation models, is the dependence on the various b_{ii} terms, even in the presence of loops that involve negative feedbacks. For example in the case of the model of Fig. 6-12, we saw that, for a triple loop, the product of the loop coefficients is multiplied by the feedback terms that do not involve this loop. These relationships may serve to indicate just how difficult it is to achieve stability in multiple-equation systems. In effect, one must build in feedback terms in numerous places in order to keep the entire system stable. The implication may be that in systems with as few as eight or ten variables absolute stability can seldom be achieved, even in the short run.[16] Nevertheless, there may be stabilizing mechanisms that are operative and that function to slow down rates of change in complex systems.

The theoretical systems discussed in the present section are far more complex than the kinds of dynamic formulations that are likely to be developed in sociology in the near future. They have involved as many as six simultaneous differential equations, which could undoubtedly be reduced in number by assuming that certain of the feedbacks were either extremely rapid or sufficiently delayed to justify their being ignored. It is perhaps true that most early attempts to develop dynamic formulations in economics have involved simple lagged recursive models of the sort illustrated by the cobweb model discussed in Chap. 5.[17] Nevertheless, it would seem helpful to keep the more general formulations in mind in order to suggest ways in which an initial theory, such as that of Hopkins, can be elaborated in order to introduce stabilizing mechanisms where they would seem most appropriate.

Illustrations

We have thus far considered only the hypothetical extension of Hopkins' theory of influence processes. In this section I shall briefly discuss two specific attempts to develop mathematical models of social processes, both of which are directly concerned with the kinds of stability conditions treated at some length in the previous sections. A simplified version of the first example on arms races has already been introduced. My purpose is not to present the

---

[16] It should be remembered, however, that our analysis has been restricted to *linear* systems which are not as satisfactory as nonlinear systems for handling saturation effects.

[17] See Wold and Jureen, *Demand Analysis*, Chaps. 1 and 3.

authors' technical mathematical reasoning, nor is it to give an extensive critique or commentary, since rather lengthy discussions of both theories already exist in the literature.[18] My objective is merely to outline how the use of simultaneous differential equations, and our knowledge of the stability conditions, can be helpful in the process of theory construction.

Richardson's theory of armament races

In a book titled *Arms and Insecurity*, which was published posthumously in 1960, Lewis F. Richardson attempted to apply actual data pertaining to arms races prior to the two World Wars to a mathematical formulation involving simultaneous linear differential equations.[19] Richardson's two-nation model is as follows:

$$\frac{dX}{dt} = kY - \alpha X + g$$

$$\frac{dY}{dt} = lX - \beta Y + h$$

(6-17)

where X and Y represent the levels of armaments in the two countries; where k and l represent "defense" coefficients; where the feedback terms α and β represent "fatigue" coefficients; and the constants g and h are referred to as "grievance" terms. It is assumed that the defense coefficients and fatigue coefficients must be positive or zero, with negative feedbacks being implied by the negative signs preceding α and β.

The basic idea is that nation X reacts to positive armament levels in Y by increasing its own arms, this in turn leading to an increase in Y's armament level. But each nation is also subject to certain limitations on its budget, and there may also be other factors that operate to restrict the levels of armaments in either nation. As previously implied, these factors are summarized in the "fatigue" coefficients. The grievance terms may be either positive or negative and constitute residual factors representing the aggregate effects of variables that can be assumed to operate independently of the actual levels of arms in the two countries. These can include actual grievances over past treatment, aggressive ambitions of leaders, general prejudices, or contentment with the status quo. A negative grievance term indicates that the nation is generally

---

[18] See James S. Coleman, "The Mathematical Study of Small Groups," in *Mathematical Thinking in the Measurement of Behavior*, ed. Herbert Solomon (New York: Free Press of Glencoe, 1960), Part I, and Anatol Rapoport, *Fights, Games, and Debates* (Ann Arbor: University of Michigan Press, 1960).

[19] Richardson, *Arms and Insecurity*.

satisfied; perhaps it is a "have" nation, or a winner of the previous conflict.

In this very simple model, each of the coefficients is taken as a constant. In short-run analyses (perhaps over only two or three years), this might be a reasonable approximation. In principle, there is nothing to prohibit one from taking each of these coefficients as a function of additional variables. That is, grievances may decay over time. Or, as Richardon suggests, the defense coefficients may be functions of the relative sizes of the two nations. Richardson also allows for the possibility that X and Y may be negative, though it is of course difficult to imagine negative armaments. He does this by taking reciprocal trade as the negative of armaments. This allows for the possibility that instability may occur in the negative direction as well. That is, nations may become increasingly friendly, engaging in ever increasing amounts of reciprocal trade. Rashevsky notes in the introduction to Richardson's work that this particular assumption—that reciprocal trade represents the opposite of arms races—is untenable.[20] We shall therefore ignore this possibility in the subsequent discussion, assuming that neither X nor Y can be negative.

Richardson derives a number of interesting propositions from this very simple model, only a few of which can be mentioned in this brief summary. He notes that unilateral disarmament cannot by itself produce stability. We know, of course, that the necessary condition for stability is that the product of the feedback terms $\alpha\beta$ must be numerically greater than the product of the "defense" coefficients kl, which are in effect measures of the sensitivity of each nation to increases in the arms of the other party. The values of the grievance terms g and h do not affect stability, since they are assumed to be constants. They do, however, help to determine the position of the system if equilibrium is reached. That is, they may affect whether or not X is greater than Y at equilibrium, and hence which nation may be in the dominant position in a stable situation.[21] Because of this, one would ordinarily expect both g and h to be positive.

To see the implications of this model for unilateral disarmament, suppose the level of armaments in country Y is reduced to zero. This will give the momentary results

$$\frac{dX}{dt} = -\alpha X + g$$

$$\frac{dY}{dt} = lX + h$$

(6-18)

[20] Nicholas Rashevsky, "Introduction," to Richardson, *Arms and Insecurity*.

[21] An additional complicating factor is that, in most instances, each nation acts so as to achieve two objectives, maximizing its own power position while simultaneously avoiding overt conflict (if the latter is expected to be disadvantageous). A more realistic model would therefore allow for the possibility that the "grievance" term is not necessarily constant.

If country X is relatively satisfied, g may be numerically small, and the right-hand side of the first equation could be negative. But the right-hand side of the second equation will ordinarily be positive (unless Y is a truly pacifist nation with l and h both zero), and there will be pressures to increase Y. This, in turn, will reintroduce a positive term into the first equation, and another arms race may be underway. Stability will then depend on whether or not the product $\alpha\beta$ is greater than the product kl. We see also that mutual disarmament (setting *both* X and Y equal to zero momentarily) will also not produce stability if the two grievance terms are positive. Richardson concludes that mutual disarmament, without mutual satisfaction, will not necessarily produce stability.[22]

Richardson also considers the interesting case of what he refers to as "rivalry" between two nations, in which each nation is motivated primarily by the *difference* between the levels of armaments. That is, nation X increases its arms in proportion to the degree that Y exceeds X, and similarly for nation Y. Richardson represents this kind of situation by the equations

$$\frac{dX}{dt} = k(Y - X) - \alpha X + g = kY - (k + \alpha)X + g$$

$$\frac{dY}{dt} = l(X - Y) - \beta Y + h = lX - (l + \beta)Y + h$$

(6-19)

Since g and h do not affect stability, we see that the necessary condition for stability is, in this case,

$$(k + \alpha)(l + \beta) > kl$$

which is automatically satisfied since we are assuming that all four coefficients are positive. Thus we reach the conclusion that "rivalry," in this specific sense, always implies that the necessary conditions for stability are met. Of course we cannot be assured that the sufficient conditions are likewise automatically satisfied. Unfortunately, also, the above model is unrealistic in at least one major respect. It requires us to assume accurate knowledge of the values of X and Y by both parties. If one nation believes that the other possesses secret armaments of unknown potential, the model is obviously inappropriate.

One important advantage of mathematical formulations is that they are

---

[22] Richardson, *Arms and Insecurity*, p. 27, notes that the League of Nations assumed that "defensive" arms are justifiable, whereas positive grievances were looked upon with alarm. According to Richardson's formulation, however, it is the former, rather than the latter, which lead to unstable armament races.

sufficiently explicit that their shortcomings are readily apparent. Therefore modifications can be systematically introduced. Richardson is well aware, for example, that two-nation models are inadequate, and that as soon as one introduces additional nations he must allow for the possibility of alliances or coalitions. He therefore develops a k-equation model and studies a number of special cases that seem reasonably analogous to real world situations. Alliances are handled by setting some of the defense coefficients equal to zero. Further simplifications are introduced by studying special cases for which the various coefficients are assigned simple numerical values, such as 0, 1, 2, or 3. Richardson then analyzes data collected for as many as ten nations.

Several interesting propositions can be deduced in the case of specific models. For example, Richardson shows that in the case of three nations, there can be pair-by-pair stability, and yet this does not necessarily imply stability in the triad. Certain types of alliances are shown not to affect stability one way or the other. Richardson also considers briefly the stability of a triadic relationship among two pugnacious nations and one compliant nation.

Explicit mathematical formulations also have the advantage that their relationships with alternative models can be systematically studied. Robert Abelson, starting with what might appear to be a very different perspective, derives the same set of equations as Richardson's.[23] In doing so, he has increased our understanding of the psychological assumptions that can be used to generate conflict models with more general applicability than Richardson's theory of arms races. Abelson considers the case of two parties, each of which reacts to the responses of the other with intensities that tend to decay with time. But since there may be a whole series of responses, these must be summed over time. Suppose Party 1 acts with intensity A_1 at time tau (τ) and that Party 2 continues to respond to this action, with the magnitude of this response at any later time t being given by

$$A_2(t) = e^{-\lambda_2(t-\tau)} \theta_2 A_1(\tau) \qquad (6\text{-}20)$$

The fact that Party 2 is assumed to forgive or forget the original act of Party 1 as time progresses is represented by the exponent of the natural constant e. The coefficient λ_2 is called the "forgiveness" coefficient of Party 2. The greater the difference between t and τ, and the greater the forgiveness coefficient, the greater the product $\lambda_2(t - \tau)$, and therefore the weaker the response. We thus see that the rapidity of the decay depends on the size of

[23] Robert P. Abelson, "A 'Derivation' of Richardson's Equations," *Journal of Conflict Resolution*, 7 (March 1963), 13–15.

the forgiveness coefficient. The factor $\theta_2 A_1(\tau)$ determines the magnitude of the initial response of Party 2 and consists of a coefficient θ_2, representing the "sensitivity" of Party 2 to the acts of Party 1, multiplied by the intensity $A_1(\tau)$ of the initial act of Party 1.

This equation only applies to a single act of Party 1 at time τ. If we imagine a whole series of such acts at different times, we might assume that the magnitude of the response of Party 2 at any particular time t would be obtained by summing his reactions to all the various acts of Party 1 at different times in the past. Of course, given the decay factor, the most recent actions of Party 1 should be the most prominent determinants of Party 2's behavior at time t. If we assume a very large number of acts over a continuous period of time, we should use an integral sign rather than a summation sign. Assuming that the initial act of Party 1 took place at time 0, this would give for the total magnitude of the response of Party 2 at time t the value

$$A_2(t) = \int_0^t e^{-\lambda_2(t-\tau)} \theta_2 A_1(\tau) \, d\tau \tag{6-21a}$$

By a similar argument, the responses of Party 1 to the numerous actions of Party 2 would be given by

$$A_1(t) = \int_0^t e^{-\lambda_1(t-\tau)} \theta_1 A_2(\tau) \, d\tau \tag{6-21b}$$

where λ_1 and θ_1 represent the forgiveness and sensitivity coefficients of Party 1. These two equations are integral equations, but they can readily be transformed into differential equations. When this is done we obtain the following familiar pair of equations

$$\frac{dA_2}{dt} = \theta_2 A_1 - \lambda_2 A_2 \tag{6-22a}$$

$$\frac{dA_1}{dt} = \theta_1 A_2 - \lambda_1 A_1 \tag{6-22b}$$

With a suitable translation of the symbols, these are of course the same equations used by Richardson, except for the omission of the grievance constants.

Thus Abelson's forgiveness coefficients λ_i appear in the role of feedback coefficients, as do Richardson's fatigue coefficients. The connotations of the terms "forgiveness" and "fatigue" are of course somewhat different, implying perhaps a different set of exogenous factors as possible explanatory variables in the two models. Similarly, Abelson's sensitivity coefficients θ_i play the same part as Richardson's defense coefficients. Here the substantive similarity is more obvious. The major point is that, by starting with a very different orientation, Abelson has derived the same equations as those used by Richardson. As Abelson notes, the interpretation in terms of time decays and sensitivity coefficients is reasonably plausible in the case of many other kinds of intergroup conflicts, including propaganda battles, racial violence, and exchanges of insults.

Simon's formalization of Homans' theory

Herbert Simon has developed several dynamic mathematical models of general group processes, three of which are presented in his *Models of Man*.[24] Only one of these involves the linear case, and I shall therefore confine the discussion to this more simple treatment. Simon's model in this instance is an attempt to formalize several propositions stated verbally in George Homans' well-known work, *The Human Group*.[25]

Simon confines the model to four group-level variables, three of which are endogenous and one exogenous. The three endogenous variables are (1) amount of interaction, I, (2) average level of friendship, F, and (3) the total amount of activity, A. The exogenous variable is the amount of activity, E, actually required by the "external system" (or environment) in order to justify the group's continued existence. Readers familiar with *The Human Group* may find it convenient to think in terms of the example of the Bank Wiring Room group, for which E would be the total amount of activity required by the company in connection with work assignments. The causal model for the theoretical system would be as indicated in Fig. 6-13, and Simon's three equations (one for each endogenous variable) are as follows:

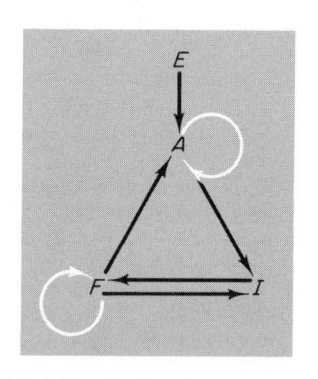

FIG. 6-13 The Simon-Homans model.

$$I = a_1 F + a_2 A \qquad (6\text{-}23a)$$

$$\frac{dF}{dt} = b(I - \beta F) \qquad (6\text{-}23b)$$

[24] Simon, *Models of Man*, Chaps. 6–8.
[25] Homans, *The Human Group*.

$$\frac{dA}{dt} = c_1(F - \gamma A) + c_2(E - A) \qquad (6\text{-}23\text{c})$$

where all of the constants are assumed to be positive (or at least nonnegative).

The first equation in the system is taken as algebraic, meaning that the effects of F and A on I are assumed to be instantaneous, or at least very rapid as compared with the feedbacks on the remaining endogenous variables. This first algebraic equation does not affect the stability of the system, and in fact will be eliminated by the substitution of $a_1 F + a_2 A$ into the second equation in place of I. We shall see, however, that the coefficients a_1 and a_2 in this equation are used to provide interpretations of the stability conditions.

Simon has also represented the feedback terms in the second and third equations in a somewhat different manner, so as to provide additional insights into the qualitative analysis of the stability conditions. Each feedback term is coupled with the nonfeedback term with a coefficient of unity. In the case of Eq. (6-23b), one may think of the feedback coefficient β as an adjustment for the difference in units between the interaction I and friendship F. We may look upon β as representing a coefficient that gives the "appropriate" equilibrium amount of friendship for a unit of interaction. Whenever $\beta F = I$, dF/dt will of course be zero. If $I > \beta F$, then the level of interaction will be greater than is appropriate for friendship, and dF/dt being positive, the level of friendship will increase. If, for any reason, F should increase by too much, so that $\beta F > I$, then dF/dt will be negative, and the level of friendship will decrease. Similar interpretations can be given the two terms in parentheses in the third equation. Since both E and A refer to the same kind of variable, activity, the feedback coefficient of the A term is taken as unity. Notice that in this third equation the total feedback term has been split into two components, one linked with F and the other with the exogenous variable E.

In order to relate the present discussion of dynamic formulations with the previous treatment of reciprocal causation in static terms, let us suppose that one assumes the system is in (stable) equilibrium, and therefore that dF/dt and dA/dt are both zero. Indeed, in terms of our verbal interpretation of the implied feedback process, and of what would happen, say, if $\beta F \neq I$, this would seem entirely reasonable. We must remember, however, that merely setting the two derivatives equal to zero does not assure one that the "equilibrium" position is a stable one. We must consider the dynamic form of the model and study the stability conditions in order to determine whether or not stability would be implied. Ideally, we would want to know the sufficient as well as the necessary conditions for stability.

Setting the two derivatives equal to zero of course gives three algebraic equations in the four variables. If we were willing to assume that the system had reached a stable position, and if only cross-sectional data at a single point in time were available, we immediately see that we would encounter an identification problem in the case of Eq. (6-23a) for *I*. This equation contains all three endogenous variables, whereas there is only one omitted exogenous variable *E*. For similar reasons, the third equation for *A* also could not be identified. If an additional exogenous variable could be introduced as a cause of *F* but not *A* or *I*, then the static system could be identified, though estimation of the various coefficients would not be straightforward because of the correlated error terms produced by the reciprocal relationship between *F* and *I*.

From the standpoint of theory building, it is convenient in this kind of example to ignore these error terms and to make substitutions as though we were dealing with exact mathematical functions. Thus one could take the three algebraic equations and express the variables as functions of each other. For example, if we represented the equilibrium values of *A*, *E*, and *F* by A_0, E_0, and F_0 respectively, we could express the equilibrium value of *A* in terms of E_0 and F_0 as follows:

$$A_0 = \frac{\beta - a_1}{a_2} F_0 \tag{6-24a}$$

$$= \frac{c_2(\beta - a_1)}{c_2(\beta - a_1) + c_1[\gamma(\beta - a_1) - a_2]} E_0 \tag{6-24b}$$

The second expression, especially, involves a rather complicated function of the various coefficients, and one might wonder whether any useful theoretical insights could be obtained by writing down these equilibrium relationships.

However, we may combine a peculiar feature of this specific model with the stability conditions to provide some interesting insights that would hardly be suggested by the verbal formulations. The peculiar feature of this model is the fact that *A* and *E* both involve activities, and we would ordinarily expect to have $A > E$. That is, if the group is to survive in its environment for any period of time, then certainly the total activities must be greater than those required by the environment. Of course there are difficult measurement problems imposed by the nature of the theory. Even if one had an adequate measure of the total activities (e.g., some output measure), how would he determine the amount actually required by the environment? One answer might be that the latter figure could be estimated by slowly reducing *A* until such a point was reached that actors from outside the group (e.g., management) began to interfere. Regardless of the measurement problem, however, one might reasonably impose the theoretical condition that *A* must be greater than or equal to *E*. Simon refers to the situation where $A > E$ as one of "positive morale," where the group engages in activities over and above the required minimum.

Looking at the equilibrium relationship (6-24b) between A_0 and E_0, we note that the first term in the denominator is the same as the numerator, and therefore for positive morale ($A > E$) we must have the second term negative.[26] Since all coefficients are positive or nonzero, this means that $\gamma(\beta - a_1)$ must be less than a_2. We shall return to this inequality after considering the stability conditions.

In order to apply the stability conditions discussed earlier in the chapter, we must first rewrite the equations in familiar terms. When we eliminate I from Eq. (6-23b) by using Eq. (6-23a), and when we collect terms, we get

$$\frac{dF}{dt} = b(a_1 - \beta)F + ba_2A \qquad (6\text{-}25a)$$

$$\frac{dA}{dt} = c_1F - (c_1\gamma + c_2)A + c_2E \qquad (6\text{-}25b)$$

Since no equation has been written for the exogenous variable E, we assume that any changes in E would occur as "random shocks" or once-and-for-all changes that would not affect the stability of the system, though they would of course affect the levels of the several variables at equilibrium. Therefore we can ignore the final term in the second of these differential equations. Making the suitable translation of coefficients gives the following inequalities for Conditions I and II:

I. $b(a_1 - \beta) - (c_1\gamma + c_2) < 0$ or $c_1\gamma + c_2 + b(\beta - a_1) > 0$ (6-26a)

II. $b(a_1 - \beta)[-(c_1\gamma + c_2)] - ba_2c_1 > 0$ or $(\beta - a_1)(c_1\gamma + c_2) - a_2c_1 > 0$ (6-26b)

since all coefficients are assumed positive and b can be canceled from both terms in the inequality for Condition II.

In order to satisfy Condition II it is necessary (though not sufficient) that $\beta > a_1$, since otherwise the expression will clearly have the wrong sign. If $\beta > a_1$ we also see that Condition I is automatically satisfied, and therefore we can concentrate our attention on Condition II. This also requires that $c_1\gamma + c_2$ be large relative to a_2c_1 unless β is very much greater than a_1. Thus large values of $\beta - a_1$ and $c_1\gamma + c_2$ aid stability, whereas large values a_2c_1 hinder stability. But we noted above that in order for A to be greater than E, we must have $\gamma(\beta - a_1)$ less than a_2, given that $\beta > a_1$ in the case of stability.

---

[26] This statement holds only if $\beta > a_1$, but it will be shown below that the condition $\beta > a_1$ is, in fact, necessary for stability.

Thus if γ is large relative to a_2, this will aid stability but is likely to reduce A below E at equilibrium. In order to have both stability and "positive morale" we must count on a large value of c_2 relative to c_1.

Even though it might be extremely difficult to obtain accurate measurements, and therefore to estimate the numerical values of the various coefficients, we can gain valuable theoretical insights by attempting to give substantive meaning to these conditions implied by this linear system. We must remember, of course, that we are dealing with necessary conditions, rather than sufficient ones. This means that if a system is observed to remain stable over a reasonable period of time we may assume that the necessary conditions are being met; we cannot, however, be assured of stability merely if these relationships actually hold.

In the absence of accurate measurements, the stability conditions provide us with only crude qualitative statements. In the case of this particular example, we have seen that stability requires that β be greater than a_1, and that stability is aided if γ is large relative to a_2 (though this may lower A below E), and if c_2 is large relative to c_1. The first question that would naturally occur to us is whether these are meaningful comparisons. This can be seen to be the case since both β and a_1 are coefficients of F, both γ and a_2 are coefficients of A, and c_2 and c_1 determine the relative weights given to the first and second terms in the equation for dA/dt.

Let us first consider the inequality $\beta > a_1$. A small value for a_1 means that interaction I is not very sensitive to changes in F. That is, it takes a rather large change in F to produce a given change in I. This might hold true in a group setting in which the amount of interaction is only to a minor degree subject to voluntary control, and is not sensitive to variations in sentiments of liking among the individuals. For example, interaction in a work setting might be primarily determined by the requirements of the job, rather than personal preferences. A large value for β of course implies a large feedback term in the second equation for dF/dt. This means that changes in friendship must be very sensitive to the level of F, relative to the amount of interaction.

Similarly, since a large γ relative to a_2 aids stability, this would imply that stability will be aided by a large negative feedback in the first term of Eq. (6-23c), as we would of course expect, or by a low degree of sensitivity of interaction I to changes in the total activity level A. That is, stability would be aided by any factors that made interaction less dependent on activity levels. For example, this might be brought about by changes in the work setting that made interaction more of an exogenous variable, being less dependent on both amount of activity and friendship levels (as would be the case if *both* a_1 and a_2 were small). As can readily be seen from Fig. 6-13, making I exogenous reduces the model to a recursive system.

But a relatively large value of a_2 has been seen necessary in order to assure "positive morale." Thus if A is to be greater than E, it is helpful to have the level of interaction sensitive to changes in total activities. This might be achieved, for example, by structuring work relationships in such a way that activities cannot easily be carried out without considerable interaction in the form of cooperative arrangements. Instability in such a system might then consist of continually increasing (or decreasing) values of the three endogenous variables as follows. Large values of a_2 relative to the negative feedback γ could mean that a slight increase in A would bring about a large and immediate increase in I. This increase in I would increase F, though with a delay as indicated in Eq. (6-23b). But if γ were relatively small, this increase in F would substantially increase A, through the first term of Eq. (6-23c). This increase in A would produce a relatively large instantaneous increase in I, and so forth.

Thus if a_2 is large compared to γ, stability will depend on there being a relatively large feedback effect as a result of the *second* term in Eq. (6-23c). This is possible provided that c_2 is large relative to c_1. If this holds, then the second term in Eq. (6-23c) will tend to dominate the first, and the relatively small size of γ will not hamper stability. But a large c_2 relative to c_1 means that changes in A must be relatively sensitive to the difference between E and A, as compared with the friendship-activity component. This means, of course, that the level of activity imposed from the outside, or required for the survival of the group, plays an important role in systems that are both stable and have "positive morale."

Homans seems to be aware of this implication when he discusses what he refers to as "disintegration" in Hilltown, a New England community that over time lost many of its independent economic functions and became virtually a "bedroom community" or satellite of a larger community.[27] Homans notes that as the requirements of the external system E decrease toward zero, so do the levels of activities, friendship, and interaction. The level of E is taken by Homans as determined by outside factors beyond the control of Hilltown residents. The question raised by Homans is that of the nature of the changes in the endogenous variables that can be expected to take place as a result of shifts in the levels of exogenous variables summarized by E.

This problem of describing changes in a system as a result of shifts in exogenous variables has been discussed in the economics literature under the label of "comparative statics." [28] One may assume that after each shift in exogenous variables the system approaches a new equilibrium level. The task is then that of studying the behavior of the "moving" equilibrium position,

[27] Homans, *The Human Group*, Chap. 13.
[28] See Baumol, *Economic Dynamics*, pp. 118–23, 373–78; and Samuelson, *Foundations of Economic Analysis*, Chap. 9.

as the system readjusts to the new conditions. The analysis is in one sense static, since the time-paths taken by the endogenous variables in the process of reaching equilibrium are of no interest. One assumes that if there is a once-and-for-all change in an exogenous variable, there will be a change in one or more endogenous variables, but the rates of change may not be measurable or of theoretical interest. In contrast, the study of dynamics is very much concerned with these differential rates of change. For example, Simon's formulation of Homans' theory involves the assumption that the changes in I produced by changes in A and F are almost instantaneous.

It has been emphasized by Paul Samuelson, the theoretical economist, that questions posed in comparative statics ordinarily cannot be answered without an explicit dynamic formulation.[29] In comparative statics, we assume that a system will readjust itself and that a new stable equilibrium point will be reached, or at least approximated, each time there is a shift in one or more exogenous variables. But in order to work with or evaluate this assumption, we must have an underlying dynamic theory to provide the stability conditions necessary to answer the kinds of questions posed in comparative statics. This will be the case even though we may have no inherent interest in the dynamic processes themselves.

Let us illustrate this very abstract notion, which Samuelson refers to as the "correspondence principle," in terms of the Homans-Simon example. The question we would like to answer in the case of comparative statics is this: Assuming that the system will approach stability, how will a change in the exogenous variable E affect the new equilibrium position? In terms of the Hilltown example, one might ask how the equilibrium values I_0, A_0, and F_0 would be affected by a decrease in E brought about by economic changes in the community.

To obtain an answer to this question, we take the derivatives of each of the endogenous variables with respect to the exogenous variable E.[30] We then try to evaluate the *signs* of these derivatives under conditions of equilibrium, where both dF/dt and dA/dt are zero, and where there would therefore be no changes in I as well. We have seen in Eq. (6-24) that when we express the equilibrium values of each of the variables as functions of the others, including E, the results involve rather complicated functions of the coefficients. The question then becomes that of determining the signs of these functions, and this usually cannot be accomplished without making use of the stability conditions provided by the dynamic formulation. This is the basis for Samuelson's claim that dynamic formulations must underlie static analyses.

[29] *Ibid.*, pp. 5, 258, 263, 284, and 350; see also Baumol, *Economic Dynamics*, pp. 122–23.
[30] If there are several exogenous variables, it will be necessary to take *partial* derivatives, holding constant all exogenous variables but one.

We shall consider only the relationship between A_0 and E_0, which is the most complex of the set. It will be recalled that setting dF/dt and dA/dt both equal to zero produced the equilibrium relationship (6-24b)

$$A_0 = \frac{c_2(\beta - a_1)}{c_2(\beta - a_1) + c_1[\gamma(\beta - a_1) - a_2]} E_0$$

We now ask whether the change in A produced by an increase in E will be positive, negative, or indeterminate. Remembering that the coefficient of E_0 is just a constant, we see that dA_0/dE_0 is equal to this same constant. Such a complex quantity would ordinarily have an indeterminate sign.

Our stability conditions indicate that the entire quantity must be positive, however. The numerator contains the positive constant c_2 times $(\beta - a_1)$ which must be positive. If we rewrite the second form of Condition II given by Eq. (6-26b), we see that this is exactly equal to the denominator of the expression for dA_0/dE_0. Since Condition II requires that this also be positive, we see that if the equilibrium is a stable one, then the new equilibrium position produced by an increase in E_0 will involve an increase in A_0. The same can be shown to hold in the case of both I_0 and F_0, and therefore we conclude that an increase in E_0 will result in increases in all three endogenous variables. But this conclusion rests on the assumption that the equilibrium is stable, and this will not necessarily be true unless the relationships among the coefficients are such that they satisfy the stability conditions for the dynamic model.

Concluding Remarks

Since this chapter has contained a number of rather technical details, it is perhaps worthwhile to emphasize the main points that have been made. It has been argued that truly dynamic formulations are necessary if one wishes to study the actual processes of change, or if he wants to answer the kinds of questions posed in "comparative statics." Fundamental in both instances are the stability conditions implied by the model. These conditions indicate relationships that must hold among the various coefficients in order for the system to stabilize at some equilibrium level. They are also necessary in determining what will happen to the equilibrium position if specific changes are made in the levels of the exogenous variables. This latter kind of question is especially important in social engineering, where one may not be particularly interested in the actual process of adjustment to new levels of the exogenous variables, but where it will be important to predict at least the signs of changes in the various endogenous variables.

There may also be an interest in situations in which oscillations or cyclical changes occur. Here, a choice must be made between difference-equation models, for which time is discrete, and differential-equation models, for which time is continuous. Where there is a definite fixed lag period, and where it is possible to "overshoot the mark," a difference-equation model is ordinarily to be preferred. If the system can be simplified to the extent that there are only two differential (or difference) equations, it may be possible to utilize nonlinear models that are somewhat more realistic than the kinds of linear systems we have considered in this book. Where multiple differential equations are more appropriate, it is possible in the linear case to study the implications of the stability conditions to gain insights as to the nature of the feedback processes that must take place for a system to stabilize. It has been emphasized, however, that one must replace the abstract feedback terms b_{ii} by specific variables, and that it is by no means inevitable that stability will be achieved in any given system. In fact, we have seen that it may be rather difficult to satisfy the necessary stability conditions in complex systems.

In dealing with simultaneous differential equations, we have not been concerned with disturbance or error terms, and the equations have been treated as though they were exact. However, whenever one attempts to estimate the various coefficients using empirical data, he will encounter the same kinds of difficult estimation problems that arise in connection with simultaneous algebraic systems. Since data must be collected at discrete points in time, least-squares procedures may be used to estimate parameters whenever the model reduces to a recursive form involving lagged endogenous variables. But autocorrelation is very likely to occur, particularly when the intervals between observations are very short. These problems of autocorrelation combine with measurement errors to produce complications in testing and estimation, problems that we have not really considered in the present work.

While it is perhaps discouraging to point to too many such complicating factors that may interfere with the theory-building process, it is nevertheless only realistic to anticipate them and deal with them as systematically as possible. Obviously, these considerations have major implications for the future of social science research. They imply that we must give much more careful attention to data collection and measurement, and to careful conceptualization.

7

Generalizations and Levels of Abstraction

Social scientists want their theories to have as wide a range of applicability as possible, while still being sufficiently specific to provide useful predictions and explanations of "middle-range" phenomena. This objective is very worthwhile and laudable, though it should be recognized that it may be difficult to formulate highly general theories that imply predictions taking us very far beyond the common-sense level of analysis. The overall strategy might be to begin with very general formulations, see what propositions these imply, and then add restrictive assumptions a few at a time until more useful specific propositions are implied.

For example, this strategy is often used in presenting mathematical theorems, though in the process of theory building, the mathematician may be more likely to begin with less abstract formulations closer to substantive fields of application. The general theory will be stated in highly abstract terms, with as few assumptions as possible as to the form of the equations, the values of the parameters, or (in the case of statistical theory) the specific distributions of the error terms. It will often be found that this very general theory cannot yield useful theorems, and so additional assumptions will be made in order to study important special cases. For example, the model may be confined to a linear-additive form, and increasingly restrictive assumptions may be made about the behavior of the error terms. Thus in order to make conventional F and t tests, one must assume that the error distributions are approximately normal.

The principal value of a highly general theoretical formulation is that it enables one to place the various special cases in perspective and to prove general theorems appropriate to them all. I rather suspect that the most usual manner in which these general theories are developed is somewhat as follows. There may be several special cases or more restrictive theories in the literature for a rather long period of time. Then it may be noticed that these theories or models contain a number of similarities, and attempts may be made to synthesize or generalize them. Once a general formulation has been developed, a number of additional special cases will be noted, including so-called "degenerate" or unusual ones. The resulting "paradigm," as Kuhn refers to it, may serve as a major stimulus to investigators to fill in the details and solve the remaining puzzles that have not been resolved by the theory.[1]

Social scientists may be tempted by the hope of developing highly general theories prior to the formulation of the more specific special cases, with the result that they may work on very high levels of abstraction too far removed from empirical data. In this concluding chapter I should like to examine several possible meanings of the notion "levels of abstraction" and the implications they may have for the process of theory building. At the risk of gross oversimplification, I would suggest that there are at least three different though related notions as to what the process of abstraction and generalization involves. I shall refer to these by the simple labels of the "element-class" perspective, the "class-subclass" perspective, and the "indicator" perspective, though it will be readily apparent that none of these can adequately be represented by single descriptive phrases. Let us first consider what I have termed the "element-class" perspective.

The Element-Class Perspective

George Homans argues that explanation consists of taking a particular phenomenon and treating it as a special case of a more general one.[2] Let us

[1] See Thomas S. Kuhn, *The Structure of Scientific Revolutions* (Chicago: University of Chicago Press, 1962), especially Chap. 2.

[2] See George C. Homans, *Social Behavior: Its Elementary Forms* (New York: Harcourt, Brace & World, 1961), p. 10; and George C. Homans, *The Nature of Social Science* (New York: Harcourt, Brace & World, 1967). Homans' usage of the term "explanation" seems to be somewhat narrower and perhaps fundamentally different from the kinds of causal explanations stressed in this book. For a discussion of this difference see David Willer, *Scientific Sociology: Theory and Method* (Englewood Cliffs: Prentice-Hall, Inc., 1967), p. 25–26.

illustrate in terms of an example used by Homans. Suppose we wish to explain the low incidence of suicide in Spain. The theoretical argument might be stated in terms of three general propositions plus two that deal specifically with Spain:

1. In any social grouping, the suicide rate varies directly with the degree of individualism (egoism).
2. The degree of individualism varies with the incidence of Protestantism.
3. Therefore, the suicide rate varies with the incidence of Protestantism.
4. The incidence of Protestantism in Spain is low.
5. Therefore, the suicide rate in Spain is low.[3]

Propositions 4 and 5 differ from the rest in that they refer to a specific case, which in this example happens to be an entire nation, Spain, but which in other examples might be an individual person, John Jones. It is true that the "explanation" of a phenomenon in Spain, or a characteristic of John Jones, is in terms of a general law connecting two variables, the incidence of Protestantism and suicide rates, but there is certainly nothing very startling about this type of explanation. It is what we do all the time in the case of regression analyses. We state a relationship between X and Y, we obtain data to estimate the appropriate coefficients, and then we "estimate" an individual's Y score from his X score. For example, we assume that if Spain has a low incidence of Protestantism (X), the value of its suicide rate (Y) will also be low because of the fact that the slope of the regression equation is positive.

More formally, suppose we let A represent the set of all nations having incidences of Protestantism defined as "low." Then there will be certain nations $a_1, a_2, \ldots, a_k$ that belong to this set of nations with low incidences of Protestantism. Proposition 4 indicates that Spain (a_1) belongs to, or is a member of, this set A. This may be written symbolically as $a \in A$, where the symbol "$\in$" can be read as "is a member of" or "is an *element* of." If we can find a statement that holds true for *all* members of set A, then we know that it must be true for Spain. In this sense, we have "explained" a property of Spain by showing that Spain also belongs to, or is an element of, another class B of nations for which all members have a given property (e.g., low suicide rates).

It should be noted that one can increase the "level" of abstraction by finding a more general class of phenomena for which A is also an element.

---

[3] Homans, "Contemporary Theory in Sociology," *Handbook of Modern Sociology*, p. 951. We have already noted that a statement such as proposition 3 does *not* automatically follow from propositions 1 and 2 unless causal asymmetry is intended (as is undoubtedly the case here) and unless perfect or very high associations are assumed.

Suppose that such a class can be referred to as α. We would then have $a \in A$, and $A \in \alpha$. It should be recognized that in the Spain example α would not be a class of *nations* but a class of classes of nations. Perhaps the shifting of levels can be more easily visualized if we take a as a person, and A as a group. Suppose a stands for John Jones, who is a member of a group A called the Hornets. Then propositions that hold true for all members of the Hornets will of course hold for John Jones. Perhaps α consists of the class of all *groups* referred to as "delinquent gangs," of which the Hornets are one. Then a proposition holding true for all delinquent gangs would hold for the Hornets, but would be on a different "level" of abstraction from that of a proposition about individual members, such as John Jones.

This seems to be one meaning that can be attached to the notion of "levels of abstraction." As we move to the next higher level, each class on the original level becomes an *element* of a new more abstract class. This is why I have referred to this perspective on the generalizing process as the "element-class" approach. The implications of this approach should be more apparent when it is compared with what I have termed the "class-subclass" approach. The "element-class" approach involves a truly major shift of focus, and it would seem as though a change in levels will ordinarily create major conceptual problems.

In the social sciences, the most familiar example of such a shift is the one already mentioned, the shift from individuals to groups as units of analysis. It may not be too difficult to develop propositions about groups as units of analysis (as in the Spain example), but the leap to propositions in which the unit of analysis is the *class* of group involves the necessity of formulating very high-level abstractions that are rather far removed from the operational level. I would therefore suggest that social scientists avoid this kind of shift in levels of abstraction, except in the case of the individual-group distinction.

The Class-Subclass Perspective

What appears to be a more generally held conception of different "levels" of abstraction involves the notion of subclasses contained within larger classes. Consider the following classes: living objects, animals, mammals, men, American men, and upper-class American men. Provided that each of these concepts is clearly defined, one may take animals as a distinct subclass of all living objects, mammals as a subclass of animals, man a subclass of mammals, and so forth. Letting these classes, in the order first mentioned, be A, B, C, D, E, and F, we may write that $F \subseteq E \subseteq D \subseteq C \subseteq B \subseteq A$, where the symbol "$\subseteq$" should be read as "is contained in" or "is a subset of." This notion of subsets should be clearly distinguished from that of elements. If William Smith is an upper-class American man, he is a member or element of F. Saying that F is contained in E means that all elements of F are also elements of E. In this example, William Smith, being in F, is also a member of all of the remaining classes. (In the previous example, Jones may be a member of the Hornets, but he is *not* a member of the class of delinquent gangs α.)

One may visualize the relationship among the sets and subsets A–F as a series of populations of decreasing membership. Any *universal* proposition about class A, that is, a proposition that holds for all members of A, will also hold for all members of the subpopulation F. Likewise the statement that no members of A are immortal implies that no members of F can be immortal. When we speak about extending the scope of our generalizations, it is often this kind of situation we have in mind.

If we begin with a class A, one way to obtain a subclass is to attach to it a qualifying adjective or set of adjectives. Thus if we begin with the class "men," we obtain a subclass by confining our attention to "American men," and a still smaller subclass by looking at "upper-class American men." Similarly, a class may consist of all societies with "class systems," and a particular subclass may consist of those societies with "closed class systems." This second meaning that can be given to the notion of raising the "level" of abstraction may therefore be conceived in terms of reducing the number of qualifying adjectives. Thus a proposition about "class-systems" in general might be considered to be on a higher level than one referring only to "closed class systems." Similarly, a generalization about upper-class American men would be on a much lower level than one dealing with all living objects.

If all propositions could be realistically stated as universals, then the process of moving from one level of abstraction to another would be relatively straightforward. As already noted, a universal proposition true of a more inclusive class must also hold for all legitimate subclasses, though the converse is of course not necessarily true. If one could state universally true propositions about upper-class American men, his next step would be to raise the "level" of abstraction to a proposition about all American men. This could be accomplished by delineating alternative subclasses of American men (e.g., lower- and middle-class American men), stating propositions about these additional subclasses, and then trying to restate a more general (and perhaps more abstract) proposition that summarized the relationships for all such classes. The process could then be repeated by examining men in other nations and again reformulating the proposition in more general terms.

This example seems farfetched precisely because we do not have such universal propositions in the social sciences. But as soon as we admit that a proposition holds only for "most" members of a highly inclusive class, we can say very little about the subclasses, unless we can also make a priori assumptions about conditional probabilities or unless we know something about the relative frequencies. Thus the proposition that most animals have a life expectancy of less than 40 years will not apply to upper-class American men. Theorists who wish to use systematic methods of relating propositions on one level to those on a higher (or lower) level will therefore find it difficult to do so without the use of statistical models involving probability distributions.

The social sciences contain many propositions that do not refer specifically to persons as units of analysis, and therefore there may be no particular population or subpopulation in mind. For example numerous sociological variables refer to behavioral acts of one kind or another. Ideally, these acts might be defined so that the class-subclass perspective would be appropriate, and so that one could move up or down the abstraction ladder by processes similar to those for populations and subpopulations. But, in fact, the basic variables may not have been defined with sufficient clarity or consensus that the generalization process can be handled in a straightforward manner. A few examples should be sufficient to illustrate the problem.

If one defines "homicide" as the taking of another person's life, and if distinctions are made between "first-degree murder," "second-degree murder," "manslaughter," killing in warfare, and so forth, then each of these latter acts can be taken as instances of homicide. That is, since any act of manslaughter is also an act of homicide, the class of all manslaughters is included in the class of all homicides. A universal proposition relating homicide to some other variable should apply to each of these types of homicides. Similarly, if criminal behavior is defined according to some definite criterion, and if delinquent behavior is defined as criminal behavior perpetrated by someone under 18 years of age, then delinquent behavior is a subtype of criminal behavior.

But many variables are not related in this simple way, though often they are implicitly treated as though they were. For example, homicide, suicide, burglary, alcoholism, and drug addiction may be conceptualized as forms of deviant behavior. Supposedly, then, a proposition about deviance could be expected to apply to these "forms" of deviance. But if suicide is defined as the taking of one's own life, rather than as a type of deviance, we encounter the obvious possibility that in some instances suicide may not be a form of deviance. Certain forms of homicide may be "normal" in some societies, as may the use of drugs. But these same acts may also be taken as "forms" of aggression or status-seeking. This point is of course obvious. What may not be so apparent is that when variables on a low level of abstraction are not defined in terms of variables at a higher level, then additional empirical assumptions must be made in moving up or down the abstraction ladder.

To illustrate this last point, suppose that murder rates (or other crime rates) are positively related to the density of the population and that a theory has been developed to this effect. The next step might be to link population density to "deviance," "aggression," or perhaps "aggressive deviance." But in order to do this, one would have to assert that murder does, in fact, constitute deviance in this particular setting. If there are varying degrees to which murder is defined as deviance, then the model may have to be conceptualized as a nonadditive one, and the argument may become much more elusive. If one author takes murder rates as an index of deviance, whereas someone else takes these rates as an index of aggression, the two may talk past each other without clearly recognizing what is taking place. The same phenomenon may of course occur if a single author uses a particular measure as an index of several different conceptual variables.

Problems of this sort border very closely on those to be discussed in the next major section, where we shall deal with unmeasured and measured variables that are linked by means of causal assumptions, rather than by definition. The processes of moving from the one "level" to the next are rather different in these two situations, as we shall see. Unfortunately, social scientists often do not define their variables clearly enough so that it is readily apparent which of the two kinds of situations actually holds. In these cases, the first step is obviously that of conceptual clarification.

Levels of generality and regression analysis

Since the regression approach has been emphasized throughout this book, it will be instructive to examine the behavior of regression equations in terms of the implications of shifts in levels of generality. Suppose we consider the single equation $Y = a + bX + u_y$. In order to use this equation we must measure the X and Y values for some class of individuals. But how broad should this class be? Suppose Y is height and X is age. Height and age of *what*? All living objects? Animals? Upper-class American men? This is of course the question of specifying the limits under which the equation is appropriate by defining the class of objects to which it applies. Ideally, we wish to state a "law" that is appropriate to a highly inclusive class, since it will then also apply to various subclasses. But we have just seen that this is difficult when we allow for less than universal relationships.

In a regression equation, the deviations from universality are handled by the error term u_y, which can be conceived as a residual component produced by all factors not explicitly considered in the model. We have seen that in order to obtain unbiased estimates of the regression coefficients, one must make certain assumptions about the behavior of this error term, and of course these assumptions may be relatively more realistic in the case of one subclass than another. For example, in dealing with upper-class American men, one may be willing to assume that extraneous factors affecting Y, and summarized in the error term, produce variation in Y that is uncorrelated with age X. Any major factors that do not operate in this manner must be incorporated into the model. But as one increases the level of generality, say by deleting the qualifier "upper-class," these assumptions regarding error terms may no longer be justified. Perhaps several additional variables must be brought into the equation, thereby making it more complex in the sense of involving more variables. This new equation, however, should also be appropriate to the subclass of upper-class American men, since it was assumed that the previously omitted variables were uncorrelated with X for this subclass. The "refined" equation should have approximately the same coefficient for X, but it will contain additional variables (uncorrelated with X in the aggregate), and therefore when the more complete equation is applied to the subclass, the error term will be smaller than in the case where only X was considered.

But as we increase the level of generality we not only have to examine the assumptions about omitted variables. We must also anticipate the possibility that the regression coefficients will change. Let us focus on the slope b relating height to age. Since growth rates will vary even within the same species, and certainly between species, this slope b should be conceived as a variable, rather than a constant. That is, we should expect b to change according to the nature of the population studied, and therefore we should expect to find statistical interaction or a nonadditive relationship between age X and whatever variables are used to define the boundaries of the population under consideration. Ideally, we might hope to locate and measure one or more explicit variables associated with the shift in populations. If this were possible, the "slope" b could be written as a function of these variables, and we would then have Y as a multiplicative function of age X times these variables affecting b.[4]

The above example is more biological than sociological, but the principle of looking for interactions as one increases the level of abstraction would seem to be very general. It would also apply when one shifts from one kind of subclass to another on the "same" level, as for example when one compares upper-class Americans with lower-class Frenchmen. The situation can be examined from the standpoint of homogeneity of subclasses. When one writes the equation $Y = a + bX + u_y$ and assumes that it is appropriate for some subclass, he is in effect assuming that the subclass is homogeneous with respect to the underlying (linear) causal processes, though of course not the levels of X and Y. That is, one would not expect all men to be of the same height and age, but it might be assumed that they are subject to the same relationship, as indicated by the coefficients a and b. It is in this sense that

[4] See Appendix A for a discussion of such multiplicative relationships.

one assumes that they are homogeneous with respect to the causal processes. If this is not true, then one would have to subdivide this class into homogeneous subclasses, within which all members are homogeneous with respect to the processes represented by the a_i and b_i for each subclass.

These subclasses could perhaps be ordered with respect to the relative magnitudes of the slopes b_i, which are now taken as variables, and one might then explicitly locate variables that could be used to explain variations in the b_i. As one increases the level of generality of a proposition in this manner, he would anticipate that certain constants in his original formulation might become variables, and that his laws would therefore become more complex.[5] If the more general theory were then applied to relatively homogeneous subclasses, corresponding simplifications could be introduced by treating certain of the variables as constants in specific special cases. Simplifications of this sort may be necessary in order to reduce the complexity of the mathematical model and to reduce the number of unknowns to the point where empirical data are sufficient to identify and estimate the remaining parameters.

Nominal scales and generalizations to populations

In the sociological literature there seems to be a tendency to overuse nominal scales and generalizations to specific populations. Both have their legitimate place in theory construction, but in many instances they seem to have been used as substitutes for careful measurement and theoretical conceptualization. As in the case of typology construction, unordered nominal scales with numerous categories lead to unwieldy theories. Likewise, cautious references to specific populations may inhibit the construction of more general theories.

There are of course valid theoretical reasons for referring to specific populations, as has been implied in the previous discussion of classes and subclasses. If one defines the limits of a class in theoretical terms (say, by specifying a list of characteristics possessed only by mammals), then there should be a specific finite population of animals corresponding to this theoretical class, and one may legitimately refer to the population of mam-

---

[5] It seems likely that whenever one raises the level of a generalization by shifting to a more inclusive *population*, he is also likely to raise the level of abstraction with respect to *variables* referring to specific behavioral acts. For example, since deviance may be defined somewhat differently from one nation to the next, a proposition referring to "hippies" in the United States may need to be generalized to similar types of deviants in other countries. This kind of double shifting of levels of abstraction would seem to preclude accurate tests and measures of interaction, thus making it difficult to state our most general propositions with any degree of precision.

mals. But often "populations" are selected primarily because of their convenience for research, as for example in the case of a social-psychological study of prejudice conducted within the confines of a nearby community. Here the "population" has no particular relevance to the limits imposed by a theoretical class (say, that of white Americans), nor are there any theoretical variables that could be used to designate this "population" as a subclass of theoretical interest. In many surveys of this type, the theoretical interest is in social-psychological processes presumed to be operating much more generally, and the reasons for delineating a specific population's boundaries are more or less arbitrary.

I do not wish to imply that specific populations are never of inherent interest in their own right. Particularly in macro-level theories, where the focus is on populations which have their own internal organization (e.g., communities or entire societies), one may wish to obtain measures for each individual population as a unit of analysis. For example, measures may be compared across populations, and generalizations about the populations may be stated and interrelated in theoretically meaningful ways. Social scientists are by no means agreed on this kind of question, and at this state in the development of theory one should probably not be overly dogmatic. It does seem safe to say, however, that the whole issue of the appropriateness of populations as units of theoretical analysis has not been sufficiently well studied. Too often, the decisions as to one's choice of population have been primarily based on research convenience, rather than careful theoretical conceptualization.

Unordered or "named" populations can of course be considered as special cases of nominal scales. Such nominal scales often appear in sociological research as "background variables" used as indicators of underlying variables of greater theoretical interest. For example, sociologists frequently compare males and females, Negroes and whites, Protestants, Catholics, and Jews, or persons who have been raised in different sections of the country. These categories are used as indicators of socialization variables. It may be assumed, for example, that on the average Negroes and whites have been exposed to different environments. Whenever the number of distinct groups or subclasses becomes relatively large, however, problems of theoretical conceptualization may become overwhelming. The result may be that no attempt is made to go beyond a simple description of the empirical results.

If the theory has been formulated in terms of underlying continua, rather than unordered categories, and if measurement has of necessity been too crude to provide an adequate test, then a weaker test can always be made. But if the theory does not encourage greater attention to the improvement of measurement procedures, then we cannot hope to advance as far as might otherwise be possible. In other words, I would prefer attempts at theory building that are in advance of present measurement practices, rather than those that take the status quo as a limiting factor.

The Indicator Perspective

Often when we refer to a theory as being highly abstract, or too distant from the operational level, we have something in mind very different from the previous two perspectives on levels of abstraction. We may be referring to the fact that the concepts in the theory may involve postulated properties or abstract theoretical constructs such as those of anomie, solidarity, or functional integration. These abstract concepts or constructs must then be linked with indicators that can actually be measured. In this sense, the notion of "abstraction" refers to the distance from the kinds of immediately sensed data that Northrop refers to as "concepts by intuition."[6]

It is of fundamental importance to realize that the movement "down" the abstraction ladder in this instance cannot be achieved by a simple process of breaking up classes into increasingly homogeneous subclasses. There will remain the problem of establishing "epistemic correlations" between the theoretical concepts and the operational indicators, and this will usually, if not always, require one to make certain a priori untestable assumptions concerning the causal linkages involved. As I have dealt with this question elsewhere, I shall only summarize the argument briefly, since it basically involves the problem of measurement which is not the primary focus of this book.[7]

A deductively formulated theory cannot be tested directly without the aid of an auxiliary theory consisting of assumptions linking at least some of the theoretical variables with operational procedures. As already noted, this auxiliary theory must also contain assumptions concerning the operation of omitted variables that produce both error terms in the equations and measurement errors in each of the variables. With respect to the assumptions required in the measurement process, one may often take a measured variable as determined or caused by the underlying variable, plus additional factors producing measurement error. In some cases, the same indicator variable may be linked to several different underlying or theoretical variables, in which case inferences will be difficult to make. For example, suicide rates may be caused not only by conditions of "anomie," but also by those producing "altruistic" or "egoistic" orientations.

[6] See F. S. C. Northrop, *The Logic of the Sciences and the Humanities*, especially Chaps. 5–7.

[7] See H. M. Blalock, "The Measurement Problem." See also Travis Hirschi and Hanan C. Selvin, *Delinquency Research: An Appraisal of Analytic Methods* (New York: Free Press, 1967), Chaps. 8 and 11.

The essential point is that the auxiliary theory linking the theoretical variables to measured indicators will contain causal assumptions that, in themselves, can never be tested directly. This means that both the main theory and the auxiliary theory must be combined in order to make definite empirical predictions. Since a number of alternative combinations can yield identical predictions, one must proceed by eliminating unsatisfactory theories rather than actually establishing a single theory as correct.

Consider the simple propositions on suicide suggested by Homans. The notion of suicide rates is reasonably close to the operational level, though there will inevitably be measurement errors involved. Therefore we may take the measured suicide rate as determined by the true rate plus additional factors. If we suspected biases in this measurement process, particularly biases that might affect the relationship between suicide rates and other variables, then the sources of biased measurement should be explicitly incorporated into the auxiliary theory. Otherwise we might assume that the remaining sources of error produce only random variation.

Similarly, we would have to obtain some measure of the incidence of Protestantism, as for example the percentage of adults actually listed as members of denominations classified as Protestant. There would once more be measurement errors that should be identified if possible. Perhaps the notion "incidence of Protestantism" refers primarily to the numbers of persons exposed to certain beliefs or values associated with Protestantism, rather than to actual church membership. Finally, we might take "individualism" or "egoism" as a completely unmeasured variable, unless independent psychological personality inventories were available.

The entire "theory" might be diagrammed as in Fig. 7-1, which combines the variables in the original or main theory with measured variables in the auxiliary theory. In this example, the auxiliary theory might also contain variables X, Y, and Z introduced because of possible distortions they might produce in the measurement process.

While this question of constructing an auxiliary theory for the purposes of testing one's main theory is logically distinct from that of operating on different levels of abstraction, there would seem to be at least one important practical connection. We would ordinarily expect that the higher the level of abstraction, in the second sense of involving more inclusive classes, the more difficult it will be to link measured indicators to these abstract concepts. Also, the wider the variety of situations to which the theory applies, the greater one's choice of indicators and, perhaps, the greater the reliance that should be placed on the use of multiple indicators. We sometimes encounter statements to the effect that a given measured variable (such as income or education) will take on different "meanings" in different contexts, or that it will be valued differently in one population (or subclass) than in another.

Generalizations and Levels of Abstraction 153

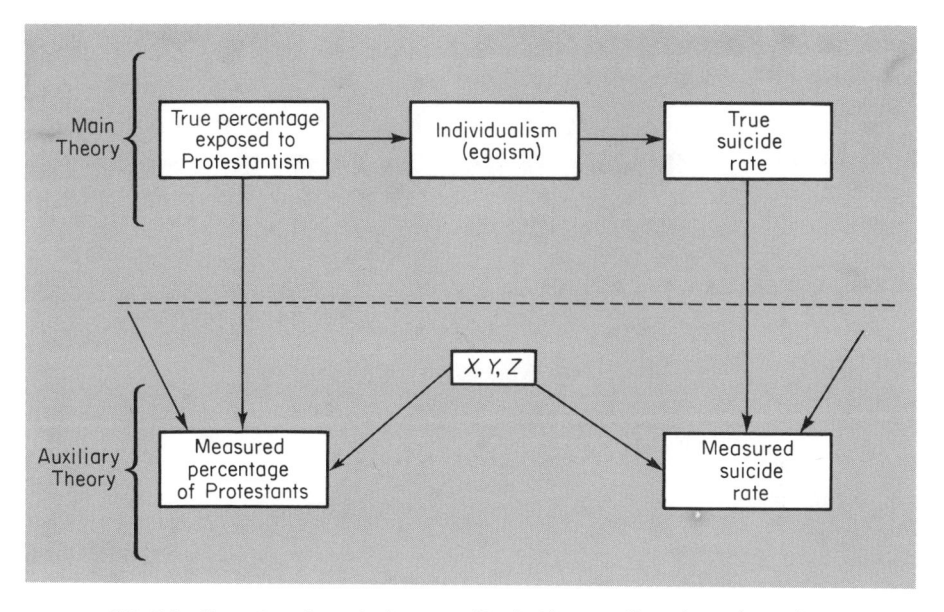

FIG. 7-1 Illustration of a main theory combined with an auxiliary theory for testing purposes.

This suggests that this particular variable is related differently to the underlying variable(s) of real theoretical interest, thus requiring a somewhat different auxiliary theory in the two situations.

One might claim that if the theoretical conceptualization were really adequate, then the variables could be measured the same way in different contexts. But the number of such contexts may become extremely large, given the fact that there will be numerous possible combinations of classes and subclasses, measuring instruments, and research designs. But if the indicators and research designs vary from one study to the next, how can one test the homogeneity assumption discussed in connection with the problem of formulating increasingly general theories?

This seems to pose an important dilemma for the social scientist. The more general his theories become, the more useful they may be, but the more difficult it will be to refine them in a precise way. If one attempts to standardize measurement procedures so that they can be used on very diverse classes, how can he be assured that they will always be linked in the same manner, and to the same degree, to the underlying or theoretical variables of real interest? Put another way, how can he be assured that the theoretical variables will be "manifested" in the same way?

There are probably no simple answers to such questions. Our only hope would seem to involve facing up to the issues by attempting to make our assumptions as explicit as possible. This will require that anyone wishing to *test* a general theory must construct an auxiliary theory appropriate for the particular population, measuring instruments, and research design with which he is dealing. Those who are more concerned with the process of theory *construction* should at least suggest the kinds of operational procedures and possible disturbing influences that should be considered in developing these auxiliary theories. Such a division of labor seems absolutely essential, given the magnitude of the task that lies ahead.

Appendix A:
Theory Building and the
Statistical Concept of Interaction[*]

Wherever one can develop a rationale for predicting interaction, one should make a conscious effort to construct and test theories that explicitly take advantage of interaction effects. The idea of interaction, as used in the statistical literature, ordinarily refers to nonadditivity, which may, of course, take many different forms;[1] here I shall discuss one particular type of non-additive model, one that involves multiplicative relationships. This kind of model is illustrated in a recent study of deviance by Palmore and Hammond, and also in motivation theory as formulated by Atkinson.[2]

---

[*] Reprinted, with the permission of the American Sociological Association, from the *American Sociological Review*, 30 (June 1965), pp. 374–80.

[1] The notion of interaction is treated most thoroughly in textbooks on experimental designs, and readers who are unfamiliar with the concept should refer to these sources. Briefly, a first-order interaction of two independent variables X_1 and X_2 on a dependent variable Y occurs when the relation between either of the X's and Y (as measured by the slope b_{yx}) is not constant for all values of the other independent variable. For example, where X_2 has been dichotomized, the interaction effect can be measured by the difference in the slopes b_{yx_1} for the two categories of X_2. Where all variables have been dichotomized, interaction may be measured as a difference of differences in percentages.

[2] See Erdman Palmore and Phillip E. Hammond, "Interacting Factors in Juvenile

In experimental designs and in the regression approach, interaction is usually handled by simply adding terms to an additive model. For example, one might begin with the model

$$\overline{Y} = a + b_1 X_1 + b_2 X_2 + b_3 X_3 \tag{A-1}$$

Interactions between X_1 and X_2, X_1 and X_3, X_2 and X_3, and all three independent variables could then be introduced explicitly. One way of doing this would be to use the cross-product terms $X_i X_j$ as follows:

$$\overline{Y} = a + b_1 X_1 + b_2 X_2 + b_3 X_3 + b_4 X_1 X_2 + b_5 X_1 X_3 \\ + b_6 X_2 X_3 + b_7 X_1 X_2 X_3 \tag{A-2}$$

This approach allows one to distinguish between the "main effects" of each independent variable and the various "interaction effects," including higher-order interactions. But when the interaction terms are large relative to the so-called "main effects," it may not be a simple matter to translate from the statistical model, represented in this form, to a theoretical conceptualization or interpretation of what the equation means. An alternative strategy is to begin with theoretical formulations that will generate equations containing interaction terms.

First-order Interactions:
Multiplicative Models

One cannot simply build theories involving interaction effects without some rationale to suggest the conditions under which nonadditive relationships might be expected. In general, additive models seem to approximate reality reasonably well, given a limited range of variation and sizable "random" fluctuations that make accurate specifications difficult. But certain more or less commonsense considerations suggest, under appropriate circumstances, specific types of nonadditive models as alternatives. The theoretical objective would be to exploit their implications as fully as possible, so as to generate predictions relatively systematically.

In a fairly common kind of theoretical situation, one assumes that a given phenomenon is most likely when two (or more) factors are both present, but that it is unlikely whenever either of these factors is absent.[3] In terms of

---

Delinquency," and John W. Atkinson, "Motivational Determinants of Risk-Taking Behavior," *Psychological Review*, 64 (November 1957), 359–72.

[3] Note that to say A and B are both necessary for C implies that C will *not* occur if *either A or B* is absent.

continuous variables, this is to assume that Y values will be large only when both X_1 and X_2 are high, but that Y scores will be small if either X_1 or X_2 approaches zero, even where the other is quite large. Of course, one need not state a proposition in absolute terms, implying necessary conditions or strict dependency; one may allow for the operation of other variables, measurement errors, and so forth, by formulating the theory in terms of statistical and probabilistic concepts.

Although crude measuring instruments may often make simple dichotomies seem advisable in handling empirical data, one can often formulate his *theory* in terms of continuous variables. The notion that two (or more) factors must both be "present" if a phenomenon is to occur can then be translated into a multiplicative model in which attributes are taken as special cases. Consider simple multiplicative models of the form $\overline{Y} = kX_1X_2$. In the case of attributes the value 0 can be assigned when the attribute is absent and 1, when it is present.[4] If all three variables are attributes, then this kind of model (with $k = 1$ and no sources of error) reduces to the very simple result that Y takes the value 1 (i.e., Y is present) only when *both* X_1 and X_2 are also present. We thus get a four-fold table where the values in the body of the table represent Y scores.

		X_1	
		Absent (0)	Present (1)
X_2	Absent (0)	0	0
	Present (1)	0	1

When the "scores" on X_1 and X_2 have been dichotomized, but there is no adequate rationale for assuming an absolute zero point, the picture can be modified rather simply. For example, we very commonly divide X scores according to whether they are "low" or "high." Presumably we can imagine some zero point, but there may be no way to determine how close the "low" scores are to this point. Even so, we can examine the nature of the Y values implied by a simple multiplicative model. Let us represent the unknown "low" and "high" values of X_1 as $X_1^{(1)}$ and $X_1^{(2)}$ respectively, and similarly for X_2. Then the model $\overline{Y} = kX_1X_2$ gives the following expected scores for Y:

[4] I shall neglect the error terms by assuming that we are dealing with expected or mean values of Y. In a more technical treatment I would have to specify assumptions about error terms and introduce these explicitly into the equations. In multiplicative models it is convenient to assume that error effects are also multiplicative, so that one may write equations of the form $Y_i = kX_1X_2u_i$, where the error term u_i is distributed about a mean of unity. In the case of interval scales a simple logarithmic transformation can then be used to obtain a linear additive model.

	$X_1^{(1)}$	$X_1^{(2)}$
$X_2^{(1)}$	$kX_1^{(1)}X_2^{(1)}$	$kX_1^{(2)}X_2^{(1)}$
$X_2^{(2)}$	$kX_1^{(1)}X_2^{(2)}$	$kX_1^{(2)}X_2^{(2)}$

We no longer get zeros in any of the cells, and the component parts of each cell are of course unknown. But taking ratios will produce some very simple results. Referring to the cells as

$$\begin{array}{cc} a & b \\ c & d \end{array}$$

note that $a/c = b/d = X_2^{(1)}/X_2^{(2)}$, and similarly $a/b = c/d = X_1^{(1)}/X_1^{(2)}$. Equivalently, the two diagonal products ad and bc should be equal, subject of course to sampling errors.[5] For example, the following set of empirical data would be consistent with this simple kind of multiplicative model:

		X_1	
		low	high
X_2	low	10	30
	high	20	60
Difference		10	30

These data would not fit an additive model, which would require that the two differences be approximately equal, as would be the case if the Y score in cell d were 40 instead of 60.[6]

---

[5] These results should not be confused with those for independence in a simple 2-by-2 contingency table, where the cell entries are *frequencies* rather than Y scores.

[6] In some instances marginal distributions may be extreme (e.g., 90 − 10), in which case percentage differences behave differently from such measures of association as ϕ. Tests for interaction generally involve comparisons of slopes rather than correlations, and therefore it would seem to make more sense in the case of nominal scales to compare slope analogues (differences in percentages) rather than measures of association. This question is much too complex, however, to be discussed here. See Leo Goodman, "Modifications of the Dorn-Stouffer-Tibbetts Methods for 'Testing the Significance of Comparisons in Sociological Data';" B. N. Lewis, "On the Analysis of Interaction in Multi-dimensional Contingency Tables," *Journal of the Royal Statistical Society*, Series A, 1962, pp. 88–117; and Hubert M. Blalock, *Causal Inferences in Nonexperimental Research*, pp. 119–24.

To illustrate additional points, I have selected two particular examples of multiplicative relationships. The first (Palmore and Hammond) reveals the implications of a specific combination of additive and multiplicative relationships, and the second (Atkinson's theory of motivation) involves higher-order interactions.

Palmore and Hammond postulate that degree of deviance is a multiplicative function of (1) barriers to legitimate opportunities, and (2) degree of exposure to illegitimate opportunities.[7] In essence, they assume that for deviance to occur two conditions may be necessary: both blockage of legitimate avenues and exposure to illegitimate ones. Put alternatively, one would expect deviance not to occur if legitimate avenues were open or if illegitimate ones were closed. This kind of reasoning, though grossly oversimplified, suggests a multiplicative rather than an additive model.

Unfortunately, as is often the case, Palmore and Hammond could not directly measure the two independent variables, access to legitimate and illegitimate opportunities. Instead, they used the following variables. Deviance was measured in terms of delinquency among a sample of somewhat over 300 lower-class New Haven youths. Independent variables (each dichotomized) included: (1) race, (2) sex, (3) success in school, (4) family deviance, and (5) neighborhood deviance. The first three (which I shall label W_1, W_2, and W_3) were taken as causal determinants of access to legitimate opportunities (X_1). Family deviance (W_4) and neighborhood deviance (W_5), on the other hand, were conceived as determinants of the degree to which the youths were exposed to illegitimate opportunities (X_2). The assumed causal model can therefore be represented as in Fig. A-1, where X_1 and X_2 are taken as having multiplicative effects on deviance (Y).

Note that since X_1 and X_2 were not measured, empirical relationships involved only the W's and Y, the dependent variable. Due to the small number of cases, the authors tended to examine only two W's at a time, looking for possible interaction effects among all possible combinations of pairs: race-sex, race-success, sex-success, and so forth. What would this particular theoretical model predict concerning interaction effects?

We have added a complication, since we are now dealing with W's (e.g., race, sex), rather than X's (access to legitimate and illegitimate avenues). This means in the case of attribute data that we can no longer expect the simple result that a/c should be approximately equal to b/d. Lacking any rationale for supposing otherwise, we may take the intervening variables X_1 and X_2 as *additive* functions of the independent variables W_i.[8] We are here

[7] Palmore and Hammond, "Interacting Factors in Juvenile Delinquency." This approach is of course suggested in Richard A. Cloward and Lloyd E. Ohlin, *Delinquency and Opportunity*.

[8] Multiplicative or other types of nonadditive relationships could also be postulated, but I shall not deal with this possibility.

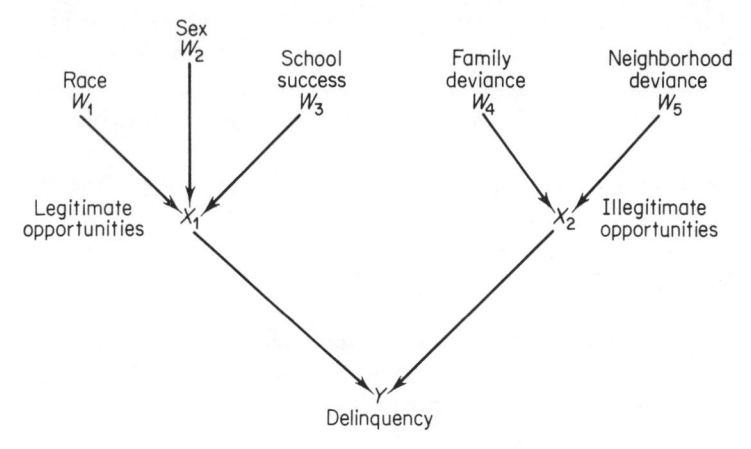

Appendix A: Theory Building and the Statistical Concept of Interaction

FIG. A-1 Causal model of the Palmore-Hammond theory.

supposing that the causes of X_1 (i.e., W_1, W_2, and W_3) are independent of the causes of X_2 (i.e., W_4 and W_5). Using linear additive models we can then write:

$$\bar{X}_1 = a_1 + b_{11}W_1 + b_{12}W_2 + b_{13}W_3$$
$$\bar{X}_2 = a_2 + b_{24}W_4 + b_{25}W_5$$
(A-3)

Obviously, $\bar{Y}$ is now a rather complex function of the W's, since we have combined features of both additive and multiplicative models. Let us examine the implications of such a model, however, in instances where we might wish to select *pairs* of W's (e.g., race and sex) to study their possible interaction effects on Y. As one can easily see, whenever the paired W's are causes of the *same* X_i their effects will be additive, whereas if they cause *different* X's their effects will be nonadditive. For example, suppose we select W_1 and W_2, both of which affect X_1 but not X_2. Under the assumption that the other W's have either been controlled or can safely be ignored, then $\bar{Y}$ could be written as a linear additive function of these two W's, as follows:

$$\bar{Y} = A + B_1 W_1 + B_2 W_2 \tag{A-4}$$

where A, B_1, and B_2 are all constants. In this case if we were to dichotomize all variables, we would also conclude that there is no interaction effect as measured by a difference of differences.

Now suppose we were to consider the effects of W_1 and W_4 on Y with the other W's constant. The equation relating $\bar{Y}$ to these particular W's would reduce to the form

$$\bar{Y} = kX_1X_2 = k(C + DW_1)(F + GW_4)$$
$$= kCF + kDFW_1 + kCGW_4 + kDGW_1W_4 \quad \text{(A-5)}$$

which contains an interaction term involving the product W_1W_4. It should be explicitly noted that equation (5) is of the same general form as equation (2). In other words the multiplicative model can be represented as an additive expression involving so-called "main effects" and "interaction effects."

Were we to dichotomize the W's into "low" and "high" scores, the simple ratio results obtained with the X's would no longer hold because of the unknown constant terms C and F. In effect this amounts to adding (or subtracting) constant values from the Y scores in cells a, b, c, and d. But the Y scores in cell d should still be substantially larger than those expected under an additive model (assuming positive relationships in all cases). For example, the Y scores might hypothetically be as follows:

		W_1 low	W_1 high
W_4	low	30	50
	high	40	80
Difference		10	30

In this particular model we have used two unmeasured variables, X_1 and X_2, to make a number of theoretical predictions concerning the relations of the various W_i to the dependent variable Y. There are in this case ten pairs of W's, four of which would be predicted to show no interaction effects and six of which should produce results similar to the hypothetical figures given above for W_1 and W_4. Thus, even though we may be confined to the crudest of measurements (i.e., dichotomies), the combination of multiplicative and additive relationships generates ten predictions that can be tested by the data. Furthermore, it would be difficult to develop *ad hoc* explanations as to why a particular set of six pairs of W's produced interactions, whereas four did not.

In the Palmore-Hammond illustration, the model predicts no interaction for the following pairs: race and sex (W_1 and W_2), race and success (W_1 and W_3), sex and success (W_2 and W_3), and family and neighborhood deviance (W_4 and W_5). The remaining six pairs should all show interaction of the predicted form. Eight of these ten predictions were reasonably well confirmed. For example, in the case of the interaction between school success and family deviance (W_3 and W_4), the following results were obtained for Negroes:

	School	
	Success	Failure
Family nondeviant	27	45
Family deviant	33	71
Difference	6	26

The figures in the body of the table (Y) represent the percentage of youths with one or more arrests or court referrals. The figure 71 in cell d is considerably higher than what would be expected under an additive model.

Higher-order Interactions:
Atkinson's Motivation Model

I shall discuss briefly a second illustration of the use of multiplicative models, primarily to point up the possibility of constructing theories that predict second- and higher-order interactions. My secondary purpose is to call to sociologists' attention the generality of motivation theories as providing the rationale for multiplicative models.

Atkinson, following Tolman and others, makes explicit a theory of motivation in which motivated behavior is taken as a multiplicative function of three general kinds of variables: (1) the strength of motives (M) or predispositions to behave, (2) expectancies (E) or subjective probabilities of achieving goals by given means, and (3) incentives (I) or the relative attractiveness of specific goals.[9] According to Atkinson, the incentive factor is often ignored in motivational theories, but it is needed to take into consideration differences in the objective environment or in the manipulations of the investigator. For example, amount of food (reward) or shock (punishment) may be varied independently of the emotional or physical state of the subject.

The three "independent" variables may themselves be interrelated. Atkinson deals with achievement situations in which he assumes that the incentive value of the activity is proportional to its difficulty, as indicated by $1 - p$, where p is the subjective probability of completing the task. The number of unknowns is thereby reduced by one, and Atkinson is then able to deduce some interesting implications that need not concern us here.[10] For

[9] Atkinson, "Motivational Determinants." For a more extensive discussion of nonadditive models in connection with motivation theories see Fred T. Schreier, *Human Motivation* (Glencoe, Ill.: Free Press, 1957).

[10] For example, he predicts that those who score high on need achievement will tend to select tasks of intermediate difficulty, for which the value of $p(1 - p)$ is maximum. Subjects

our purposes it is sufficient to point out that simple additive models would not have produced these predictions.

Note that this model is sufficiently general that it may be used to account for numerous types of behavior of interest to sociologists, including the phenomenon of deviance. To speculate a bit, it may be possible to link "blockage of legitimate opportunities" with the M component, and "exposure to illegitimate opportunities" with expectancy or the E component. Possibly, also, incentives may be linked with alternative forms of deviance, with one type of deviance having more reward value than another. I do not want to push the analogy with the Palmore-Hammond model too far, but it may not be coincidental that multiplicative models such as these turn out to be appropriate in a number of situations. The implications of Atkinson's very general formulation are that motivated behavior will not take place in the absence of any *one* of three kinds of factors: internal driving mechanisms (motives, needs), a perceived probability of success, and some incentive or object in the environment. I am suggesting that this kind of reasoning will generate multiplicative models appropriate for a wide range of phenomena.

I have introduced the Atkinson model for another purpose as well, however. Notice that motivated behavior is taken as a multiplicative function of three variables instead of two. This would lead us theoretically to look for *second-order* interactions. A second-order interaction means, essentially, an interaction of an interaction. As previously indicated, if one is dealing with interval scales a first-order interaction will show up as a difference in slopes. With attributes, it will consist of a difference of differences in proportions. A second-order interaction will involve, then, a difference of differences in slopes or a difference of differences of differences in proportions. Conceivably, one might postulate still higher-order interactions, to be similarly interpreted.

Let us illustrate the notion of a second-order interaction with the Palmore-Hammond data. The table cited shows an interaction between school success and family deviance *for Negroes only*. That is, for Negroes there is a difference of differences amounting to 26 − 6 or 20, indicating that deviants are especially likely among youths who are from deviant homes *and* do poorly in school. But this same difference of differences may not hold for whites. Since the data are not given, we do not know what the comparable interaction effect is for whites, but let us assume that this second difference of differences turns out to be 8. Then the second-order interaction would be 20 − 8 = 12, which constitutes a difference of differences of differences.

Such second- and higher-order interactions are ordinarily not anticipated

---

with high anxiety about failure, however, will select either extremely easy or extremely difficult tasks.

in sociological research, and an investigator who finds them is apt to conclude that generalization is nearly hopeless. But note that a very simple multiplicative model such as Atkinson's leads one to predict this kind of result. For example, imagine two experiments, one of which involves a very small food reward and the second a much larger one. In both experiments one studies the interaction between motives (e.g., hunger) and subjective probabilities, as they affect the strength or intensity of effort. With incentive (e.g., amount of food) held constant, one might predict that the greater the expectancy the steeper the slope between hunger and effort. This first-order interaction would be measured by differences in slopes for several levels of expectancy. But when we compare *across* experiments we would also expect the *interaction* between motive and expectancy to be stronger in the experiment where the food reward was larger.[11]

Let us suppose that Y is a multiplicative function of X_1, X_2, and X_3, which in turn are caused by a number of W_i. If X_1 and X_2 are functions of W_1, $W_2, \ldots, W_5$ as before, whereas X_3 is a linear additive function of W_6 and W_7, we can then make a number of predictions similar to those made for the Palmore-Hammond data. In examining *triplets* of W's, we would expect second-order interactions whenever all three X's were involved, first-order interactions among pairs of W's whenever only two were involved, and no interactions if the W's caused the same X_i. If the interactions between family deviance and school success proved to be different in the case of Negroes and whites, then we might interpret this to mean that the original model should be modified. This might suggest adding a third X variable, perhaps tapping the incentive notion, and linking one or more of the five measured variables to this third intervening variable.

Concluding Remarks

Though formulated in terms of continuous variables, multiplicative and other forms of nonadditive models can generate predictions which may be tested even where measurement has been very crude. Furthermore, provided the theoretical variables can be linked with a sufficient number of measured indicators, it becomes possible to develop a series of predictions that would not readily be suggested by common sense or alternative theories. In the Palmore-Hammond data, for example, the particular model used predicts six

---

[11] This kind of prediction follows from the equation $\bar{Y} = kX_1X_2X_3$. Let X_3 (incentive) take on the values 1 and 2 in the two experiments. Then in the first case $\bar{Y} = kX_1X_2$, whereas in the second $\bar{Y} = 2kX_1X_2$. If we now compare slopes relating Y and X_1 for several levels of X_2, we will obtain larger differences of slopes in the second of the two experiments because of the factor $2k$.

interactions of a specific type and four situations where interaction would not be expected. With slightly more complex models, such as Atkinson's, second-order and possibly even higher-order interactions can be predicted.

It may be premature to hope for fully developed theories predicting such interaction patterns in advance of data collection. *But the same procedures are useful for theory building.* The approach used here suggests working with relatively simple theories, such as multiplicative models, to study the kinds of predictions these imply. Such predictions, hopefully, would be helpful in ordering what might otherwise appear to be rather chaotic empirical findings.[12]

Alternatives to simple multiplicative models exist, of course; many such possibilities should be explored with a view to locating general conditions under which a given type of model is most appropriate. Thus we may be able to develop relatively general laws (e.g., a theory of motivation), of which certain others (e.g., a theory of deviance) are special cases. For example, if the same form of nonadditive relationship worked for two very different sets of data, one might be led to look for similarities or more general principles operating, while with simple additive relationships this sort of approach to theory building would not appear nearly so fruitful.

---

[12] For a number of reasons, apparent interaction may be found in a sample where none exists in a population. One obvious possibility is that of sampling error. Additional considerations include the possibilities of unequal measurement errors and nonlinearity, and situations in which values of the dependent variable are approaching an upper or lower limit imposed by the nature of the measure used. The case of unequal measurement errors is discussed in Hubert M. Blalock, "Some Implications of Random Measurement Error for Causal Inferences," *American Journal of Sociology*, 71 (July 1965), 37–47.

Appendix B:
Some Elementary Calculus

In order not to distract the reader's attention from the major substantive and methodological arguments of Chap. 5, I have reserved for this appendix a brief discussion of some very elementary principles of differential and integral calculus. Readers who are completely unfamiliar with the calculus should read this appendix before attempting to digest the second half of Chap. 5. Others may wish to review these materials briefly after a first reading of Chap. 5.

Although we shall later use a notation involving time t and a number of variables X_i that may vary over time, let us generalize the situation a bit by referring to *any* variables X and Y. We shall follow the convention of taking Y to be the dependent variable, and X independent. Later, time t will play the role of X, and the X_i will replace Y. Consider any function of the form $Y = f(X)$, which has been represented as a smooth curve in Fig. B-1. The rate of change in Y with respect to X need not be a constant, as is in fact only the case for a straight line. We must therefore define what we mean by the rate of change in Y, with respect to X, at a given point (X_0, Y_0) on the curve. The rate of change in Y with respect to X is defined to be the slope of the *tangent* to the curve at the point (X_0, Y_0).

166

Appendix B: Some Elementary Calculus 167

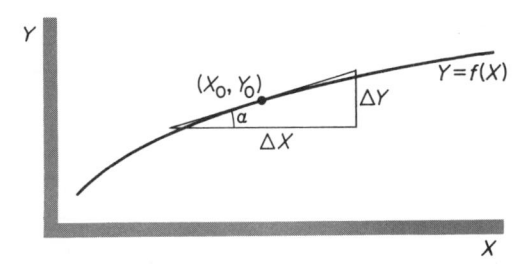

FIG. B-1 Curve showing slope of tangent.

We can draw a small right triangle, having this tangent as its hypotenuse, and having the base ΔX and height ΔY. The slope of the tangent is then given by the ratio $\Delta Y/\Delta X$, which is of course also the tangent of the angle α. We can now imagine a series of such triangles at different points along the curve, and we might wish to study how the slopes of these tangents vary along the curve. Furthermore, we can imagine approaching a limit in which the triangles become smaller and smaller so that the ratio $\Delta Y/\Delta X$ approaches dY/dX, which therefore can be conceptualized as the slope of the tangent line at a single point.

An important kind of question is the following. Suppose we are given that Y is a particular function of X, say the polynomial $Y = a + bX + cX^2 + dX^3$. What can be said about the slope of this function at different points on the curve? Another question might be: How fast is the slope *changing*, or what is the "acceleration" in the curve? The first of these questions reduces to the problem of finding an expression for dY/dX, whereas the second involves a rate of change in dY/dX. Alternatively, one might be given that dY/dX is some function, and he might be asked to "solve" for Y. These are the kinds of considerations ordinarily treated in courses on elementary calculus. Before we attempt to deal with the question of *why* they are important in the study of change, we first need to know some rules for obtaining dY/dX in the case of simple types of functions.

Polynomials

If we are given the general polynomial

$$Y = a + bX + cX^2 + dX^3 + \cdots + kX^n \tag{B-1}$$

we can obtain dY/dX, the derivative of Y with respect to X, by the following rules:

1. proceed by taking the derivatives of each successive term;
2. the derivative of a constant is zero;
3. to find the derivative of any term kX^n, multiply the coefficient k by the exponent n to which X has been raised and reduce the exponent of X by one.

Thus in the given example the derivative of the constant a is zero. Proceeding to the next term, we multiply the constant b by the power of X (unity), and reduce this exponent by unity, obtaining (1) $bX^0 = b$. The derivative of cX^2 is $2cX$, and so forth. Thus

$$\frac{dY}{dX} = b + 2cX + 3dX^2 + \cdots + nkX^{n-1} \tag{B-2}$$

For example, if we were dealing with the parabola $Y = 5 + 12X - 4X^2$ we would have $dY/dX = 12 - 8X$. Similarly, in the case of the third degree equation $Y = 7 + X - 2X^2 + X^3$, we get $dY/dX = 1 - 4X + 3X^2$.

Recall that an nth degree polynomial can generally (except for a few degenerate cases) be represented by a curve with $n - 1$ bend points. Thus a second degree polynomial has one bend point, a third degree polynomial has two bend points, and so forth. If we know the derivative we can describe the behavior of any polynomial without having to go through the tedious procedure of plotting the curve for numerous values of X. Consider the curve in Fig. B-2, which has four bend points and therefore represents a

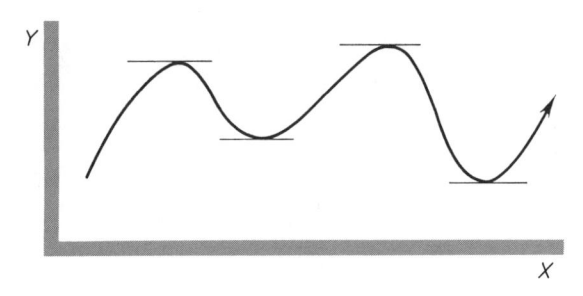

FIG. B-2   A fifth degree polynomial.

fifth degree polynomial. It is evident that bend points represent local maxima or minima, and that, furthermore, the slopes of the tangents at these bend points must be horizontal. This means that the value of dY/dX at each bend point must be zero, and thus by setting the derivative equal to zero we can locate the maxima and minima.

Next consider one of the two maximum points in Fig. B-2. As we proceed from left to right toward these maxima we notice that the slope dY/dX must be *decreasing* toward zero. Put another way, Y itself is increasing at a decreasing rate. After we pass the maxima the slope continues to decrease, becoming negative, until we reach some point to the right of the maximum point, where the (negative) slope then begins to increase to zero, becoming positive after it passes the minimum points. In the case of this particular curve, the slope to the left of the first maximum is always positive, and that to the right of the second minimum is likewise positive. The important and general point is that maximum points can be recognized from the fact that the rate of change in dY/dX is negative in the vicinity, whereas the rate of change in dY/dX will be positive near a minimum point.

This suggests the desirability of obtaining the rate of change in a derivative, or what is referred to as a *second derivative* of Y with respect to X. This can be written symbolically as

$$\frac{d}{dX}\left(\frac{dY}{dX}\right) \quad \text{or more simply as} \quad \frac{d^2Y}{dX^2}$$

It should be noted that the operator "d" is merely a shorthand symbol. Obviously the expression d^2Y/dX^2 does *not* mean that we multiply d^2 by Y and then divide by d times X^2. The entire expression indicates that we have taken successive derivatives. An alternative way to look at it is to replace the symbol dY/dX by Z and then to ask about the derivative of Z with respect to X. For example, a change in distance over time is commonly given the name "velocity." "Acceleration" can then be defined as either a change in velocity or as a change in the change in distance over time.

The rule for obtaining a second derivative is straightforward; one merely applies the same rules as were applied to the expression for dY/dX. For example, we previously obtained the result, Eq. (B-2):

$$\frac{dY}{dX} = b + 2cX + 3dX^2 + \cdots + nkX^{n-1}$$

Therefore

$$\frac{d^2Y}{dX^2} = 2c + 6dX + \cdots + n(n-1)kX^{n-2} \tag{B-3}$$

Notice that the exponents in the original polynomial have been reduced by two, and the coefficients a and b have disappeared. We shall have to pay attention to this second fact when we later deal with the question of inferring the original relationship from the expressions for dY/dX or d^2Y/dX^2. In effect, we lose information about the constant terms whenever we take derivatives, and when we travel the reverse route from dY/dX to Y we shall have to introduce unknown constant coefficients.

Consider the parabola (second degree equation) $Y = 5 + 12X - 4X^2$. We have seen that in this case $dY/dX = 12 - 8X$. Suppose we wished to determine the single bend point and to ascertain whether this is a maximum or minimum (and therefore whether the parabola opens downward or upward). Since we know that the slope must be zero at this bend point, we set $dY/dX = 0$ and solve for X, getting $8X = 12$, or $X = 1.5$. We then take the second derivative and note the sign of this quantity at the bend point (where $X = 1.5$). Thus

$$\frac{d^2Y}{dX^2} = -8$$

which is of course negative not only at $X = 1.5$ but at all points. Therefore we have a maximum point and the parabola opens downward. We note, incidentally, that parabolas have the interesting property that the "acceleration" or rate of change in the slope will always be a constant, the sign of which is determined by the coefficient of X^2 in the original equation.

In the case of the third degree equation $Y = 7 + X - 2X^2 + X^3$ we obtained $dY/dX = 1 - 4X + 3X^2$ which, when set equal to zero, gives $(3X - 1)(X - 1) = 0$, and thus $X = \frac{1}{3}$ and $X = 1$ are the X coordinates of the two bend points. Next we find the second derivative as follows:

$$\frac{d^2Y}{dX^2} = -4 + 6X$$

When $X = \frac{1}{3}$ the second derivative takes on the value -2, and therefore we have a maximum point. When $X = 1$, on the other hand, the value is 2, and the second bend point is a minimum. The height of the curve can be determined for various selected points such as for $X = 0$ (where $Y = 7$); the maximum point $X = \frac{1}{3}$ (where $Y = 7 + 4/27$); and the minimum point $X = 1$ (where $Y = 7$). For values of X that are negative we note that all of the terms in X are negative, and hence Y will decrease from 7 on the Y axis to minus infinity. As X increases beyond 1.0 the cubic term dominates the polynomial expression, and Y will increase indefinitely. Thus the curve can be plotted as in Fig. B-3.

Problems of maximization and minimization are exceedingly important in many applied fields, and these simple principles of calculus can often be used to solve these problems. For example, in order to obtain formulas for the least-squares estimates a and b in the equation $Y = a + bX + u_y$, one first formulates an equation for the quantity to be minimized (i.e., the sum of

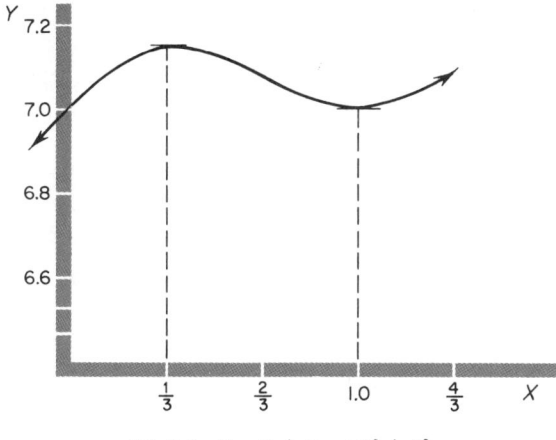

FIG. B-3 $Y = 7 + X - 2X^2 + X^3$

the squared vertical deviations from the line), takes derivatives with respect to a and b and sets them equal to zero, and then solves for the estimators a and b. Second derivatives may then be computed in order to check to see whether the solution is actually a minimum. Although you will need more knowledge of the calculus to solve specific problems of this nature, the principles involved are always the same.

Exponential functions

There are of course a number of relatively simple functions that are not polynomials. Certain of these functions have very simple derivatives that need not be discussed further in the present context. For example, the derivative of $\sin X$ is $\cos X$; that of $\cos X$ is $-\sin X$; and the derivative of $\log_e X$ is $1/X$. I shall confine the discussion to exponentials of the form e^{bX}, where e is an important natural constant approximately equal numerically to 2.718. This expression has the very simple derivative $b\,e^{bX}$. To find the derivative of $Y = k\,e^{bX}$ one merely multiplies the constant k times the coefficient of X in the exponential, leaving the expression e^{bX} unchanged. Thus the derivative of e^X is e^X, as is the second derivative. The derivative of $5\,e^{2X}$ is $10\,e^{2X}$, and that of $2\,e^{-X}$ is $-2\,e^{-X}$.

Recall that a negative exponent can be written as a denominator having a positive exponent. Thus $X^{-3} = 1/X^3$ and $e^{-X} = 1/e^X$. We shall shortly return to situations in which X is the time variable, and where our interest is in tracing the path of a curve as time passes. Whenever we encounter an expression such as e^{-t} or e^{-kt}, where k is positive, we know that this expression must approach zero as t increases, since we will be raising a number greater than unity (i.e., 2.718) to a negative power which becomes numerically large. Thus in the expression $1/e^{kt}$ the denominator becomes extremely large, and the entire term approaches zero. Terms of this sort will therefore drop out of the picture as time progresses, and we can use this fact to study equilibrium behavior.

Exponential functions frequently appear in solutions to simple differential equations, as we shall see later. This results from the fact that in the case where $Y = e^X$ we have $dY/dX = e^X = Y$, and for $Y = e^{bX}$ we get $dY/dX = b\,e^{bX} = bY$. Thus whenever we have occasion to write dY/dX as a function of Y itself, we can expect exponential functions to result.

The rule for taking derivatives term by term applies to exponential functions, and also to mixed functions. Thus if

$$Y = 5 + 3X^2 - 8X^5 + 3\,e^X - 5\,e^{3X}$$

then

$$\frac{dY}{dX} = 6X - 40X^4 + 3\,e^X - 15\,e^{3X}$$

Note, however, that we have not considered more complex functions in which terms have been multiplied together, or divided by one another. Thus we have not given a rule for finding the derivative of $(X^2 + 3X)(5X - 6)$, although in this simple case one could expand by multiplying out the parentheses, and then he could apply the term–by–term rule. Finding the derivative of a fraction would not be so simple, however. Since we shall deal only with the simplest types of equations there is no need in the present context to discuss derivatives of such slightly more complex functions.

Integration

We have dealt with situations in which Y is given as a function of X and where the objective is to find dY/dX. But there are also a number of situations in which one is given a function involving dY/dX, or higher-order derivatives, the task being that of expressing Y as a function of X. This task is referred to as that of "solving" differential equations, which may of course be much more complex than simple linear equations of the first order (i.e., those involving only dY/dX and not d^2Y/dX^2 or more complex expressions). In general, it is often difficult to solve complex differential equations, and only the more simple types have explicit solutions at all.

How does one work backwards to obtain expressions for Y if he is given dY/dX? In some cases simple inspection or trial and error will work. For example if we are given that $dY/dX = 5$, we know that one solution is

$Y = 5X$. This is true because when we differentiate Y with respect to X, the equation $Y = 5X$ gives $dY/dX = 5$. But so does the equation $Y = 5X - 6$, or the general equation $Y = 5X + C$. This latter equation is referred to as the "general solution" to the simple differential equation $dY/dX = 5$, whereas $Y = 5X$ or $Y = 5X - 6$ are "particular solutions." The objective is to find general solutions, and then to obtain particular solutions that satisfy certain initial conditions or other restrictions. For example, if we are told that when $X = 1$ then $Y = 11$, we may insert these values into the general solution $Y = 5X + C$, obtaining $11 = 5 + C$, giving $C = 6$.

A more systematic procedure will in general be necessary, however. This procedure is referred to as "integration," and the field of study as "integral calculus." Once one learns how to integrate individual expressions he can then handle more complex differential equations. We shall again deal with only the simplest cases in order to illustrate the general strategy. Fortunately, it does not seem necessary at this stage for most social scientists to concern themselves with more than these simple types of equations.

If we are given the equation $dY/dX = k$, we may multiply both sides by the expression dX, obtaining $dY = k\,dX$. This means that a very small change in X, represented by dX, is associated with a small change in Y, namely dY, according to the above equation. In the present context we will not be concerned with the problem of causal asymmetry, though such a problem will immediately arise whenever one attempts to interpret the meaning of the equation *substantively*. We now introduce the symbol $\int$ (like an archaic "S" for "summation") to represent integration, or the reverse process from that of differentiation. This integration sign followed by some expression times dX (or dY) means that we are to reverse the process of differentiation by adding up all of the small quantities dX over some interval, say from a to b.

The meaning of the expression $\int f(X)\,dX$ can be interpreted geometrically as an area under the curve $Y = f(X)$, as indicated in Fig. B-4. If one wishes

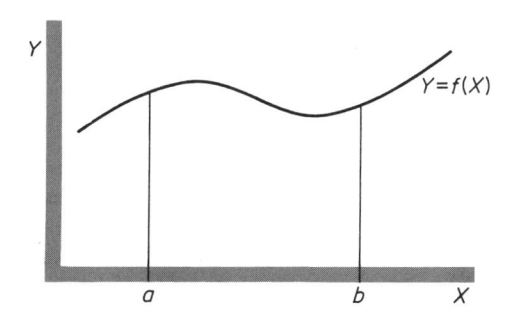

FIG. B-4   Area under curve from a to b.

Appendix B: Some Elementary Calculus

to specify the limits in order to obtain particular numerical values, these can be written at the bottom and top of the integral sign. For example the expression $\int_{-\infty}^{\infty}$ would indicate that one wishes to obtain the total area under the curve, running from "minus infinity" to "plus infinity." The expression $\int_{a}^{b}$ would indicate that we are to find the area between the ordinates a and b.

For purposes of illustration, suppose we are given the cubic equation

$$Y = c_1 + c_2 X + c_3 X^2 + c_4 X^3 \tag{B-4}$$

and are asked to find the area under this curve between a and b. This area could be approximated by a series of rectangles (see Fig. B-5), each with

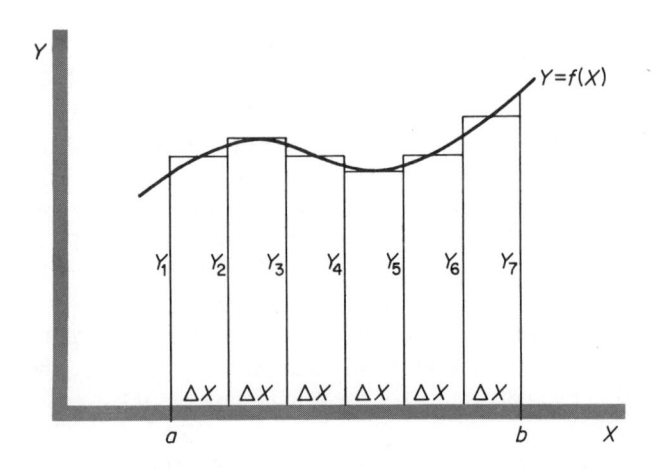

FIG. B-5 Area under curve approximated by areas of rectangles.

width ΔX but with heights adjusted to the heights of the curve at the midpoints of each interval (i.e., $Y_1, Y_2, \ldots$). The area of each rectangle would be $Y_i \Delta X$, and we could approximate the total area by using the sum $\sum_{i=1}^{k} Y_i \Delta X$.

We now imagine that the rectangles have narrower widths, and of course that more and more rectangles are used to approximate the heights at each point on the curve. It can then be shown that the area under the smooth curve can be approximated to within any desired degree of accuracy. In the limit, the widths become indefinitely small, and we replace ΔX by dX. The heights of course vary, but at any given point on the X axis they are given by the value Y. Finally, we replace the summation sign by an integral sign, writing the area as

$$\int_a^b Y\, dX = \int_a^b (c_1 + c_2 X + c_3 X^2 + c_4 X^3)\, dX \tag{B-5}$$

This gives the rationale for representing an integral sign as an archaic "S". It may be conceptualized as an addition of an indefinitely large number of very small quantities.

The rules for integration are generally more difficult to apply in practice than are the rules for differentiation, but for simple expressions we shall not encounter any special problems. For polynomials, as illustrated above, one may proceed term by term, *increasing* the power or exponent of X by unity, and adjusting the coefficient by *dividing* by the *new* exponent. Several simple examples should illustrate the procedure. Recalling that the derivative of an unknown constant C will be zero, we have:

$$\int k\, dX = kX + C$$

$$\int kX\, dX = \frac{k}{2} X^2 + C$$

$$\int kX^2\, dX = \frac{k}{3} X^3 + C$$

$$\int (k_1 + k_2 X)\, dX = k_1 X + \frac{k_2}{2} X^2 + C$$

$$\int (k_1 + k_2 X^3 + k_3 X^8)\, dX = k_1 X + \frac{k_2}{4} X^4 + \frac{k_3}{9} X^9 + C$$

Each of these results may of course be checked by differentiating the right-hand expressions.

Now let us consider two somewhat more complex equations. Suppose we are given that the rate of acceleration in some variable X is a constant. As we have already seen, this will be true in the case of a parabola, but let us see how we could derive this result beginning with the differential equation

$$\frac{d^2 X}{dt^2} = K \tag{B-6}$$

Let us first write an expression for the velocity, $V = dX/dt$. Differentiating V

we get $dV/dt = d^2X/dt^2 = K$. Therefore, multiplying both sides by dt,

$$dV = K\, dt$$

and

$$\int dV = \int K\, dt \quad \text{or} \quad V = Kt + C_1 \tag{B-7}$$

But $V = dX/dt$ or $dX = V\, dt = (Kt + C_1)\, dt$; therefore

$$X = \int dX = \int (Kt + C_1)\, dt = \frac{K}{2} t^2 + C_1 t + C_2 \tag{B-8}$$

Notice that there are now two arbitrary and unknown constants C_1 and C_2 appearing in the general solution. We see that the path of X through time is parabolic, but we cannot obtain the exact position of X at any given time without knowing C_1 and C_2 as well as K. If the initial position and velocity were given, these pieces of information would be sufficient to solve for C_1 and C_2 and to obtain a particular solution. Notice, also, that we did not specify time limits, such as a and b, over which the integration was to be carried out. This is because the nature of our problem did not refer to such limits, but sometimes it is desirable to obtain specific numerical results within fixed time limits.

As a second example consider the equation $dX/dt = bX$, the solution of which will involve the exponential e^{bt}. Let us see how this result can be obtained by integration. We have

$$\frac{dX}{dt} = bX \quad \text{or} \quad dX = bX\, dt \quad \text{or} \quad \frac{1}{X} dX = b\, dt \tag{B-9}$$

Here we have separated terms in such a way that X and dX appear on one side of the equation and dt (and any pure function of t) appears on the other. Though this procedure will not be possible in more complex equations, whenever it can be done this makes it possible to carry out a simple integration of both sides, as was also done in the previous example. Thus, recalling that the derivative of $\log_e X$ is $1/X$, we have

$$\int \frac{1}{X} dX = \int b\, dt$$
$$\log_e X = bt + C \tag{B-10}$$

It would of course be possible to introduce constants on both sides of the equation, but this is unnecessary since we may always take $C = C_1 + C_2$. Thus integration of both sides results in a single constant, rather than two.

In order to express this result in exponential form, recall that logarithms are exponents, and that if one were to take antilogs of both sides he would obtain

$$X = e^{(bt+C)} = e^{bt} e^C = k\, e^{bt}, \quad \text{where } k = e^C \qquad \text{(B-11)}$$

Such a simple result would not have been possible had logarithms been taken to a base other than the natural constant e. This shows why this quantity is such a convenient number, and why it occurs so frequently in differential equations.

As a check, we may always take the derivative of X with respect to t, obtaining

$$\frac{dX}{dt} = bk\, e^{bt} = bX$$

and it can be seen that this result holds regardless of the value of k. If we are given the value of X when $t = 0$, we can solve for k. Representing the value of X at time zero as X_0, we must have $X_0 = k\, e^0 = k$, and thus k represents the initial value of X.

Index

Abelson, Robert P., 130–32
Abstraction, levels of:
   class-subclass perspective, 144–51
   element-class perspective, 142–44
   indicator perspective, 151–54
Acceleration, 167, 169–70, 175
Alker, Hayward R., Jr., 5, 60–61, 66–69, 81
Areas under curves, 173–74
Armament races, 90, 96–97, 109, 127–32
Asymmetry, causal, 13–15, 19
Atkinson, John W., 37, 155, 156n, 159, 162–65
Autocorrelation (*see* Error terms)
Axioms, 10–26

Barton, Allen H., 30
Baumol, William J., 51n, 78, 85n, 86n, 96n, 101n, 106n, 107n, 137n, 138n
Bernd, Joseph L., 60n
Blalock, Ann B., 5n
Blalock, Hubert M., 5n, 7n, 11n, 12n, 15n, 19n, 28n, 37n, 47n, 50n, 69n, 70n, 151n, 158n, 165n
Blau, Peter M., 8n

Block-recursive systems, 29, 36, 42, 63, 65, 71–74, 114, 120–21
Buckley, Walter, 76n, 106

Calculus, 88, 90, 166–77
Canonical correlation, 42
Capecchi, Vittorio, 30–31, 35n
Causal systems, 80
Chains, causal, 16–17, 20–21, 43–45
Change rates, 91–97
Christ, Carl F., 51n, 55n, 59n, 65n, 67n, 69n, 71n, 84n, 98n
Cloward, Richard A., 37, 159n
Cobweb models, 84–87, 96
Coleman, James S., 6n, 7n, 11n, 91n, 94n, 95, 97–100, 101n, 122, 127n
Comparative statics, 137–39
Constructed types (*see* Typologies)
Correlations, 17, 21, 23, 42 (*see also* Covariance statements)
Correspondence principle, 138
Costner, Herbert L., 13, 15–16, 17n
Covariance statements, 11–19

Dahrendorf, Ralf, 14
Derivatives, 88
  partial, 138n
  rules for, 167–69, 172
  second, 169–71
Determinants, 109–10, 116–17
Deutsch, Karl W., 76n, 106
Dichotomies, 31, 33–34, 157–58 (see also Typologies)
Difference equations, 78–88, 95–96, 140
Differential equations:
  versus difference equations, 88, 95–96, 140
  general solutions of, 173, 177
  multiple equations, 100–140
  single equations, 88–99, 172–77
  stability conditions in, 92–96, 106–26
Duncan, O. Dudley, 8n, 16n, 21n
Durkheim, Emile, 29
Dynamic theories, 26, 59 (see also Difference equations, Differential equations, Stability conditions)
  nature of, 77–78
  simultaneous-equation, 100–140
  single-equation, 76–99

Easton, David, 76n
Endogenous variables:
  in general model, 59–66
  lagged, 48, 62, 68, 75, 78–87, 140
Equilibrium, 51, 57, 81–82, 86, 92, 94–97, 132–35, 137–39
Error terms, 7, 48–49, 55
  autocorrelation of, 49, 83–84, 97–100, 140
  covariances among, 70, 72–73
  and generalization, 147–48
Estimation, 3, 58–59
Etzioni, Amitai, 32n
Exogenous variables, 35, 40
  in block-recursive systems, 73–75
  in differential equations, 94, 96, 109, 114, 119–22
  and identification, 55–66, 78–79
Explanation, concept of, 142–43
Exponential functions, 171–72, 176–77 (see also Differential equations)

Factor analysis, 41
Faris, Robert E. L., 1n
Feedback, 21–25, 50
  in block-recursive systems, 71–74
  loops, 46–47, 60–61, 79, 112, 115, 118–19, 122–25
  mechanisms, 102–6
  in simultaneous differential equations:
    k equations, 106–8, 116–26
    three equations, 109–16
    two equations, 108–9
  in single differential equations, 95–97
Fisher, Franklin M., 49n, 55n, 59n, 63n, 65n, 71, 84n
Frideres, James, 38–39

Generality (see Abstraction, levels of)
Generalization (see also Abstraction, levels of):
  to populations, 145–46, 149–50
  and regression analysis, 147–49
Gibbs, Jack P., 16, 17n, 20
Glaser, Barney, 8
Goodman, Leo A., 45n, 158n
Gordon, Robert A., 71n

Hammond, Phillip E., 37, 155, 159–61, 163–64
Harmon, Harry H., 41n
Hempel, C., 30
Hirschi, Travis, 42n, 151n
Historical systems, 80
Hodge, Robert W., 7n
Homans, George C., 1, 13–14, 87, 109, 132–39, 142–43, 152
Homogeneity of subclasses, 148–49, 151, 153
Hopkins, Terence K., 21–25, 46, 61, 66–68, 79–83, 95, 101–5, 112, 126

Ideal types (see Typologies)
Identification:
  and difference equations, 78–85
  in general model, 59–66
  necessary and sufficient conditions for, 64–65, 67, 69
  overidentification and testing, 68–69
  in recursive systems, 70–71
  in supply and demand equations, 50–59
Independent variables, 35–36, 40 (see also Exogenous variables)
Indicators, 4, 36, 150–54, 164
Integral equations, 131
Integration, 172–76
Interaction, statistical, 6n, 34–35, 43, 45, 148, 155–65
  first-order, 156–62, 164
  higher-order, 162–64
Intervening variables, 36–40, 159–61
Inventories:
  of causes, 35–40
  of effects, 41–43

Janowitz, Morris, 41
Johnston, J., 59n, 67n, 71n
Jureen, Lars, 49n, 83n, 85n, 126n

Kemeny, John G., 7n
Keyfitz, Nathan, 89n
Klein, Lawrence R., 54n, 75n, 84n
Kuhn, Thomas S., 142

Lagged variables (see Endogenous variables)
Lasswell, H. D., 30n
Lazarsfeld, Paul H., 30
League of Nations, 129n
Least squares, ordinary, 49, 58, 67, 70, 79, 97–99, 140, 170

Leik, Robert K., 13, 15–16, 17n
Lenski, Gerhard E., 41, 70n, 71
Lerner, D., 30n
Lewis, B. N., 158n
Li, C. C., 21n
Loops (see Feedback)
Lotka, A. J., 89n

McGinnis, Robert, 7n
McKinney, John C., 30–34
Martin, Walter T., 16, 17n, 20
Maximizing, principle of:
    in calculus, 168–71
    and feedbacks, 103–4
Measurement error, 5n, 12, 84, 99, 140, 152, 165n
Merton, Robert K., 1, 31–32, 34, 37
Minimizing (see Maximizing, principle of)
Motivation theory, 162–63
Multicollinearity, 71n
Multiplicative functions, 37, 40, 155–65 (see also Interaction, statistical)

Nominal scales, 149–50
Nonadditivity, 5–6 (see also Interaction, statistical)
Nonlinear models, 71, 86–87, 101, 126n, 140, 165n
Northrop, F. S. C., 11n, 151
Nye, F. Ivan, 38–39

Ohlin, Lloyd E., 37, 159n
Oppenheim, P., 30

Palmore, Erdman, 37, 155, 159–61, 163–64
Parabolas, 170, 175–76
Parameters (see Structural parameters)
Path coefficients, 44
Polynomial functions, 91, 167–71, 175
Population growth, 89–90
Populations (see Generalization)
Prediction (see Estimation)

Rapoport, Anatol, 127n
Rashevsky, Nicholas, 128
Reciprocal causation, pairwise, 112–16 (see also Feedback)
Recursive systems, 19n, 46, 48–50, 69–71, 78–85, 119–22 (see also Block-recursive systems)
Redfield, Robert, 31
Reduced forms, 56
Regression equations, 143, 147–49, 156 (see also Least squares, ordinary)
Richardson, Lewis F., 90, 96–97, 109, 127–32

Ross, Shepley L., 106n

Samuelson, Paul A., 51n, 78, 80n, 82n, 88n, 96n, 103, 137n, 138
Saturation effect, 105, 126n
Schreier, Fred T., 162n
Selvin, Hanan C., 42n, 151n
Servomechanisms, 76, 105–6
Siegel, Paul M., 7n
Simon, Herbert A., 76n, 87, 88n, 101n, 104, 105n, 109, 132–39
Snell, J. Laurie, 7n
Solomon, Herbert, 127n
Stability conditions, 77
    in difference equations, 81–82, 85–87
    in simultaneous differential equations:
        k equations, 106–8, 116–26
        three equations, 109–16
        two equations, 108–9
    in single differential equations, 92–96
Static theories, 76–78, 137–39
Status inconsistency, 69–71
Strauss, Anselm, 8
Strotz, Robert H., 55n, 83n
Structural parameters, 50
Supply and demand, 50–59, 84–87
Sutherland, E. H., 37n
Symmetry (see Asymmetry, causal)

Tangent, slope of, 166–68
Testing theories (see Theory)
Theorems, 10–26
Theory (see also Dynamic theories, Static theories):
    auxiliary, 5, 151–54
    concept of, 1–2
    testing of, 3, 10–11, 68–69
Thompson, Gerald L., 7n
Tolman, Edward, 162
Typologies, 2, 30–35, 149

Udy, Stanley H., 32–33
Universal propositions, 145–47

Velocity, 169, 175–76

Weber, Max, 29, 32–33
White, Lynn, 38–39
Willer, David, 142
Wold, Herman, 49n, 55n, 83, 85n, 126n
Wright, Sewall, 21n

Zero restrictions, 65n, 74
Zetterberg, Hans L., 1–2, 12–13, 15, 18–20, 35n